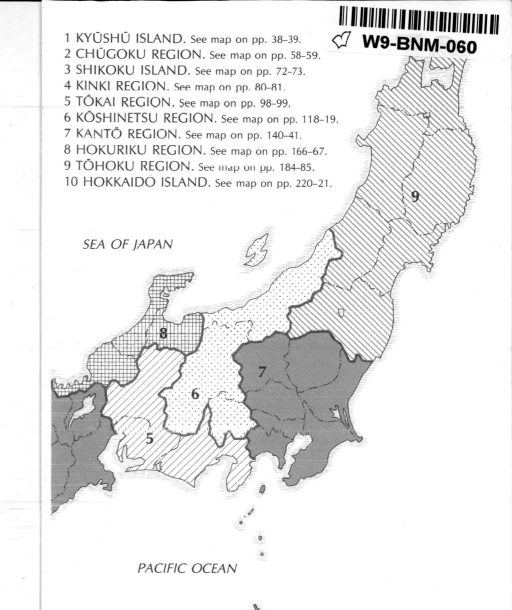

SEA OF JAPAN

PACIFIC OCEAN

MAP OF JAPAN

A Guide to
JAPANESE HOT SPRINGS

A Guide to
JAPANESE
HOT SPRINGS

by Anne Hotta
with Yoko Ishiguro

KODANSHA INTERNATIONAL
Tokyo • New York • London

Note on name order: Japanese personal names are given in the Japanese order—with surname first—except in the preface and on the title page.

The front cover shows a riverside pool at Takaragawa Hot Spring superimposed with the Japanese characters for *onsen* (hot spring). The back cover shows an indoor bath at Hōshi Hot Spring.

Photo credits: jacket, front, Dandy Photo; back, Heibonsha; 1, 3, Bon Color; 2, 6, 8, 9, 11, Fujitake Shōei, 4, Sekai Bunka Photo; 5, 7, 12, Japan Travel Bureau; 10, Koshinoyu.

Maps by Kojima Michio

Distributed in the United States by Kodansha America, Inc., 575 Lexington Avenue, New York, N.Y. 10022, and in the United Kingdom and continental Europe by Kodansha Europe Ltd., 95 Aldwych, London WC2B 4JF. Published by Kodansha International Ltd., 17-14 Otowa 1-chome, Bunkyo-ku, Tokyo 112-8652, and Kodansha America Inc.

LCC 85-40066
ISBN 0-87011-7203
ISBN 4-7700-1220-9 (in Japan)

First edition, 1986
99 00 01 02 15 14 13 12

CONTENTS

PREFACE

You might imagine writing a guide to Japanese hot springs meant a lot of sitting around in thermal tubs sipping from cups of saké as they floated past on waterproof trays. That's not quite the case, although if you chose your springs carefully you could dip your way around a lot of Japan in such select surroundings. Hot-spring bathing is one of the great pleasures of the Japanese and one of the country's best offerings—it was primarily this which prompted me to do something about getting foreign visitors into the tubs of Japan.

A rough calculation shows that if you visited one hot spring a week, it would take forty years or so to sample them all—a daunting fact that proved a major problem in selecting springs to include in the book. How does one choose from the more than two thousand possibilities, a figure that doesn't include the vastly different bathing facilities offered by the various inns and hotels in each area? As you'll see, less than ten percent have been included. These were selected according to location, type of bath, and personal experience. I have tried to cover all the main hot-spring areas, the main types of baths (both indoor and out, natural and man-made), and springs in areas foreigners frequently visit, since many travelers will fit a spring into their travel plans but not vice versa. This means springs near sites of cultural, scenic, and historical interest have been specially included. As further enticement, medicinal waters, quiet, remote springs, and those suited to first-time dippers have also been covered.

This book couldn't have been written unaided. (Forty years is a bit long to spend on research!) My deepest appreciation goes to my friend and collaborator Yoko Ishiguro, whose unstinting research and support made the project feasible. Without her native sense of what should be and her knowledge of Japan, a far less accurate interpretation of this aspect of Japanese culture would have resulted. To her go all the gratitude words can muster.

Two more people played a vital role in advising and insuring accuracy throughout. I wish to thank Fuyuto Noguchi and Setsuko Takemura of Gendai Ryokō Kenkyūjo for giving their knowledge and time so generously to this project. Their many years of visiting and writing about hot springs have made them unrivaled experts in the field. They only ask that foreign visitors come to know Japan better by knowing hot springs better.

To Chinami Ebina, Peter Goodman, Martin Roth, and Jules Young I would also like to express gratitude for their enthusiasm and advice. When all the logistics had been worked through and the manuscript written, an expert hand was needed to put it together for publication. Fortunately for us, Pamela Pasti, our editor, was given the task. Not only did she work above and beyond the call of duty, but she never let us think we'd embarked on an impossible task. Her support and professional assistance made the out-of-the-tub research a far less arduous undertaking.

Finally, behind the scenes, there were two husbands (Shigeru and Jōji) and three children who had to take a lot of baths, wait for a lot of meals, and generally put up with all that goes with involuntary involvement in such a project. Yoko and I greatly appreciate their understanding.

Even if the first bath leaves you overheated, red-faced, exhausted, and tingling, don't despair. Relax, have a beer, and wait 30 minutes. Then take another peek in the mirror. There will be a radiant, wrinkle-free (or at least stress-free), new person determined to spend much of his or her spare time bath-hopping about Japan.

Here's to tubbing and all its trappings! Never let it be said that the frazzles of Japan can assault your nerves unchallenged!

1. Riverside bathing in rock pools at Meotobuchi Hot Spring (98).▶

2. One of seven outdoor pools at Renge Hot Spring (81),
a favorite among hikers.

3. An open-air bath at Nakabusa Hot
Spring (72) in the Japan Alps.

4. Outdoor bathing by a pounding river
at Yunotaira Hot Spring (87).

5, 6. The central riverside pool at Takaragawa Hot Spring (90), said to have the best outdoor baths in Japan—in winter (*above*) and autumn (*right*).

12

7. The high-ceilinged communal bathhouse at rustic Hōshi Hot Spring (89).

8. The medicinal waters of Tarutama Hot Spring (12) at the foot of Mount Aso.

9. A steamy open-air bath set in a traditional Japanese garden at Yumura Hot Spring (37).

10. A jungle bath at Katsuura
Hot Spring (42).

11. A bath with a bay view at Katsuura Hot Spring (42), one of many springs on tiny Nakanoshima Island.

12. Attendants covering "bathers" with thermally heated sand at Ibusuki Hot Spring (7).

1
THE
BATHER'S
HANDBOOK

THE GODS' BATHHOUSE

A Brief History

*Cleanliness is one of the few original items
of Japanese civilization. Almost all other
Japanese institutions have their root in
China but not tubs.*
—Basil Hall Chamberlain,
Things Japanese, 1890

On the surface there's barely a ripple; everything is calm and reassuring.
This is Japan. Underneath, things are brewing, bubbling, getting ready to
surface. This is also Japan—the fragile chain of volcanic islands that plays
wary host to twenty thousand thermal springs. With two massive volcanic
zones—the east and west belts—straddling practically the whole country,
Japan perches gingerly atop the Ring of Fire (circum-Pacific mobile belt).
But the inhabitants of the land dedicated to the fire of the sun above (the
Sun Goddess, Amaterasu, was worshiped as the "grandmother" of the first
mythical emperor of Japan and the sun was revered as the highest Shinto
deity) made the best of their thermal fires below. No nation more respects
the attainment of a bodily state likened to that of "boiled octopus" (*yude-
dako*), and no people are more devoted to the rituals of cleanliness and tub
camaraderie. Indeed, the Japanese have often been called *ofuroholics*, or
bath fanatics.

It's hard to say how far back the discovery and subsequent use of thermal
springs go in Japan. Some myths tell of the gods splashing about, and there
are ancient stories about springs like Dōgo (in Shikoku), Arima (Hyōgo Prefecture), and Shirahama (Wakayama Prefecture). Apparently the indigenous
Ainu people used springs for healing: their legends are associated with many
thermal areas. But since their lore and culture were only transmitted orally,
there's no written account of when or how they took to dipping.

Although human beings played a large part in the development of thermal springs (called *onsen* in Japanese), animals also did their bit. In fact, from one side of the globe to the other, observers ranging from kings to swineherds were all equally fascinated by the antics of animals that rolled about in foul-smelling mud and steam trying to relieve smarting wounds. In Japan such animals, and birds as well, were often called messengers from the gods, come to show man where the healing, purifying waters were. From the majestic white heron dipping daintily to the brown bear splashing clumsily, animals must be given credit for many hot-spring discoveries. Many of these first bathers have been enshrined and ornament the rooftops and lobbies of bathhouses today.

Even when they were afraid of the bubbling mud in oozing gray pools, human beings were able to overcome their fear long enough to find that the more approachable pools of hot water could heal their bodies, clean their clothes, and cook their food. Later, of course, they realized the miraculous waters could also purge their souls. But never did they take these places for granted; hot springs were always revered for the sacred, god-given waters they were. Even today these ideas are preserved in the religious statues overlooking some springs and in rituals, such as the presentation of hot water to the shrine spirits at the Nasu Yumoto spring, that show the links of man and nature and the respect due to one from the other.

In A.D. 552, Buddhism was introduced into Japan. Buddhism and bathing were natural bedfellows. Like Shinto, this religion taught purification through immersion; not only would the body be rid of the sins that plague the flesh, but sevenfold luck would be bestowed upon the cleansed bather. At this time the custom of charity baths began, further linking the spring and the temple. Famous as the saint of charity baths is Empress Kōmyō, an eighth-century lady who spent a lot of time bent over the gnarled, hideous forms of beggars, washing them. Old prints show her in Hokkeji Temple, in Nara, immersed in her act of charity, her voluminous black hair cascading to the bathhouse floor. It was a time when hosts could cleanse their guests' bodies and souls and carry out a pious act, all in the same tub.

Meanwhile, out-of-doors, Buddhist and Shinto priests climbing about the mountains in search of enlightenment and remote places in which to pray were also instrumental in discovering and promoting hot springs. It's not clear which or how many springs they actually discovered since townsfolk loved to name their springs after these revered men. Three who were particularly well known were Kōbō Daishi, Gyōki, and En no Ozuno. Their teachings and names are foremost in the annals of hot springs. These men were often led to thermal sites by supernatural creatures that came to them in dreams as they lay napping by the wayside. Lowlier folk also had such visions, sometimes seeing an image of Buddha himself.

But by no means has bathing always been an entirely sober, religious undertaking. Warm water makes even the most pious men smile and stretch out, especially if a chilly wind whistles around the bath or mounds of icy snow roll right down to the edge of the pool. And it seems that people bereft of their clothes and other trappings can't help but unwind, however serious their bathing intentions. So the bath was naturally a happy, social place where tired farmers, fed-up fishermen, and gossip-starved mountain dwellers got together and whiled away the hours in a spirit of warmth and bonhomie. The roads leading to hot-spring towns saw many a holiday maker, his rice and *miso* (bean paste), pots and pans, and bedding weighing him down as he wended his way to a long-awaited soak. Such people lodged at inns and healed their weary bodies and souls in the baths for as long as farm chores would allow. There was no place on earth quite like the bath with friends.

Poor folk weren't the only ones who were partial to a spot of soaking. Many springs proudly exhibit the tub that held the water that cleansed the emperor of some century past. Daimyo, samurai, and shogunate officials all liked to slip off to select springs to heal their battered bodies or egos. One such warrior was the great daimyo Takeda Shingen (1521–73), who kept several springs for the exclusive use of his men. Off-the-track springs are still known as *Shingen no kakushi yu* (Shingen's hidden baths).

To cope with the social chaos of classes mixing in the bathhouse, some hot springs had separate baths for the samurai, who weren't keen on tubbing with the merchant class at the bottom of the social ladder. In farming areas or fishing villages such problems didn't really arise. In fact, in general, people of the same class naturally went to the same bathhouse. Men and women were not segregated, however, and even if a bit of peeking did go on, it never caused the havoc it did in the West. The bathhouse frolics of Victorian England (and Europe) left Japan unscathed—so natural, neutral, and everyday was the custom of mixed bathing. Men who wanted women to bathe and service them in the bathhouses could hire female attendants, but there were private baths or other rooms in the bathhouse building set aside for this purpose.

This situation didn't last however. In 1853 the West, in the form of Commodore Matthew Perry from America, dropped anchor. Some of Perry's men looked in on the local bathhouses and emerged shaken and horrified. By 1870 "wrong" was righted and a law prohibiting mixed bathing was enacted. Tubs were divided and bath inspectors were dispatched to check the new designs. This proved to be a difficult task; some bathhouse proprietors couldn't afford to build partitions and others couldn't afford to offend their patrons, many of whom couldn't fathom the new law. When inspectors drew near, logs and pieces of rope were thrown across the water, giving women one-third and men two-thirds of the space. This sufficed until the logs and the inspectors drifted off and things returned to normal.

Nowadays segregated bathing is the norm, except in remote country areas and outdoor pools (again ones off the beaten path). Young Japanese women in particular no longer relish the thought of sharing their bath water with men, and despite what popular magazines or television may show, all-in-together is not generally the case. The West will have to wait; the laws they once enforced, and now may wish they hadn't, will take a long time, if not for ever, to change back again.

The twentieth century has seen big changes in Japanese hot springs. The coming of the charter bus, the bullet train (Shinkansen), the all-inclusive weekend package tour, and affluence have all had considerable impact on the development of thermal regions. Resort springs began the drive to attract city workers as early as the 1920s. Their success is well known. Hakone and Izu near Tōkyō, Arima near Ōsaka, and Jōzankei near Sapporo were some of the areas that began catering to large groups of primarily men, bent on sweating the city and company protocol out of their pores in thermal baths over the weekend. Traditional Japanese inns, or ryokan, at these resorts became fortresses guarded by rows of buses waiting patiently for their white-collar warriors to return from their well-deserved R and R.

The fierce competition among these establishments means that many hot springs today resemble the spa playgrounds of fashionable nineteenth-century England and Europe—minus the debutantes and their matchmaking mamas. Accommodations are luxurious, meals (especially dinner) are sumptuous affairs where the middle-aged warrior, his stomach protruding impressively over the hip sash of his cotton kimono, sits and eats and drinks with no thought of calories or cholesterol. Geisha move about, lighting cigarettes, singing, dancing, flattering, and cajoling until the worries of work and home have all disappeared and just the glow of camaraderie and good living remains.

Japanese springs are heading in several directions at the moment. The above-mentioned pleasure resorts are expanding their exotica and après-bath activities (night entertainment, sports facilities, and the like) in the hope of boosting business. Medicinal springs are also increasing in number as the health benefits of mineral water are reassessed, and combinations of both pleasure and medicine are being offered as a third alternative.

Around the world hot springs and spas are gaining popularity as places for physical and mental rehabilitation. In Japan, people suffering from nervous disorders, skin complaints, stomach problems, arthritis, and rheumatism are being referred to hot-spring hospitals by local doctors. Based on German models of recuperation in a total environment, some Japanese springs are now offering programs of coordinated bathing routines, exercise, and relaxation in calm, beautiful surroundings conducive to complete rest. These places are called *kuahausu* (from the German "kurhaus"), and there are many all over Japan. Below is a list of kurhaus:

Futtsu Kankō Hotel (Chiba Pref.) (0439)87-2111
Goten (Yamagata Pref.) (0237)56-3351
Hotel Kunitomi (Nagano Pref.) (0255)57-2111
Kakeyu (Nagano Pref.) (02684)4-2131
Kikusuikan (Shizuoka Pref.) (05583)2-1018
Listel Inawashiro (Fukushima Pref.) (0242)66-2233
Meitetsu Sunnyland (Mie Pref.) (05944)5-1122
Nozawa (Nagano Pref.) (0269)85-3184
Getō Onsenkan (Iwate Pref.) (0197)64-6989
Shirakawagō (Gifu Pref.) (05769)5-2314
Takenoyu (Nagano Pref.) (0261)72-4832
Tochiomata (Niigata Pref.) (02579)5-2216

It's hard to say whether the younger generations will continue to be lured to springs, given the choice of leisure pursuits available today. But providing the custom of bathing doesn't yield to the three-minute shower, the diminishing size of apartment baths might drive younger Japanese back to the more roomy hot-spring baths. Current health booms are also working for hot springs. Not that it's such a problem: every year an estimated hundred million people check in at hot-spring ryokan or hotels in Japan, so there's no need to pull the plug out yet!

SAND, STEAM, SALT, OR SULPHUR

Types of Baths

A hot-spring bath can cure anything but love.
—Kusatsu folksong

Natural thermal baths are found in all sorts of places in Japan: from the heights of Takamagahara, 2,284 meters above sea level in Toyama Prefecture, to sandy beaches in Beppu and Ibusuki in Kyūshū. Springs emerge from flowing rivers and dry riverbeds, out of the sides of mountains, up from the floors of deep ravines, out of rocks on the beach, from fields of snow, sand, or ash, out of urban backyards, from caves, from cliff faces. The site is rarely volcanic gray, powdery, and spooky, like something out of a science-fiction movie; rather it's usually in idyllic, scenic environs, further enhancing the delights of bathing. If you keep an eye on the weather and falling leaves or blossoms, it's impossible to go wrong aesthetically when you choose a hot spring in Japan. Even pleasure resorts have quiet nooks and ryokan offering garden settings and views, especially those off the main thoroughfares. The wealth of options can be overwhelming. Not only must you choose among the reds of autumn, the pinks of spring, and the greens of summer as a backdrop, but you have to decide on the kind of thermal water your body and spirit most need. The kinds of bath water are nearly as diverse as their settings.

A good place to start is with the Japanese description and classification system for hot springs. Nowadays the temperature is not taken into account when defining a spring as a spring. What counts is whether it has a certain chemical composition—namely, at least one constituent from a group of nineteen, at or above a fixed proportion. The group includes gases as well as dissolved minerals. Thermal water can be artificially produced but it isn't as efficacious as natural spring water. In Japan there are over two thousand spring areas, all of which produce thermal water of different composition and temperature.

Once a spring is classified as a spring it is further grouped according to temperature: over 42° C (108° F) is "very hot," 34°–42° C (93°–108° F) is "hot," 25°–34° C (77°–93° F) is "warm," and under 25° C (77° F) is "cool." The temperatures are hotter on the average than in Europe. Water is also classified by pH according to its osmotic pressure in relation to the amount of solutes it contains and its freezing point, and then classified as acidic, neutral, or alkaline. A further grouping according to the softness of the water—soft or hard—indicates whether it is good or bad for delicate skins. After this, all that remains is a closer analysis of its chemical content. The categories used in this book are: sodium chloride, simple thermal, carbon-dioxated, hydrogen carbonate, sulphate, sulphur, acidic, iron, and radio-active. The chemical content determines a spring's therapeutic value —what maladies or physical complaints it helps remedy.

Most thermal water in Japan is sodium chloride or simple thermal. This water heats the body very effectively, is good for digestive problems when imbibed, and helps those suffering from hypertension. A lot of thermal water also falls in the category alkaline, which is good for the skin. Iron works on the blood, especially women's, and sulphur on the bronchial tubes. Sulphur is also of some assistance to those plagued with syphilis. (See Appendix 1 for a detailed listing of other health benefits of the various water types.) There's a lot of research yet to be done on the medicinal properties of thermal waters, although it's widely accepted that bathing in hot springs is mentally relaxing and physically rejuvenating. This is quite pertinent when treating patients who no longer feel any relief from conventional medication. The Japan Health and Research Institute in Tokyo (3274-2861) offers free counseling to those considering thermal-water cures. Certainly you must take cures with a grain of salt; don't expect miracle cures in just two days.

A short cut to understanding the more scientific side of thermal water is to examine the name of the hot spring, which quite often contains a reference to the type of water. Slimy alkaline waters, for example, are often named *unagiyu*, or "eel water." Iron springs, which can turn your towel a reddish orange, often contain *aka* (red) somewhere in their names—for example, Akakura or Akagawa. Salty water could mean a name like Shiobara, Shio-no-yu, or Enzan, since *shio* and *en* mean salt. *Hari* (needle) implies the water pricks, *atsu* means it'll be hot, and references to parts of the body will mean the water is good for illnesses or aches in these areas. *Me-no-yu* is for your eyes (*me*), and *ta-no-yu* will cure ringworm (*ta mushi*).

Then there are the less scientific, more romantic waters where beautiful women with milk white skin and red, cupid's-bow mouths bathed. These springs claim their water will make you beautiful too (*bijin-ni-naru yu*). Likewise, *wakagaeri-no-yu* is the magic water of eternal youth. So a lot of the work has been done for you. Read the name carefully, consult your body, and see which bath you both need.

Once you've considered the setting and the water, there's only one more question to resolve—how you want to experience the water you've selected. Do you fancy the pummeling of a hot cascade (*takiyu*) and its very thorough massage? Or do you like the sound of the waves on the shore and the taste of sea air? If so, you need the sand bath (*sunayu*), which sees you buried in warm, snuggly, mineral-rich sand. A bit more exotic-minded? Then possibly the "body facial" is for you—the mud bath (*doroyu*), where you stick encased in gray, clinging mud and concentrate on smooth skin. A bath that is a bit more familiar and not so sticky is the steam bath (*mushiyu*), which is much like a sauna. In the past there was also the do-it-yourself "hot spring": herbs, heated stones, and ordinary water all thrown into a trough.

The most exciting bath, if you can take it, is like that found at Kusatsu in Gunma Prefecture. It is the time bath (*jikan-yu*)—a bath so hot it must be stirred for half an hour by attendants, who sing and beat the water rhythmically with long boards until it's time for the bathers to make a will and get in. Once in, you can scream, chant, curse, or do whatever you like to try to forget the heat. (Keeping still helps everyone stay "cooler.") But you can't get out until 3 minutes are up. Obviously you will emerge the boiled lobster—spanking red—but you'll soon recover, usually just in time for the next round! This bath will probably send you off in search of a sub-thermal bath where the water is relatively cool and you can sit comfortably for hours, or even all night long if you want.

If you tire of "serious" bathing and feel like something a bit more decadent, rest assured: there are so many possibilities you could spend a lifetime bathing on the wild side. Such possibilities include baths in cable cars, baths entered via slippery dips or waterfall curtains, and baths constructed about whirlpools, Jacuzzi-type tubs, and fountains. You can sit and contemplate fish flitting around in floor-to-ceiling aquariums or traditional gardens landscaped to the bath's edge. Some tubs meander through simulated jungle tangles or through caves, around statues, under shrine gates—all designed to tempt you in. With special lighting effects, taped music, floating trays bearing saké and nibbles, there's not much missing.

It all adds up to two things: every bath is unique and anything you desire is bound to exist somewhere in Japan. So provided you don't expect your spare tire to float away, your complexion to become baby-soft overnight, and your old football injuries to immediately drown themselves, you won't be disappointed wherever you bathe.

To help you choose from the many types of baths and bathing environments, the symbols below are used at the beginning of hot-spring entries in this book. (Note that on Japanese maps and signs, the most common symbol for a hot spring is ♨ .) Bear in mind that many hot springs offer a wide variety of bathing facilities, so that, when you go, you may find other types of baths in addition to those indicated.

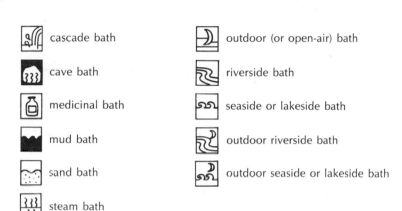

cascade bath

cave bath

medicinal bath

mud bath

sand bath

steam bath

outdoor (or open-air) bath

riverside bath

seaside or lakeside bath

outdoor riverside bath

outdoor seaside or lakeside bath

HELP!

Making Travel Plans

*If landscape beauty is to be regarded as a
factor in hot spring cure[s], then Japan is un-
questionably a country most abundantly
blessed.*

—K. Fujinami,
Hot Springs in Japan, 1936

Once you've worked up the courage and curiosity to try a hot spring, how
do you get from your apartment to the tub? If you've read this far, you know
what kind of spring and bath you would like and now it's a matter of zoom-
ing in on one of the several hundred possibilities. Just what sort of town
and in what kind of place do you want to be?

Think of sites near the sea, up in the mountains, on riverbanks, areas with
sports facilities, cultural nooks, religious sites, festival seasons, culinary once-
in-a-lifetimes, regional arts and crafts, and so on. The aim is to get the best
possible combination of personal interests, visual panoramas, and appealing bath water. Provided it's not peak season and your dream destination
isn't the same as several thousand other bathers', you're ready to reserve
your room.

Congestion is an important consideration, particularly if you're thinking
of traveling to areas near major cities. Not only can road traffic complicate
getting to your destination before the weekend is over, but it can mean tubs
overflowing with bodies, and crowded, expensive accommodations—all of
which herald disaster where quiet, long-awaited holidays are concerned.

There is no lack of lodgings at most Japanese springs except during the
peak seasons, summertime, and the New Year holiday. Depending on the
size of the spring and town, the choices will range from deluxe Western
and Japanese hotels or inns (ryokan) to minshuku (pension-type accommodations with a family), kokuminshukusha (government-sponsored lodges), and

youth hostels. The last three don't always have thermal water piped in even in big resort areas. But you can lodge and eat at the cheaper accommodations and go elsewhere to bathe—public baths, where available, cost about ¥250 to enter and many large ryokan and hotels allow the public to use their tubs for around ¥500 or less before 5:00 P.M. This type of arrangement extends your options to staying at business hotels and campsites as well. It would be wise, however, to limit your public bathing to the baths recommended in this text or make inquiries about the baths at the local tourist office or at your hotel, youth hostel, or whatever; public baths have not always been kept up and can be dirty and dilapidated, the haunts of loyal local folk only. To avoid disappointment or worse, ask for details about unknown and out-of-the-way public baths. Many are the best places to bathe in town, but quite a few are not.

Costs for lodgings of the same standard don't vary much throughout Japan. On weekdays during the off-season, the simpler table fare and availability of smaller rooms will reduce costs for those on budgets. You can negotiate the cost yourself at the local reservation center or at the inn door, but it is not possible to do this through city reservation offices or tourist agencies. You can often get discounts by saying, for example, you'll settle for a small room, a room with no view, or no meals. The best hotels or ryokan, or combinations of both (ryokan that offer Western bedrooms in a traditional Japanese setting), start from around ¥10,000 (including breakfast and dinner) and go up and up. Just once, though, every bather should experience the service, facilities, atmosphere, and table fare of a first-class ryokan. It's an unforgettable experience. Ryokan of "lesser" standards are priced accordingly, with some almost as cheap as minshuku—about ¥4,000. Kokumin-shukusha range around ¥4,000 and include two meals and service as do all of the above. Business hotels start at ¥5,000 (meals excluded). Youth hostels and campgrounds are the cheapest and vary according to the facilities provided. Note that while credit cards are often accepted in cities and at the more expensive hotels and ryokan, you should plan to pay in cash at smaller or remote inns.

If you want a touch of the past, an old ryokan is probably the best choice. These Japanese inns have a long tradition of serving hot-spring visitors. Many new, modern ones are, like Western hotels, very comfortable and may be good places for beginners since there are many signs in English and the staff isn't afraid of foreigners. In the following chapters specific accommodations are recommended, and you will find a complete list of their names, addresses (in English and Japanese), telephone numbers, and price ranges in Appendix 2. The same appendix also lists major tourist and minshuku information centers to help those not wanting to deal directly with a ryokan. Wherever you go, however, you'll find local offices able to supply information and arrange accommodations. City tourist offices will do all this too, but you must know what you want. Personnel in these offices will not give personal recommendations or try to influence you, even when you're dying for someone to make a decision for you. All questions are answered but extra information is rarely volunteered.

If time is not a problem and it's not summer, the New Year holiday, or festival time, there's nothing wrong with finding a place to stay when you actually get off the train. Station squares, newsstands, and passers-by are always fountains of travel information and may be your only source if there's no local tourist, minshuku, or ryokan center in the town. Sign language and neck and face contortions will suffice when your Japanese fails or when the local dialect doesn't sound like Japanese at all. Or turn to the mini-language guide in Appendix 3, which is tailored to fit such hot-spring dilemmas.

DON'T PULL OUT THE PLUG!

Etiquette

Hadaka to hadaka no tsukiai.
(Bathing buddies are the best of friends.)
—Japanese saying

You've found the right ryokan in the right town, checked in, finished your welcome cup of green tea and rice crackers, and are eagerly anticipating a look at the bath you've heard so much about. The maid chatters on, pointing this way and that. You catch the word *"furo"* (bath) and try to connect it to one of her gestures. Suddenly she bows low, shuffles to the door, and slips out, leaving you no better informed on how to get to the bath. You're on your own and unless you want to use the small, plain-water tub *en suite,* you'll have to locate that *furo!*

A good place to start is with your yukata—literally, "bath (*yu*) garment (*kata*)." (*Yu* also means hot water or hot springs, so it is commonly used in hot-spring names.) This starched, cotton robe will be together with a small hand towel on the tatami-mat floor or in the closet. (The towel is yours to keep but don't pack the yukata.) This is the most comfortable way to go to and from the bath and saves struggling with bits and pieces of Western dress when you're overheated and exhausted. Now, armed with your hand towel (a very valuable possession as you will soon see), shampoo, a bath towel for your hair, a toothbrush, and any other après-bath secrets you use, you're set for the bath. Moisture lotions are not necessary, as spring water doesn't dry out your skin, providing you don't wash it off with tap water. If you have a *furoshiki* (a square cloth) you can use it as it was meant to be used—for carrying things to the bathhouse. It was also used as a wraparound skirt in emergencies. In the corridor look for these signs:

Bath: 浴室 yokushitsu or 風呂 furo

For men: 男性 dansei or 大浴場 daiyokujō

For women: 女性 josei

Family bath: 家族風呂 kazoku-buro

Usually baths are in the basement or on the first floor. If you can't smell the sulphur or see the steam, look for people with red faces and clinging wet hair and ask them or guess where they came from. There are always plenty of such people wandering the maze of passageways many ryokan include in the price of bed, breakfast, and dinner.

Large ryokan often have a "family" bath for the use of small groups. No questions will be asked if your family consists of you and your other half; as long as the room is empty, it can be used by anyone. In a minshuku, you'll use the proprietor's bath if it's a small establishment. If it's bigger there will be segregated baths. Nowadays, as previously mentioned, most baths are segregated. The women's is the smaller, less ornate one. If you're way off the beaten track or thinking of dipping outdoors, or in a place that has a large pavilion-type enclosure, then you might want to find out whether the entrances marked "women" and "men" actually lead to the same pool where male and female aren't separated at all. If you don't like all-in-together surprises, it's best to check before reserving or checking in (or worse still, emerging unawares through the entrance). *"Naka wa kon-yoku desu ka?"* (Is it mixed bathing?) should get a shake or a nod for you to decipher. One alternative for the modest bather is the hot-spring swimming pool—the only type of mineral pool where clothing (a swimsuit) is required.

Once in the dressing room, place your clothes and belongings in an empty clothes basket or on a shelf. (Jewelry shouldn't go near the bathroom; the metal could tarnish or alter chemically.) After shedding your yukata, place your hand towel strategically (about where you see the black spot in censored films in Japan), take your shampoo, and head for the steam. If you're foreign you might have all eyes on your entrance and it can be a bit daunting. Sometimes there's a falter in the across-the-bath conversation, especially in country towns. With all the heat and billowing vapor you may be momentarily thrown off balance and even consider a fast exit, but don't—the feeling passes. Locate the hand dippers and stools, and take one of each in an assured manner. By this time no one will be obviously interested in you and you can commence the serious business of washing, unperturbed. If you feel cold or the hand showers or taps are crowded and you have to wait a bit, you can sit near the bath and splash yourself and then get in to warm up. Many Japanese bathers do this prior to washing themselves.

To wash, sit on your stool in front of a tap and use your hand towel like a washcloth. You can use water straight from the tub if you like, but never let soap suds get near the bath water. Japanese people take quite a lot of time to wash themselves, so if you can, spin the scrubbing out a bit . . . it makes you look like an old hand. Don't wash out your undies or brush your teeth in the bath room. Such activities should be done in your room or in the dressing room. Shaving your legs is all right, though you'll rarely see a Japanese woman do it. After you've scrubbed for what seems like forever, rinse away your suds, rinse and replace your dipper and stool, and you're ready for the real thing.

Ease yourself in gently if you're worried about the temperature. (Your hand towel wrung out and placed on your head or forehead will supposedly stop you from fainting.) Now is the time to unwind, forget about your cares, lose yourself in the scenery, whether inside or out, and reap all the benefits a hot-spring bath offers. There may be a waterfall to try or a bubble bath or a pool of an unusual color. When you get too hot or bored you should move somewhere different. This is when many foreigners wonder what to think about next and wonder how Japanese people can spend so long just sitting in the bath. If you've exhausted the walls, ceiling, and fellow bathers, and have nothing to look at and can only think of getting out, then that's all you can do. This is one reason why you shouldn't bathe alone—the pleasures of bathing with friends are among those which Japanese people have always found most enjoyable. The bath is also a place where you can start up conversations with strangers without worrying about standing on ceremony. If your Japanese prohibits this, then you need a friend or you're stuck talking to yourself. (I once heard a foreign couple having a conversation back and forth over the top of the partition separating the men's bath from the women's. It's one possibility, but secrets spilled in the bathhouse have undone many a bather. . . .)

When enough is enough, it's time to get out. Three baths in twenty-four hours is recommended. Don't wash or shower the mineral water off; just wipe yourself with the wrung-out hand towel. This will help soften your skin. You probably feel drained and will stagger back to your room and collapse on the tatami floor with a cold beer or some mineral water until dinner time. (People with high blood pressure, pregnant women, children under one, and people with certain skin problems should seek a doctor's advice before taking hot-spring baths.)

Before closing the subject of bathroom etiquette, let me add one final word of reassurance. Those, women in particular, who dread being scrutinized in the bath room should know that some Japanese feel it too. The stares many of you provoke as a fair nymph soaping up in a room full of your dark, usually slimmer, Oriental sisters are not meant to offend. They're generally just the result of natural curiosity, which soon passes, especially if you can make some remark about the temperature of the water or the weather outside. If you like to bathe in silence and not discuss the merits of spas in your own country, then a smile and an "I'm not much of a talker, at least in Japanese" look on your face will lighten the atmosphere, and you can settle back and relax. I have never found this aspect of bathing in Japan to be a real problem. I don't know what goes on regarding this in the men's bath, but I've heard stories about comparisons being made between the races in the tub!

Next let's consider ryokan etiquette. Ryokan at hot springs are somewhat different from other Japanese inns. The atmosphere in the surrounding town is quite informal and the streets are often splashed with the blue and white of ryokan yukata, since guests like to go out walking after their baths. Wearing your *tanzen* or *haori* (topcoat) if it's cool outdoors and the geta (wooden clogs) waiting at the inn's entrance, you should try it. It'll revive you in preparation for a typically grand ryokan dinner and, later, another bath. Ryokan and minshuku serve dinner early, usually around six o'clock.

Ryokan at hot springs are the venues for everything from weddings to weekend study sessions, but their main purpose is to serve as a place where people can let their hair down. This is sometimes done with a vengeance, so if you can't outsing the group next door (who are armed with a microphone and taped music), then try the bath again, and when that wears off just remember that carousing is a universal custom that goes way back and you can't fight it. Put your head under the futon cover and think quiet thoughts.

Often ryokan staff will try to Westernize things for you—bedding, food, where you eat (dining room instead of your own room), and so on. If you don't want this to happen, make it clear from the beginning that you want the usual treatment. Of course if you don't like raw egg, rice, and soy sauce for breakfast, join a lot of the Japanese guests and have toast with ham and eggs instead.

Happy soaking! May your wrinkles float away with your worries and may you emerge refreshed and closer to the heart of Japan!

2
THE
HOT
SPRINGS

1 KYŪSHŪ ISLAND

Colorful Gateway to Japan

Blue: Blue is the sea which shimmering and bold seems ever present in Kyu-shū. Whether as the haven for the scraggly, magnificent Amakusa Islands or as the cool edge to the hot, steamy southern coasts, it begs for attention. Not that it's always nice: annually typhoons sweep through Kyūshū wreaking havoc. Kagoshima is known as Typhoon Ginza (_Taifū Ginza_), such a thoroughfare is this area for these natural menaces. On the other hand, it was a typhoon that sent Kubla Khan and his invading ships back home in 1281. That particular typhoon was called _kamikaze_—the divine wind.

The sea also carried in visitors who blessed and cursed Japanese soil over the centuries. Merchants from Europe came in the sixteenth century and missionaries arrived soon after. The first Korean potter, Lee Sanpei, was brought to the Arita area in 1592. Many others followed, creating exquisite pottery for the tea ceremony and in time establishing Imari, Karatsu, and Satsuma ware as world-famous ceramics.

Blue is the sky, and from somewhere above Kyūshū came the forebears of Amaterasu, the Sun Goddess, who is credited with founding Japan since it was her grandson who alighted on Mount Takachiho in Kagoshima Prefecture and became the first of the unbroken line of emperors who have ruled the nation.

Red: Red is the blood that has been shed in Kyūshū. When Japan's gates were closed and Christianity banned in the 1600s, the northwestern regions of Kyūshū became battlegrounds for and against the foreign religion and

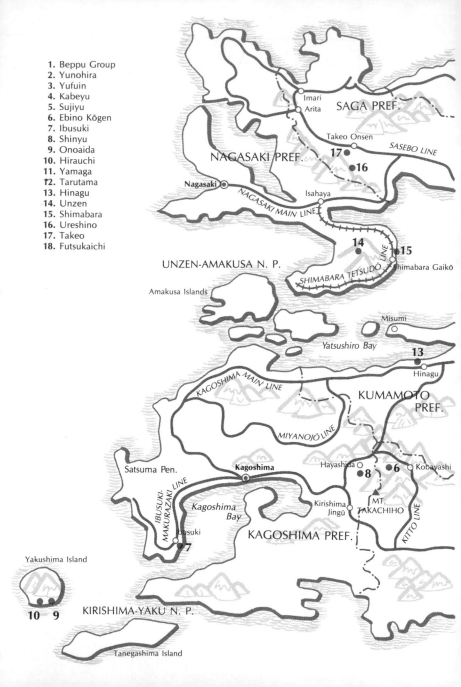

1. Beppu Group
2. Yunohira
3. Yufuin
4. Kabeyu
5. Sujiyu
6. Ebino Kōgen
7. Ibusuki
8. Shinyu
9. Onoaida
10. Hirauchi
11. Yamaga
12. Tarutama
13. Hinagu
14. Unzen
15. Shimabara
16. Ureshino
17. Takeo
18. Futsukaichi

1 KYŪSHŪ ISLAND

Hakata

Fukuoka

18 Futsukaichi

Saga

TŌKAIDŌ-SANYŌ SHINKANSEN

FUKUOKA PREF.

Kurume

NIPPŌ MAIN LINE

Setaka

KYŪDAI MAIN LINE

11

Bungomori

Kumamoto

HŌHI MAIN LINE

4 Era
Hōsenji Bungo-Nakamura
Yamanami Yufuin
Highway 3

12

2

MT. ASO

5 Yunohira

Tateno

OITA PREF.

Aso Shimoda TAKAMORI LINE

1

Beppu

Ōita

Usuki

MIYAZAKI PREF.

NIPPŌ MAIN LINE

Miyazaki

all it stood for. Bloody conflicts broke out, and the persecution that followed was ferocious and thorough. Christianity went underground, and trade with the West was limited to a handful of merchants permitted residence on Dejima Island in Nagasaki Bay.

Ironically, Kyūshū was also a battleground for old customs. In 1877 a force of conservative samurai made their last stand in Kagoshima. Led by Saigō Takamori, these men were protesting their loss of status, income, and way of life that resulted from reforms of the new Meiji government. Their final battle against the government army occurred at Shiroyama, where, rather than surrender, they chose death. A lot is said about this incident. It's often related to the brave, chivalrous nature of present-day men from Kagoshima. To an outsider such Kyūshū attitudes may appear macho and sexist, but recent surveys show that in Kagoshima more women than men think men are superior beings.

Red is fire, and Kyūshū with its summer sun above and thermal fires below is a hot place. Volcanoes like Mount Aso and the one on Sakurajima and the steam spirals of Beppu and Unzen are mind-boggling geothermal sightseeing spots, vivid reminders of the turbulence below. Such dramatic activity in Kyūshū's past, both above and below ground, might explain the character of its inhabitants: emotional, individualistic, and at the same time more easygoing than natives of other parts of Japan.

Green: Green forms the backdrop for some of the most beautiful views of Kyūshū. It lines gorges like Takachiho or contrasts richly with bright red-orange shrine gates, or it slopes down to the sea, merging with the blue. It's gentle on the eyes and sets off the pinks and purples of spring azaleas and the reds of summer hibiscuses.

Gold: Gold flashes about in the numerous festivals where it's part of a dragon costume, or it glitters on lanterns and shrines, also often involved in festival frivolity. In a more somber vein it adorns armor, ceramics, and religious statues.

All the colors appear somewhere on plates in the form of garnishes, morsels, and tidbits to wind your tongue around. Tropical fruit is bright . . . yellow, orange, touches of shiny black. Fish is abundant. In Nagasaki it is served with vegetables on a platter, a sight the eyes don't want the tongue to disturb, so lavish and colorful it is. This dish, called *shippoku*, consists of crabs, prawns, lobster, fish eggs, and red, pink, and silver slices of raw fish. Chinese noodles, distilled liquor (*shōchū*), eel, gigantic radishes, and the succulent undersides of *shiitake* mushrooms make up the white part of Kyūshū's table fare.

1 Beppu Group

LOCATION: Beppu is in Ōita Prefecture on the northeastern coast of Kyū-shū. You can take one of several routes to this city. The Nippō Main Line connects northern Kyūshū cities with Beppu, the Kyūdai Main Line in combination with the Nippō Main Line connects western cities, and ferries travel from mainland Japan to Beppu. By bus you travel from the west to Beppu via the picturesque Yamanami Highway. The Shinkansen (bullet train) connects with the Nippō Main Line, making the trip from Tōkyō a fast one. By air you travel to Ōita Airport, which is near Beppu.

THE WATERS: Beppu is very old and very famous—a real vintage hot-spring area albeit a gaudily packaged one. The waters are sparkling, hot, mineral-rich, and multicolored and work miracles on body, skin, and spirit. There are 3,800 springs and wells at work bubbling in and around Beppu; it is one of the most thermally active places in the world. The Beppu group of springs (*Beppu onsen kyō*) is divided geographically into Beppu proper, Horita, Kannawa, Myōban, Kankaiji, Hamawaki, Shibaseki and Kamegawa. Beppu is a hot-spring buff's water wonderland and, as well, a good place for beginners to hit the water for the first time. Some possibilities: ■ BEPPU KAIHIN SUNAYU: This sand bath (*sunayu*) opened in 1986. It was modeled after the Kamegawa sand bath, which is no longer in operation. Change into a yukata and lie on the sand. While you watch the sea gulls flying overhead, an attendant will shovel sand on top of all but your head. (You may want to tie your locks up with a towel to keep the sand out.) It's certainly a gritty sensation, and hot, so grit your teeth and bear it for a while and then with the attendant's help get out and shower off. The fee, which includes use of a yukata and both sand and hot-water baths, is ¥600. The sand bath is at Shōningahama Beach, about 15 minutes by bus from Beppu Station. The sand bath soothes stiff joints, tired muscles, and frazzled nerves. The best way to top it off is to stretch out on tatami with a cup of green tea. This you can do above the Takegawara sand bath (in Beppu proper). In this indoor sand bath you can see the hot water circling through the sand so you know it's clean, and the women who work here have had many years of experience and know how to pack the sand exactly where you need it. Just tell them what ails you. ■ MYŌBAN: This quiet spring is famous for the giant, melon-sized oranges that float from winter to early spring in the waters of the Okamotoya Ryokan tubs. Called *zabon*, they turn the water into a skin softener and add a nice fruity aroma to the bath. You can also watch them bobbing about if you get bored, though that is unlikely given the scenic outdoor setting of the "orange" tub. Myōban is known for its thatched huts used for collecting sinter, which is sold for making do-it-yourself hot springs in your home bath. Above the thatching, spirals of sulphur fumes rise—another visually appealing touch to this out-of-the-limelight spring. ■ KAN-

NAWA: Kannawa has a steam bath (*mushiyu*) open to the public for a small fee. You crawl into a cavelike chamber and lie on racks covered with *shekishō*. Breathing in steam bearing this herb is said to help your rheumatism and treat your nose. The bath is called Shiei-mushiyu and is in the center of Kannawa. ■ HONBŌZU JIGOKU: Although this bath in the Kannawa area is a mud-pool "hell" (*jigoku*), there is a disguised touch of heaven here in the form of a *doroyu* (mud bath) designed to give your skin a new lease on life. For a minimal fee, you can have a body "facial" in a murky, sticky pool. Put your hair up, keep your face out, and sink down. Don't let the mud dry, as it works best when wet. When you think you've been a bog creature for long enough, get out and wash it off. The more adventurous may want to try the mud at the Hoyōland bathing complex at Kōya Jigoku. There you will find cloudy green baths whose minerals complement mud; they say it's good to follow the gray with the green. ■ EXOTIC BATHING: In the glittering, shimmering tourist resort that is Beppu, there is a mind-boggling array of exotic tubs, some of which you should at least peek into. For a spot of dipping on the wild side you might try the Dream Bath or the Flower Bath at the Suginoi Hotel. For about ¥1,000 you, and one thousand friends (of the same sex), can wallow in a fantasyland of sculptured tubs, rainbow fountains, bubbles, landscaped jungle, and soft lighting. A similar playground for once-in-a-lifetime tubbing is the Hoyōland complex of baths, which also has an open-air communal bath.

AROUND AND ABOUT: Beppu is a fascinating place, with baths even the most foolhardy wouldn't go near. These are the *jigoku*, or "hell," pools—a series of weird and wonderful geothermal eruptions. In this geologist's paradise you can ponder burping, blood-red mud (Chi-no-ike) or water that looks cool and green but is simmering at 85° C (185° F) and is used for boiling eggs (Umi). As well there are geysers that shoot up steaming and punctual daring anyone to stop them (Tatsumaki). It's not all nature's fault, however; when you come to the crocodile hell (Oniyama), the slimy reptile hells, and other hells landscaped with garish caricature-like statues, you realize enterprising man had a hand in creating this hell land. Away from all this drama, there are parts of Beppu (Kannawa is one) having cobbled, winding streets lined with fragile-looking, wooden ryokan that give you the feeling you're in an old, old hot-springs town. Further away still are the mountains, which sit quietly surveying the hubbub that bubbles below.

ACCOMMODATIONS: Beppu has it all—from deluxe Western and Japanese lodgings to minshuku, business hotels, and a youth hostel. Oniyama Hotel and the ryokan Kannawa-en, both in Kannawa, are two good places to stay. The first is modern and in the hills near Yamanami Highway. The second is traditional and has a teahouse and an open-air bath set in a rock garden.

HELL: The concept of *jigoku* was introduced with Buddhism. *Jigoku* consisted of six hells, including one of fire and another of boiling water, so you can imagine the fear that puffs of steam must have caused those who first stumbled across Beppu. In the past, animals and birds often perished near *jigoku*, usually due to the noxious fumes emitted. Even today threats of banishment to the hell places are not taken lightly, especially by children.

2 Yunohira

LOCATION: Yunohira is on the Kagono River near the Handa Highlands in central Ōita Prefecture. From Beppu take the Nippō Main Line to Ōita and then the Kyūdai Main Line. Get off at Yunohira Station and it's another 10 minutes by bus to the spring.

THE WATERS: Yunohira is the oldest potable spring in Japan. Even though it's classified as salty (sodium chloride) the water has a pleasant taste—not at all like drinking brine. Bottling this delicacy is now a lucrative business, rivaling Perrier some say. The bottlers distribute the water throughout the country and receive many letters from grateful drinkers, testimony to its good effects. It treats, among other ailments, indigestion, heartburn, constipation, and gastroenteric complaints. Ryokan proprietors serve this water instead of green tea, and if you drink it with *shōchu* (a Japanese liquor, especially good in Kyūshū), you'll never be hung over the next day. The water here is superb and has always had a good reputation for its medicinal effects, which explains why you'll see the bathers wandering about the town, kettles in hand, stopping to drink at a fountain and swap hot-spring gossip. A poet, Noguchi Ujō (1882–1942), wrote a poem praising the sweet fragrance that lingers on your skin for days after bathing at Yunohira. A favorite bathing village in the Edo period (1603–1868), protected and patronized by high officials, Yunohira is now a registered National Health Resort.

AROUND AND ABOUT: Yunohira is a serene away-from-it-all mountain retreat. Like traditional mountain springs, ryokan and public baths tumble over each other up the sides of twisting, steep streets. Some of the public baths are Kin-no-yu, Gin-no-yu, and Naka-no-yu.

ACCOMMODATIONS: Migimaru Ryokan is small, has good views from the tubs, and welcomes families. Shimizu Ryokan has a cave bath, a Japanese garden, and mountain views from the guests' rooms.

3 Yufuin

LOCATION: Yufuin is in the center of Ōita Prefecture, west of Beppu and near Yunohira (2). It sits at the foot of Mount Yufu on the picturesque Yamanami Highway. Take the Kyūdai Main Line from Ōita to Yufuin Station; then walk 20 minutes. The bus from Beppu takes 40 minutes.

THE WATERS: Like Yunohira, Yufuin goes way back as a medicinal spring.

It has also been a great boon to local women, who have used the hot water for cooking rice and washing clothes. The alkaline simple thermal water now serves several public baths and outdoor pools (*rotenburo*). The temperatures range from 42° C to 65° C (108°–149° F) and are particularly beneficial to those suffering from stress and in need of relaxation. The mineral water here rivals Yunohira's and is a rare vintage. Imbibing is very popular. A public bath worth trying is Shitanyu with its thatched roof and view on one side of Lake Kinrin. Here, as you soak, you can see women washing clothes in the lakeside springs even today. If you want to join them, you can. The cost is about ¥50 for as many loads as you have. The bath, too, is cheap: put ¥100 in the poolside box (payment is on the honor system) and a misty morning bath, or an evening bath lit by fireflies flitting over the lake, is yours.

AROUND AND ABOUT: As part of a strong movement here to preserve the past, the local people oppose high-rise hotels, nightclubs, and the like and urge landowners not to sell their land to city entrepreneurs. Instead, they advise, buy a cow to stave off financial hardship. Tourists are welcome, nevertheless, as long as they settle for small crafts shops (the town's something of a folk-crafts village) in place of sophisticated night life. There is, however, a modern film festival held every summer on the third Wednesday of August, the town's way of getting around building a movie theater and jazz bars, which would have been out of keeping with the traditional atmosphere. With its horse-drawn carriages, thatched roofs, quiet farms, ancient cedar trees, cows, and bamboo crafts, Yufuin is delightful and getting to be the destination of more and more summer holiday-makers. Go now while you can.

■ USUKI: The city Usuki, southeast of Ōita City, boasts a series of sixty Buddhist images (*sekibutsu*) carved into a rock face. It was obviously an important religious site at some time, although no one today is sure of the origins of these stone monuments. ■ RENT-A-BICYCLE: A great way to get around Yufuin! They are ready and waiting for you right near the train station.

ACCOMMODATIONS: Kamenoi Bessō is a series of deluxe cottages, patronized most frequently by writers. A quiet ryokan is Tama-no-yu Ryokan.

4 Kabeyu

LOCATION: This spring is in Ōita Prefecture, near Hōsenji and west of Yunohira (2) and Yufuin (3) springs. Take the Kyūdai Main Line from Ōita to Bungomori (2 hours) and then a bus to Kabeyu—about 30 minutes.

THE WATERS: Kabeyu, a lonely cave bath overhung with ivy and matted green ferns, was presumably found by a deer sometime in the eighteenth century. At first glance the water looks dark and one wonders what lurks inside. But once you're in, looking out down the crystal-clear Machida River, which runs past the cave, everything appears bright and sunny. It's definitely

Mother Nature experimenting with thermal sights. As you sit and soak there's a lot to think about. For example, it's said the bath was used at sunrise every morning by a wrinkled old seer who lived in the nearby mountains. One morning she suddenly disappeared; the local people say she went to heaven directly from the cave bath. Or possibly you'll meet the pretty young girl who comes every day to bathe wearing a white glove. It hides her burned, deformed hand, and like many people, she believes the water is good for burns. (There is a hospital for such patients near Kabeyu.) The simple thermal water contains sodium chloride, which, besides burns, treats rheumatism, neuralgia, and stress. The cave is for mixed bathing; in such a setting anything else would be unnatural.

AROUND AND ABOUT: Verdant in summer and somewhat snowy in winter, this mountain-encircled area is known as the roof of Kyūshū. Hōsenji Hot Spring is a mere kilometer away—handy for when Kabeyu seems a little too remote from things. Not that Hōsenji is very big or brassy. Tradition has it that when the monk Kūya came here he struck the ground with his staff. The staff then grew into a tree, and from its base a hot spring began to gush. People who like the outdoor life might note that very near Hōsenji is the well-known Jizōbaru campsite.

ACCOMMODATIONS: It's simple: there's only one choice in Kabeyu. The ryokan Fukumotoya is a small, no frills place that isn't as expensive as most ryokan. Hōsenji has more to choose from. You can hire fishing gear at Fukumotoya (as well as purchase bath tickets for the cave) and fish in the river while you bathe in the cave.

5 Sujiyu

LOCATION: This spring is very near Kabeyu in the Handa Highlands region of western Ōita Prefecture. To get there, take the Kyudai Main Line from Ōita or Kurume (in the west) to Bungō-Nakamura Station. From there it is 1 hour by bus to the spring.

THE WATERS: The water is very hot: 93° C (199° F) at the point of emission. A good deal of cold water is added before it gets to the tub, however. Containing sulphur and carbon, the water is good for skin complaints and nervous disorders in particular. Because of the voluminous flow, cascade baths (*takiyu*) have been installed. The water is piped in through open bamboo pipes that end just above the bathers' heads. The combination of minerals, heat, and force have made these bathhouse waterfalls very popular with physicians and others treating mental patients. Spas specializing in mental illnesses were usually built in remote, hidden places. In Sujiyu the spring came first and the town followed, mainly to meet the needs of the growing number of people interested in the water's therapeutic benefits. It was, and still is, largely a *tōjiba*—a serious health spa. By positioning your own aches and pains under any of the cascades in any of the three public baths, you'll go a long way toward relief. If you don't ache anywhere, it's still a good way to get a muscle massage.

AROUND AND ABOUT: Sujiyu is nicely positioned in a sunken basin on the plateau where most of the springs in this area are located. Of this Handa Highlands group, it is said that Sujiyu is the most picturesque, especially when viewed from the base of the cascades.

ACCOMMODATIONS: This is a small spring, so accommodations are limited. Asahiya is a small, comfortable inn. For more luxury and somewhat Western-style accommodations try Sujiyu Kankō Hotel.

NIGHT LIFE: There's very little night life and therefore, so the locals say, very few beautiful women in Sujiyu. Beautiful women only appear at night, you see.

6 Ebino Kōgen

LOCATION: This spring is located at the foot of Mount Karakuni, in the middle of Kirishima-Yaku National Park, Miyazaki Prefecture. To get there from Miyazaki take the Nippō Main Line to Kirishima Jingū Station. The spring is 1 hour by bus from the station. The hot spring can also be reached by bus (a 1-hour ride) from Kobayashi Station on the Kitto Line.

THE WATERS: The water is acid-aluminum sulphate and good for just about anything. If you drink it, it will help you conquer digestive troubles, although with the clear mountain air skating on and Lake Byakushi it's hard to see how anyone could be suffering from such problems, especially in winter. In summer, bathers watch birds between baths—again an activity not likely to induce heartburn. The water will also ease your bruises if the ice causes any spills. There is a public bath, near Sainokawara, which is a rock pool.

AROUND AND ABOUT: Kirishima means "Island of Mist" and is an unusual blend of nature's prowess above and below ground. Above ground the mountain peaks rise out of the sulphurous clouds generated below ground. The peaks look like islands in the sea. In winter the view is even more impressive with trees dripping icicles and skaters in bright colors twirling across the ice. This entire area is called Ebino Kōgen and it's a nature park through which you can walk or ride on a bus to gorges, rivers, extinct volcanoes, deer, foxes, birds, and flowers. ■ KIRISHIMA SHRINE: To the south is Kirishima Shrine, originally constructed fourteen hundred years ago and reconstructed several times since. This building, shiny black and bright red with fussy carvings in gold, pink, red, and green, is well worth visiting. The grounds wind about ancient cedars and all is quiet and calming, despite the incredible blend of paints. The shrine is dedicated to Ninigi no Mikoto, a descendant of the Sun Goddess, who chose nearby Takachihonomine as the place to first set foot on Japanese soil.

ACCOMMODATIONS: The main choice is Ebino Kōgen Hotel. There are also a kokuminshukusha and a separate camping village with cabins for summer, though not much else. Ebino Kōgen Hotel's bath is open twenty-four hours a day, and the hotel serves *tengu nabe* (a stew of meat and mountain vegetables).

7 Ibusuki

LOCATION: Ibusuki is on the eastern side of Satsuma Peninsula in Kagoshima Prefecture. To get to this popular honeymoon resort, take the Ibusuki-Makurazaki Line from Kagoshima City to Ibusuki Station. From the station, the various ryokan are a walk or taxi ride away.

THE WATERS: Ibusuki used to be called Yubushuku, or "Inn of Rich Waters." There's still plenty of hot salty water coming out of the six hundred odd sources Ibusuki boasts. What doesn't go into tubs is used to grow vegetables and fruit in hothouses made of plastic. For a bit of dipping on the tropical side, try Ibusuki Kankō Hotel. Here you'll be asked to choose from fifty-nine tubs, one of which is a very fancy man-made jungle tub complete with hanging vines—not for swinging on though, as it might be too shocking for Venus, who stands demure and white in the center of the pool. After the love dip, try the delectable, tantalizing banana, papaya, and litchi tubs, each a genuinely decadent feast of a bath. Visitors not staying at the hotel are welcome. ■ SAND BATHING: Ibusuki and *sunayu* (sand bath) are practically synonymous. The sand bath has long been its main attraction, although the tropical Hawaiian atmosphere has been so well developed that it more than rivals the other little Hawaiis of Japan. The public *sunayu* is on Surigahama beach, and here you'll lie in your warm sand bed under a brightly colored umbrella to keep the sun from drying out your face. The warm weight of the sandy security blanket is calming and the sound of the waves washing up at your feet adds to the feeling. Don't bake too long if it's the first time or if you have especially sensitive skin. The color of it all—parasol, attendant's yukata, sea, and sun—make this one of the gayer baths you'll have.

AROUND AND ABOUT: As noted above, there is a little Hawaii—an indoor "beach" complete with Diamond Head—for desperate lovers not soothed by Venus. The bougainvillea, palms, and junglelike tangles make an ideal setting for a tropical paradise. It's not until you stir from the hotel and venture out into the streets for the summer festivals that you see the Orient. These dizzy affairs with dragons, street dancing, and fireworks are unmistakably Japanese. Try to make the hot-spring festival, which is held on the last weekend of July.

ACCOMMODATIONS: Ibusuki Kaijō Hotel and Hakusuikan are two deluxe, Western-style hotels that have good facilities and suit the modern resort atmosphere of Ibusuki.

8 Shinyu

LOCATION: Shinyu is in the Kirishima group of springs (*Kirishima onsen kyō*) in northern Kagoshima Prefecture. From Nishi Kagoshima Station in Kagoshima City take a bus (a 2¼-hour ride) to Hayashida Onsen, or take the Nippō Main Line from Kagoshima to Kirishima Jingū Station and then a bus (a 40-minute ride) to Hayashida Onsen. From Hayashida take the bus for Ebino Kōgen as far as Minami Geito (15 minutes). From this stop the spring is a short walk.

THE WATERS: This spring is unparalleled in its powers to heal athlete's foot and other skin diseases. It is even patronized by skin specialists with such problems, so efficacious are its waters. The sulphur water is very strong and emits a lot of hydrogen sulphide so the windows are always open in the baths. The spring was patronized by people seeking skin cures as far back as the eighteenth century, when it was used for treating leprosy. Some of the afflicted lived in makeshift huts around the pools. There's little left of those times now, except for the water and the beautiful surroundings. You will find two superb tubs crafted from hemlock with a step carved into one side—an aromatic way to soak up the benefits of Shinyu. Folks without serious problems will find the water good for nervous tension and aches anywhere on the body.

AROUND AND ABOUT: From the open-air tubs you can look up and around this untouched, mountain haven. The slopes are covered in dense green, and pink and red azaleas bloom around the tubs in spring. It's quiet and rustic.

ACCOMMODATIONS: The solitary inn, Shinmoesō, now a kokuminshukusha, has cook-it-yourself facilities. The owner/manager started the inn to help the local community—a poor one which had suffered severe typhoon damage.

9 Onoaida

LOCATION: Onoaida is on Yakushima Island, which is almost directly south of Kagoshima. A pleasant way to get there is by sea. In Kagoshima City take a ferry from Kagoshima Pier. The journey takes about 4 hours, and ferries dock at Miyanoura. From there it's a 1-hour bus ride to Onoaida. To go by air, take the TOA domestic airlines flight that shuttles from Kagoshima to Yakushima in 35 minutes. The bus from Yakushima Airport to Onoaida takes about 45 minutes.

THE WATERS: Onoaida water contains acid-aluminum sulphate and is mild and odorless. It is good for heart problems, diabetes, and athlete's foot. But whatever else it cures, bathing in this idyllic spot makes you feel like new. This is especially true if you take the round-the-island bus to Hirauchi Hot Spring, 10 minutes away. This spring is just a rock pool on the beach open to the public. You need only bring a swimsuit (if it's crowded), and watch that the tide doesn't come in and cut you off while you soak unawares. **AROUND AND ABOUT**: Yakushima Island has picturesque and craggy cliffs, clothed in rocky outcrops and cedar trees old enough to be national treasures. There are hidden ravines, kept dark by steep slopes. At the bottoms of the ravines, you're likely to find fast-flowing streams and perfect camping spots. The islanders are few and far between and live in fishing villages clustered around clear-water inlets. The island's a favorite destination of hikers, who can be seen stocking up on supplies at local markets. **ACCOMMODATIONS**: Onoaida has several ryokan, minshuku, and one kokuminshukusha. Sasakisō, is comfortable and inexpensive.

10 Hirauchi

This hot spring is no more than a rock pool where you can soak at low tide; high tide cuts it off from the path. The pool is west of Onoaida, 10 minutes by bus, on the coast of Yakushima Island. You can do your wash in the spring water and then sit in another pool in the sun, soaking up the minerals while waiting for your glad rags to dry. It's one of those delightful hibiscus and papaya heavens on a lonely coast that you dream about over summer cocktails in Tōkyō hotels.

11 Yamaga

LOCATION: Yamaga is north of Kumamoto City, Kumamoto Prefecture. From Kumamoto take the Kagoshima Main Line to Setaka Station and then a bus for 1 hour to the hot spring. Or you can take a bus from Kumamoto Station to Yamaga Hot Spring, which also takes an hour.
THE WATERS: This old riverside spring is said to have been discovered by a cold or wounded deer. The alkaline simple thermal, moderately hot waters have never been in short supply and were used in the past for washing clothes. A public bath called Onsen Plaza combines segregated saunas, swimming pools, and baths all in one building—an inexpensive, relaxing way to spend the day.
AROUND AND ABOUT: Yamaga was formerly a travelers' way stop so it has a bright and breezy past of strangers stopping off to bathe, talk, and make merry before moving on. Some of this atmosphere remains in the old merchants' quarter where you can still see streets that look like a samurai movie set. The local Kabuki theater—Yachiyoza—also adds to the nostalgia, though it's no longer used. For a different, somewhat Chinese experience, attend the annual Yamaga Lantern Festival held on August 15 and 16. During this bright, sparkling extravaganza, kimono-clad maidens dance through the

streets wearing the famous Yamaga *dōrō* on their heads. These are intricate, gold paper lanterns with lighted candles inside that send shadows and reflections dancing. In Nabeta (a short bus ride from Yamaga) are some interesting hillside caves (Nabeta Yokoana), the homes of primitive tribes in ages past. The drawings on the walls aren't like any found elsewhere in Japan.

ACCOMMODATIONS: This is a hot-spring resort, so there are ryokan, Western-style hotels, and combination hotel-ryokan in abundance. However, Kumamoto, which is close, is a cheaper base for tourists and has a vast range of accommodations. One in Yamaga that is small and comfortable is the ryokan Asanoya.

FOOD: This area is known for its horse sashimi in case you're so inclined. Horse sashimi is horse meat served raw with sauces. Or you can test your mettle with *karashi renkon*—very spicy lotus root.

12 Tarutama

LOCATION: This spring is located at the foot of Mount Aso, one of the world's largest craters, in Kumamoto Prefecture. From Kumamoto City take the Hōhi Main Line to Tateno. Transfer to the Takamori Line and get off at Aso Shimoda Station. From there it is 20 minutes by bus to the spring.

THE WATERS: The water is acidic sulphur, good for skin irritations in particular. Tarutama is considered a medicinal spring, which means people come to bathe for a period of time, and often to imbibe the waters, on doctors' orders. The water replenishes dwindling acid supplies in the body when drunk (but only under supervision, please).

AROUND AND ABOUT: From the open-air tub the view is in tune with the soothing powers of the water; few signs of habitation mar the natural setting of rocks, trees, a waterfall, and steep cliffs cradling the spring in the valley. In summer you can hear frogs croaking in the river. In winter you can ski on Mount Aso, spectacular under its snow mantle. It's the only ski slope in Kyūshū. ■ MOUNT ASO: Though opinions vary as to whether it's beautiful, fascinating, or just plain ugly, Mount Aso is a Kyūshū "must." The outskirts are pastoral with grazing cows and rich green pastures, the crater lip is dirty and smoky with expanses of dusty gray desolation, and the eruption shelters scattered about the top, albeit not reassuring, are fascinating in an unsettling way. Mount Aso will put you in your place as a tiny defenseless speck on the edge, literally, of infinite natural power.

ACCOMMODATIONS: There's just one choice, Yamaguchi Ryokan, which is comfortable and suits the quiet surroundings.

13 Hinagu

LOCATION: This spring is situated on the western coast of southern

Kumamoto Prefecture. It sits on Yatsushiro Bay facing the beautiful Amakusa Islands. Take the Kagoshima Main Line from Kumamoto City to Hinagu Station. The spring is a 10-minute walk from the station.

THE WATERS: The simple thermal water has been praised for curing many things over the years. At the moment it is recommended for hypertension. Discovered in the fifteenth century, the spring was a favorite with government officials during the Edo period (1603-1868).

AROUND AND ABOUT: The town of Hinagu is split by a highway that divides it into old public baths and ryokan on the mountain side and modern ferroconcrete additions on the sea side. This kind of layout is typical of hot-spring resorts. In summer the town buzzes with talk of the fire balls, called *shiranui*, that roll across the sky around September 20. Many people come to see this strange phenomenon, which can now be explained in terms of weather and light reflections but which used to give great inspiration to storytellers (see below).

ACCOMMODATIONS: The ryokan Kinparō is traditional and old, suited to those who favor the romantic version of the fire-ball event. The ryokan Ichifuji is old, small, and inexpensive.

ROMANTIC FIRES: The fire balls, which move 10 kilometers across the horizon and then disappear, have been given countless supernatural interpretations. One which suits the mood of the area is the Urashima Tarō tale. Urashima Tarō, walking along the seashore, sees some children teasing a turtle and steps in to rescue the poor creature. To show his gratitude, the turtle takes the man down below the waves to a fabulous castle complete with beautiful princess. Naturally, he falls madly in love with her and forgets about life on land. Eventually he drags himself away and goes back to the beach where he first met the crab. He carries a gift from his princess, which he was told not to open. He can't resist for long, however, and opens the present only to release fumes that turn his hair gray, making him the lovesick laughingstock of the village. The fire balls, it is said, are reflections of the gorgeous palace under the sea.

FESTIVALS: At the beginning of August, fireworks are set off over the sea and eel is eaten to ward off the lethargy of the dog days. The hot-spring festival is held on November 15.

14 Unzen

LOCATION: Unzen is in Unzen-Amakusa National Park in the center of Shimabara Peninsula, Nagasaki Prefecture. From Nagasaki City take the Nagasaki Main Line to Isahaya Station. It's a 90-minute bus ride from there to Unzen. There are also many ferry routes in this area, so it's possible, for example, to take a ferry to Shimabara and then a bus (40 minutes) to Unzen.

THE WATERS: Unzen consists of three springs—Furuyu, the oldest, discovered by Katō Yoshizaemon in 1653; Shinyu, formerly the summer haven of well-to-do foreigners living in various parts of Asia; and Kojigoku, supposedly the least touristy, with an unusual, beautiful ceramic tub in its public bathhouse. The water in the area is hot and plentiful and classified as acidic hydrogen sulphide—good for treating rheumatism and skin diseases among other maladies.

AROUND AND ABOUT: The area is characterized by its strong association with Christianity and its beauty, the latter providing no hint of the violence that accompanied the former. Side by side stand the brilliant reds and pinks of spring azaleas and the bubbling pools that were once used as boiling pots for hapless Christians. Morning wafts in the shimmering blue mists the Unzen area is known for, and evening brings the no-less-spectacular sunsets of the Amakusa Islands. In summer the springs in this area are crowded. People come to bathe, play tennis, and watch the summer fireworks in mid- or late July.

ACCOMMODATIONS: Kyūshū Hotel has the appearance of a traditional Japanese-style structure, though it is a modern building.

FOOD: The local delicacy is tea-leaf tempura. You should also try the dark brown mushrooms called *shiitake*, which are found throughout Japan but are especially good in Kyūshū.

HELLISH TALES: This area has some bad memories, some of which are reflected in the names of the hell (*jigoku*) places. Daikyōkan Jigoku was named for the rumbles that rise from its thermal depths. Presumably they are the futile cries for help uttered by the Christians who were killed here. Seishichi Jigoku was named after Seishichi, a Christian killed on the day this thermal spring first appeared. He had refused to step on the image of Christ. Oito Jigoku was named after a woman who, together with her lover, killed her patron. On the day she was beheaded and her head was dragged through the streets, this spring erupted into life.

15 Shimabara

LOCATION: This spring is in the southern part of the port city Shimabara, on the eastern side of Shimabara Peninsula, Nagasaki Prefecture. Take the Shimabara Tetsudō Line from Isahaya Station to Shimabara Gaikō Station. It's a short walk from there to the spring. Ferries to Shimabara leave from Misumi—a junction for traffic heading west from Kumamoto through the Amakusa Islands region. The ferry takes about an hour.

THE WATERS: The water, sodium hydrogen-carbonate with calcium, isn't very hot—only 31° C (88° F)—so it's heated for the baths. Hospitals here use the water in treating surface cuts, bruises, and burns.

AROUND AND ABOUT: A port town situated across the way from Nagasaki, Shimabara naturally has a colorful past. Frequented by diverse foreigners—

from Portuguese and Dutch traders to Jesuit missionaries, all of whom were regular visitors by the end of the sixteenth century—Shimabara functioned as one of the East-meets-West crossroads of Kyūshū. Shimabara is most famous for the bloody Shimabara Uprising of 1637-38. At that time 37,000 men rose, fed up with the cruelty of the local daimyo, who, among other things, had forced workers to cart stones for building a new castle. In addition, they were overtaxed, and many were Christians who resented the increasingly harsh persecution of their brethren. Led by Amakusa Shirō, they took over the castle, a siege that ended only when they had all been slaughtered by the shogun's men. This area is second to none in Japan's religious past in terms of tragedy, valor, and civil conflict. Today all is still, and the only reminders of the past are the Christian burial grounds and the wind sighing through the pines.

ACCOMMODATIONS: The ryokan Kunimitsuya is large but has a hot-spring resort atmosphere about it. There is a garden and in winter they serve a shellfish dish they call *shiranui* (fire ball) barbeque. Nanpūrō, a ryokan, is on the seaside with a garden overlooking the waves. The Grand Hotel will, upon request from a group, add *doburoku* (unrefined saké) to your bath water. If the fumes don't make you merry enough, they'll give you a wee cup to sip while a-soaking.

A SAD STORY: During the Meiji and Taishō eras (1868-1926) the poor people of this area used to sell their daughters to prostitution houses throughout Asia. The tragic results of this came to light in a novel released in 1972 (*San dakan Hachiban Shōkan* by Yamazaki Tomoko). The women lived miserable lives abroad, pining for a country to which they could only return in disguise to protect their families from the shame. Though most died outside of Japan, the headstones on their graves face the land of the rising sun.

16 Ureshino

LOCATION: Ureshino is northeast of Nagasaki City in Saga Prefecture. To get there take the Sasebo Line from Saga City to Takeo Onsen Station. From there it's 35 minutes by bus to the spring.

THE WATERS: Ureshino's water is famous as the first to be introduced to the West: a Dutch doctor mentioned the water of Ureshino in a travel book he wrote in 1700. Now the spring is more of a resort, although the water is still studied for its curative powers. It is very hot, 96° C (205° F) at the point of origin, contains salt, and is classified as good alkaline water (sodium hydrogen-carbonate). There are three separate bathing areas: the oldest is Furuyu and the newest are Motoyu and Arayu. You can choose traditional or modern tubs, as you fancy.

AROUND AND ABOUT: Ureshino has a lot of charm, due in no small part to the low, smooth, sculptured rows of tea bushes that surround it. Mountains are visible in the distance, and small pottery workshops in the vicinity produce the famous Arita ware (*Arita-yaki*). Tea and pottery, combined with excellent water, make for a very attractive place to visit.

ACCOMMODATIONS: Wataya Bessō is a large Japanese-style inn on the Ureshino River. The food served includes sea bream *nabe* (stew), "Viking" (all-you-can-eat) breakfasts, and, for those wanting some night life, an international dinner-dance show. The deluxe Ureshino Kankō Hotel Taishōya features baths overlooking a waterfall. This ryokan serves special tofu dishes and offers Western-style rooms as well as Japanese ones.

FOOD: Using the spring water, boil up some tofu and chicken and feast on an Ureshino delicacy. Remember: there's no need to add salt.

DEVIL'S DANCE: For a fee, you can have the *menfuryū* dance performed for you. This local dance originated a hundred years ago during a war with a neighboring clan. The Ureshino men were faring poorly so they decided to use psychological warfare. They put on devil's masks and frightening clothing and tied drums to their stomachs. Then, shrieking and beating their bellies in the manner of devils, they went forth to engage in battle once more. Of course the opposition split ranks and fled in terror. Now anyone can witness this tactic and judge its effectiveness for himself.

17 Takeo

LOCATION: Takeo is west of Saga City, Saga Prefecture, and near Mount Hōrai, which is northeast of Nagasaki City. Take the Sasebo Line from Saga City to Takeo Onsen Station. The various ryokan are a 10-minute walk away.

THE WATERS: The water is alkaline simple thermal and treats burns and surface wounds very effectively. It is also good for physical exhaustion. There are several public baths—one with a wooden tub is behind the Chinese gate at the entrance to the town (you can't miss it). There are also wooden tubs in several ryokan. Takeo is a medicinal spring, so you can join those staying and bathing over a period of several days if you feel the need. It has been a favorite with tourists for centuries; during the Nara period it was a popular stop en route to Nagasaki City. Legend attributes the discovery of Takeo variously to an empress with a divining rod or to a heron with a cold.

AROUND AND ABOUT: The bright red-orange Chinese-style entrance gate is a sight in itself as it towers in stark contrast to the surrounding greenery. At night it is brilliantly lit and the hot-spring symbol on the gate shines out of the dark. The gate was designed by the architect Tatsuno Kingo, whose work includes such famous landmarks as Tōkyō Station. Takeo is near the famous pottery towns of Arita and Imari, which were heavily influenced by Korean potters. So with the Korean influence in the pottery, the Chinese gate, and the Japanese-style ryokan, Takeo is a place of diverse Oriental charm, color, and style. If you do spend the day pottery-hunting and have some extra cash and an eye for the finest, seek out Kakiemon ware in Arita. Its distinctive decoration—red on white with touches of blue—is exquisite to behold; just be sure to put it down before you read the price tag! For a more calming experience, take a stroll in Mifuneyama Park, which was laid out by the leader of the Nabeshima clan.

ACCOMMODATIONS: The ryokan Kagetsu is quiet, subdued, and traditional and has a very pleasant garden.

FESTIVALS: On May 3 and 4, a Chinese dragon crazily wends it way through the streets in the Hakata Dontaku Festival. It's bright, noisy, and fun.

18 Futsukaichi

LOCATION: This spring is about 15 kilometers south of Fukuoka City, Fukuoka Prefecture. Take the Kagoshima Main Line to Futsukaichi Station. The spring is a 5-minute walk from the station.

THE WATERS: This spring goes back fourteen hundred years. Its radioactive water, long used for skin complaints, today is used in treating burns, surface wounds, and sore limbs caused by anything from too much strenuous hiking to serious accidents. It was found by a man named Toramaru who saw an image of Buddha in a dream and was told by the image where to go. A rich man, he had the time and money to develop a resort as it was done in those times. The result was very popular with the government officials who lived in Fukuoka in the eighth to twelfth centuries. They built a shrine to the spring, which still remains, although not untouched. There is only one public bath here and it's a good one. Housed in a wooden building, the clean tiled bath occupies a large room with high ceilings. You can just drop into town, take a bath here, and continue on if you want.

AROUND AND ABOUT: Futsukaichi is a serene spot where willows hang lazily over the river dragging their tresses in the water. The ryokan-lined river runs through town and narrow streets wind away from the river. If you want action you can go to Fukuoka, whose bright lights have robbed Futsukaichi of some of its clientele, leaving the hot-spring town all the more peaceful. In fact, the activity local residents are best known for is bowing; apparently, they do it even more than most Japanese.

ACCOMMODATIONS: The ryokan are Western-style, modern buildings, constructed to attract city folk. One such inn is Enjukan, which is comfortable and has good bathing facilities.

2. CHŪGOKU REGION

Kaleidoscope of Light and Shadow

The Chūgoku Region is divided geographically down the middle by the for-midable Chūgoku Mountain Range. The southern side, known as Sanyō, comprises Okayama, Hiroshima, and southern Yamaguchi prefectures. The northern half, Sanin, is made up of the rest of Yamaguchi, Shimane, and Tottori prefectures. Sanin (literally, "Mountain Shadow") is considered the shady side and Sanyō ("Mountain Light") is presumably in the sun. But life is not so simple. Despite the apparent division of roles, each side of the Chū-goku Mountains is a kaleidoscope of light and dark.

Sanyō: Much of Sanyō borders on the beautiful Inland Sea, with its jagged bays and inlets, tiny islands, tangled waterways, and water-bound rocks. It boasts Miyajima, or Shrine Island, near Hiroshima, which is so revered that, in times past, births and burials were not allowed on its soil. Even to-day burials are not carried out here. The graceful, vermilion torii, or shrine gate, that stands in the water a short distance from the shore seems to rock on the waves. In the sixth century this original shrine was transferred from its location atop the highest peak on the island. In 1875, during vast reconstruction, the present torii was built. No less traditional and moving are certain sections of Kurashiki City, also on the Inland Sea. Its willow-lined canals, cobblestone streets, tiled storehouses, and displays of folk crafts recall former eras and lifestyles.

Light seems to imply art. Bizen ware—simple, earthy, unglazed pottery made in Bizen, near Okayama City—has been produced in Sanyō for more than a thousand years. Hiroshima produces a vast number of the shiny black-lacquered altars (*butsudan*) used in private homes, but it seems that most of the old arts of Sanyō have given way to industrial expertise. This region was responsible in no small way for the economic miracle worked in Japan in postwar years.

Shade is the other side of the economic coin: pollution of the Inland Sea and construction of belching factories and refineries, crowded and ugly apartment blocks, and vast webs of crisscrossing steel line to carry ever faster trains.

Shade also conjures up images of war. Japan's emergence as a military power began and finished in Chūgoku. Hiroshima was home port to the fleets that sailed successfully against China in 1894 and Russia in 1905. And it was the home of the thousands who died there on August 6, 1945—the day the bomb fell. Further back in time at Shimonoseki, where Sanyō and Sanin converge, East and West met once more. The fiery Chōshū clan, who opposed the gains made by the foreign barbarians and traders in the latter half of the nineteenth century, took a stand here and fired on foreign vessels passing through the straits. The result was a combined display of strength by the English, French, Dutch, and Americans, which settled the matter once and for all in 1864. The Genji and Heike families also fought each other at Shimonoseki in the twelfth century. The Genji (Minamoto) defeated the Heike (Taira), and Lady Nii no Tsubone of the Heike jumped into the waves of Dan-no-ura with the young emperor Antoku in her arms—a noble act worthy of a samurai woman whose time had run out.

Sanin: Light is plentiful in Sanin. There's the sparkle of the very blue Sea of Japan, and its miles of spectacular coastal beauty. A prominent example is the stretch of white sand dunes at Tottori that, whirling and swirling, artfully rearranges itself hourly. Lakes also abound in this region, some barely separate from the brine. One is Lake Shinji, where the sun rises and sets with great panache. Lake Togō is a similar visual extravaganza with beaches fringed in scented, green pine and the sound of the sea just over the ridge.

Sanin's natural light doesn't only flow from water: the mountains inland are equally beautiful. The Daisen area is a perfect example of solid earth displaying all its best features. Awesome, impervious, mist-shrouded, and foreboding from a distance but serene, protective, and seemingly hospitable from the vantage of its slopes. Like the Oki Islands off Matsue City, nature seems unaccustomed to man but offers delights many men don't think exist in Japan anymore. Sanin offers religious light too, although its very famous Izumo Taisha Shrine at first glance seems on the shady and dark side. This ancient site of worship, with its blend of stone, wood, plaited rope, eaves, curves, and solitude, is uplifting and instills a feeling of respect for man's creations. It seems the obvious place for the shrine gods to meet annually;

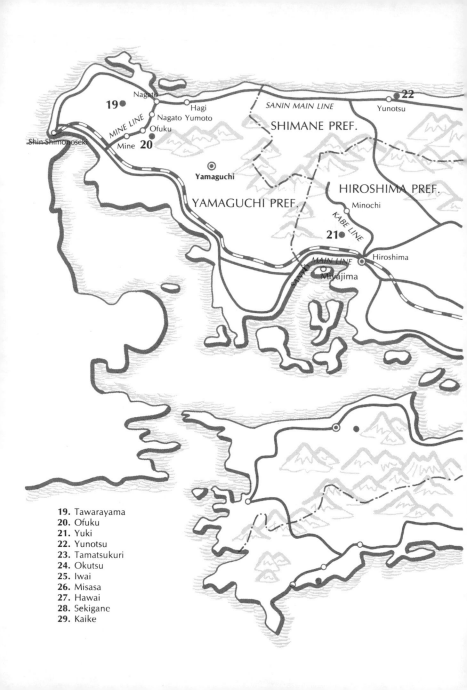

19 ●

Nagato

Hagi

19

MINE LINE

Nagato Yumoto

Ofuku

Shin-Shimonoseki

Mine **20**

SANIN MAIN LINE

Yunotsu

● 22

SHIMANE PREF.

◉ **Yamaguchi**

YAMAGUCHI PREF.

HIROSHIMA PREF.

Minochi

KABE LINE

21 ●

Hiroshima

SANYO MAIN LINE

Miyajima

2 CHŪGOKU REGION

to Oki Islands

SEA OF JAPAN

Izumo Taisha Shrine

L. Shinji

Matsue

Tamatsukuri Onsen

23

29

Yonago

MT. DAISEN

Iwami

27

Matsuzaki **Tottori**

Kurayoshi

26

28

25

TOTTORI PREF.

24

KISHIN LINE

Tsuyama

Hayashino

to Himeji

Yunogō

OKAYAMA PREF.

TSUYAMA LINE

TŌKAIDŌ-SANYO

SHINKANSEN

Kurashiki

Okayama

INLAND SEA

it's believed the gods from all over Japan journey to Izumo during October or November. Izumo Taisha is near Matsue City, Shimane Prefecture. Also in Matsue is the former residence of Lafcadio Hearn, the British writer who shed a lot of light on Japan and the Japanese in his extensive writings at the turn of the century.

This supposed land of shade was not plagued by war as much as Sanyō was, at least in modern times. Perhaps the residents of Sanin have been too caught up in their battles against the bitter winters of this side of Japan.

Shade and light meet at Shūhōdō, a series of limestone caves in Yamaguchi Prefecture that run for several kilometers under the earth. Magnificent caverns full of nature's sculpture, they are at the same time cold and eery sanctuaries for shade. Similarly, Hagi ware, pottery made in Hagi, Yamaguchi Prefecture, embodies both shade and light. It was first made by Korean potters brought to Japan in the sixteenth century. Despite its grim past, its soft, translucent, off-white glazes are beautiful.

Chūgoku—its customs, people, and history,—poses a wealth of contradictions unless you remember that everything—even the earth itself—has a light and a dark side.

19 Tawarayama

LOCATION: Tawarayama is northwest of Yamaguchi City in Yamaguchi Prefecture. Take the Shinkansen (bullet train) to Shin-Shimonoseki Station and then a bus (1 hour 20 minutes) to the spring. Or, take the Mine Line from Nagato Station to Nagato Yumoto Station. From there it's a 25-minute bus ride to Tawarayama.

THE WATERS: "If you want to have fun, don't come to this spring," warns one guidebook. In one way this is true: Tawarayama is a quiet, medicinal spring, unlit by neon and with just country-town vistas and accommodations to offer. The bathers who come are the serious type who like the public baths of old. Even if they stay at ryokan with thermal bathing facilities, they often go to the public baths to dip, so you'll find them at the public Machino-yu, Kawa-no-yu, Sato-no-yu, and Masa-no-yu soaking up the alkaline simple thermal water in hopes of healing rheumatic twinges, nervous problems, sprains, breaks, and obesity.

AROUND AND ABOUT: This town was made for clip-clopping geta (wooden clogs), strolls in yukata, and riverside hand claps to entice the carp nearer. In autumn you can add picking and eating juicy, purple grapes to the list of suitable activities, and in summer yellow-green pears can also be gathered and eaten.

ACCOMMODATIONS: The ryokan Fukuzumi is homey and has a rock garden. It is small, but at dinner time the chefs skillfully combine mountain vegetables from the area with seafood from the coast nearby. In addition, several inns offer rooms with cooking facilities, a viable option with the almost-daily markets selling local produce.

FESTIVALS: On the third weekend of April there is a Kabuki performance staged by an all-female cast. During these few festive days the townspeople dress up and parade about singing and eating *saru manjū* (steamed monkey cakes), a local delicacy with a story (see below).

LEGENDS: Tawarayama was discovered by a hunter, or so they say. According to the story, he shot a white monkey one day while out hunting. The monkey limped off leaving a trail of blood, which the man followed the next day. At the end of the trail he found the monkey, badly wounded, not far from where it had been shot. The hunter shot it again. It disappeared into thin air and in its place was a thermal spring. While the local bean cakes may no longer be steamed over the waters of this hot spring, their name—monkey cakes—is a good reminder of their connected past.

The next story, dating from 1551, one can only hope is fiction. . . . The lord of Yamaguchi Castle, Ōuchi Yoshitaka, was betrayed by a retainer and forced to flee. He was caught near Tawarayama, whereupon he killed himself. His son, hoping to escape, disguised himself as a woman. Unfortunately he fared little better than his father: when he was discovered, his manhood was cut off. Not all of the villagers thought well of this and some of them, to register their disapproval, placed a stone shaped like a penis in the temple there. Today this temple, Mara Kannon, and the stone are still there—along with other stones and pieces of wood, all penis-shaped and called Konsei-sama by those who make regular visits to the temple. The purpose of their pilgrimages? To pray for children—for the stones, ironically enough, have become symbols of fertility. Mara Kannon is a 30-minute walk north of Tawarayama.

20 Ofuku

LOCATION: Ofuku is in western Yamaguchi Prefecture, in the northern part of Mine City. Take the Mine Line from Mine to Ofuku Station and then walk for a few minutes to the ryokan. The Mine Line connects the Sanin and Sanyō lines.

THE WATERS. The water is radioactive simple thermal and is heated. It is good for hardening of the arteries, lazy blood, stiff joints, and neuralgia.

AROUND AND ABOUT: This small hot spring has only four ryokan. Situated in a basin near the Furuya River, it's a perfect base for exploring the Akiyoshidai fields and the Shūhōdō limestone caves. It is also a convenient steppingstone to Ōmi Island, a good place to go for solitude and fishing. The limestone caves consist of a 10-kilometer-long series of caves entered by way of a never-ending, slowly descending stairway. Down under it's a damp, fascinating world of smooth, deformed rock sculpture. The safety lights throw eery shadows around, and although the stalactites and stalagmites are beautiful, they are cold and their names, taken from Buddhist deities, are unnerving. You exit via an elevator—a necessity since you've descended quite far—which deposits you in the Akiyoshidai fields, a bright, sunny, wild-flower-strewn contrast to the caves below.

ACCOMMODATIONS: Ofukusō and Fukuya Ryokan are two small inns where mountain vegetables and freshwater fish are menu highlights.

21 Yuki

LOCATION: This hot spring is west of Hiroshima City in Hiroshima Prefecture. Take the Kabe Line from Hiroshima and get off at Minochi Station. The bus ride from there takes 40 minutes.

THE WATERS: Hiroshima Prefecture has only two thermal springs, Yuki and Yunoyama. The other springs contain minerals but are less than 25° C (77° F) at the source, so they must be heated artificially. These "cool" springs are called *kōsen*. Yuki is a National Health Resort. The radioactive water helps to ease the pain of gout and rheumatism and treats surface wounds and, if imbibed at the same time, indigestion. This spring is called Hiroshima's *okuzashiki*, or "parlor in reserve"—a place where people from Hiroshima can entertain and relax on special occasions. It is a special, well-cared-for retreat more than a thousand years old.

AROUND AND ABOUT: After the Ōsaka Expo in 1970, the Vietnamese pavilion was transported here lock, stock, and barrel. So don't be surprised if wandering through the streets in your yukata after your bath, you come upon a superb collection of Asian artifacts. Another of Yuki's exotic touches is its *yamafugu*, or "mountain blowfish." As anyone in Japan will gleefully tell you, blowfish is the fish that gourmets will literally die for—its liver, a rare delicacy, can be lethal if prepared by a novice. "Mountain blowfish" is sliced *konnyaku* (a jellylike substance with no taste or calories, derived from the devil's-tongue plant). It takes its bizarre name from its texture, which is said to be chewy like blowfish. Other things around Yuki are not so startling—edible mountain plants in spring, croaking frogs and fireflies in summer, and colorful maples in autumn. There is also a picturesque walking trail from Yuki through Sandan Gorge that, after 20 kilometers or so, takes you to Hiroshima City. Don't leave without visiting the Peace Memorial Park and Museum in Hiroshima. It is open from 9:00 A.M. to 4:30 P.M. except during the New Year holiday. A sobering place, it details the dropping of the atomic bomb here in 1945.

ACCOMMODATIONS: Kajikasō is a comfortable ryokan. Kokuminshukusha Yuki Lodge is famous for its good service and food.

22 Yunotsu

LOCATION: This spring is in northern Shimane Prefecture. It is a 10-minute walk from Yunotsu Station on the Sanin Main Line. Note that a car is very useful in getting around in this region of Japan.

THE WATERS: The water contains sodium chloride with calcium sulphate—good for rheumatism, neuralgia, high blood pressure, and whiplash. Yunotsu really flourished in the Edo period when it was a silver-shipping port. But times have changed. Today, this historical port is likened to an old man—wrinkled and experienced and a bit wistful when he thinks back on his wild, carefree days as a youth. The loss of the silver glitter has meant a concentration of energies on improving the spring's other attractions; the public baths, the ryokan facilities, and the table fare are all meant to make up for the loss of the silver industry.

AROUND AND ABOUT: When you enter this town you'll first be struck by the orange-tiled roofs. The tiles are Iwami ware, a style of ceramics much prized in the area. Near Ryūomae Shrine in the center of town you can see it being made. You'll also notice the narrow streets winding circuitously about the town's buildings; these were once trails trod by horses on their way to Edo (Tōkyō) carrying loads of ore. In the shade of an old-fashioned roof you can sit and eat *soba* (buckwheat noodles in broth) served in heavy ceramic bowls and listen for the clomp-clomping of weary animals going by. Other reminders of the past are the white-plastered, thick-walled storehouses (*kura*)—sturdy, boxlike structures with high, impenetrable windows that are used for storing food, clothing, and treasures. Garden lovers will want to see the beautiful garden at the Gangyōji Temple, and everyone should try sea bream (*tai*), a local specialty.

ACCOMMODATIONS: Masuya is a small, comfortable ryokan where the staff prides itself on a homey atmosphere. They offer to cook any fish you may catch for your evening meal.

23 Tamatsukuri

LOCATION: Tamatsukuri is 10 minutes by bus from Tamatsukuri Onsen Station on the Sanin Main Line. It's situated on the Tamatsukuri River, a short distance from Lake Shinji. Shin ("New") Tamatsukuri Hot Spring is on the lake front. Both are in Shimane Prefecture.

THE WATERS: Said to be the oldest hot spring on record in Japan, Tamatsukuri was mentioned in writings dating as far back as the early eighth century. In those days it was a lively place where people bathed in the open-air hot pools and then sat around eating what they had caught in the lake. You can still do this; there are seven varieties of fish in the lake, all good for grilling. The water in the pools is known for its softness. The first dip will make you look good and the second will make you feel good, or so they say. Although the water's always been called "water from the gods," chemists will tell you it's just plain calcium sulphate with sodium chloride, good for treating skin diseases and neuralgia and whitening sallow complexions and freckles. Outdoor pools are still very popular here: there's a public one and the ryokan Chōrakuen boasts the biggest one in Japan. This Olympic-size communal pool covers 3,600 square meters and is walled in by stonework resembling the foundations of a castle with a tangle of surrounding green peeking over the top. The pool is open to the public for a fee.

AROUND AND ABOUT: Matsue City, just a bit further around the lake counterclockwise, is well worth a few-hour visit. Matsue Castle, built in 1611, is a foreboding, seemingly impenetrable fortress. Inside, yellowed scrolls depict daily life and glory in splashes of red, blue, and green. ■ IZUMO TAISHA: This is another place you would regret not visiting on your Sanin tour. This very old, gray-brown, wood-and-stone shrine is a muted delight. From the huge, plaited ropes hanging across the sanctuary entrances to the bamboo water ladles, it's understated, tranquil, and a suitable place for the shrine gods from all over Japan to gather once a year, around October or November. The only sounds heard are an occasional drum thud, the swish of a priest's robe, or the hand claps of a suppliant. The god of the shrine, Enmusubi, is said to do good deeds for unmarrieds over thirty who are looking for mates. If this doesn't work, take a stroll near Lake Shinji around sunset; its sunsets are said to be the most beautiful in Japan and should move even the most unromantic souls.

ACCOMMODATIONS: Chōrakuen is nice—both garden and architecture are quite attractive—but not inexpensive.

24 Okutsu

LOCATION: Okutsu is on the Yoshii River, in northern Okayama Prefecture. Together with Yubara and Yunogō, it makes up the Mimasaka group of hot springs. Take the Kishin Line from Himeji or the Tsuyama Line from Okayama to Tsuyama Station. From this station the spring is 1½ hours by bus.

THE WATERS: The romantic and hopeful consider this a beautifying spring, or *bijin-ni-naru yu*. They bathe to acquire milky white complexions and rosy cheeks. The more pragmatic are inclined to see this water as merely weak alkaline, simple thermal, a bit slimy, and no doubt good for the skin but.... They will stress its benefits for those with rheumatism, insomnia, and asthma. Lending support to the romantic view, fresh-faced young women in traditional garb can be seen stamping on clothes soaked in hot-spring water. This is how they do their wash on Sundays and on public holidays for tourists. On Sundays they wear country-style kimono of blue-and-white fabric called *kasuri* with bright red undergarments and white scarves tied about their heads. Their sleeves are tied up and out of the way with red sashes (*tasuki*). On weekdays the women wear jeans and use washing machines. There's a good reason for their standing posture when doing the wash in the spring water: in the past, when bears wandered about freely, a person bending over could be eaten unawares.

AROUND AND ABOUT: The Okutsu Gorge is a scenic spot with a river running through the center and cliff faces sculpted by ages of erosion. The wavy, smooth stretches of stone are pitted here and there with small cavelike indentations. This display of natural art is protected, so don't chip off samples to take home. There's not much in the way of entertainment at Okutsu. If you can afford it, you can hire a *yatona* to pour your saké for you. This woman visits inns to perform this service for guests wanting some real pampering. There are few *yatona* left, so don't wait too long to indulge in this old custom.

■ YUNOGŌ'S "REVENGE" BATH: Near Okutsu on the Yoshii River is Yunogō Hot Spring's renowned "revenge" bath—a women's outdoor pool that overlooks the men's pool. Women who feel that hot springs have given men all the peeking rights in the past can now get their own back. This is part of the bathing fare offered by the ryokan Chikutei. So for a bit of spicy revenge, drop in for a peek. To get to Yunogō, take the Kishin Line from Tsuyama Station to Hayashino Station (25 minutes), then a bus to Yunogō Hot Spring (10 minutes).

ACCOMMODATIONS: Kawanishi Hotel, on the river, has a large open-air bath and serves various turtle (*suppon*) dishes. The ryokan Okutsusō is old and traditional in structure.

25 Iwai

LOCATION: This hot spring is east of Tottori City, Tottori Prefecture. Take the Sanin Main Line to Iwami Station. The spring is a 10-minute bus ride from there

THE WATERS: Iwai has its own special bathing ditty (called *Yukamuri uta*). This ditty is part of a bathing routine that, if followed correctly, will do wonders for sluggish blood, sallow complexions, and stiff joints. The water contains calcium sulphate and sodium chloride. To learn the routine, first of all you need to find a local bather who knows the words to the song (best found at the public bathhouse). Then place your hand towel on your head, take a bamboo dipper, and settle down in the tub. Together with the other bathers, you then commence singing and, in time to the song, alternately beating the water and pouring it over your head. This is all so confusing that you'll forget about the heat of the water and soak yourself for longer than you would otherwise, thus letting the healing minerals work their maximum wonder cure.

AROUND AND ABOUT: Iwai is a small town with a river, the Gamō River, running through its center. Places to visit, like the hot-spring shrine built in 811 in the Heian period, are equally tranquil and slow-moving. You'll feel compelled to visit the famous sand dunes (*sakyū*) a 30-minute bus ride away, and for those craving a bit of the Sahara complete with camels, it's worthwhile. The white sand does swirl into unusual patterns in the wind, but by and large it's just sand. The nearby Uradome Coast is more spectacular, if not so well publicized, and bereft of exotic animal life.

ACCOMMODATIONS: The ryokan Akashiya has a communal outdoor bath with a view and serves oyster sashimi and crab meat in season. Hanaya Ryokan also provides comfortable accommodations.

FOOD: Around Iwai in fall you can pick and eat the famous Twentieth Century (*nijū seiki*) pears. These round, succulent light-green pears can be found in many orchards here open to the public.

RAIN DANCE: At the end of the Edo period Inaba, as this area was then known, was experiencing a severe drought. An old man called Gorosaku came along and offered to remedy the situation. Taking rice straw, he wove a lot of wide-brimmed, flat-topped hats, like the ones you see in samurai movies, and then started to dance using the hats. He danced for three days and three nights and sure enough the skies opened up and it poured. This dance, called *Inaba kasa odori*, is still performed at the summer Bon Festival.

26 Misasa

LOCATION: Misasa is situated on the Misasa River in the center of Tottori Prefecture. Take the Sanin Main Line to Kurayoshi Station. The spring is a 30-minute bus ride from there.

THE WATERS: This radioactive water contains the most radium of any spring water in the world. Such water is very good for chronic skin diseases, high blood pressure, hardening of the arteries, rheumatism, and neuralgia. Imbibing aids digestion and will get you ready for the seafood delicacies served for dinner. Misasa was discovered by a retainer of the famous general Minamoto Yoshitomo. The retainer, when praying on holy Mount Mitoku, received divine word on the presence of a thermal spring nearby. The discovery happened in 1164 and the spring and mountain remain as they were then. The popular outdoor public bath, often pictured in postcards and scenes of Misasa, is a rough, rock-enclosed pool almost in the river itself. You could probably catch your dinner while you bathed. From the pool you can watch the river or the people walking across a bridge a little way upstream. Small lanterns top the bridge's balustrades and glow like miniature houses at night.

AROUND AND ABOUT: Although Misasa is known as a pleasure resort, there's too much mountain green around to let the city slickers' greenbacks have too much of an effect. The river is clear and sparkles, and many of the ryokan have put a lot of effort into making attractive gardens that anyone can observe on a quiet stroll. But the tourist trade is not ignored, as evidenced by the sale of "radium" cookies and "radium-flavored" steamed cakes! These delicacies will not make you a walking toxic-waste dump; the unfortunate name comes from Misasa's unsurpassed merit as a radioactive spring. Similarly, a bust of Madame Curie mounted in the park and the annual "radium" festival in August, to which the French ambassador to Japan is always invited, are tributes to the waters.

ACCOMMODATIONS: Misasa's accommodations are conveniently arranged: the expensive ryokan and hotels are grouped together on the north bank, the cheaper ones on the south bank, and the medicinal ones for long-term patients at the top of the river. One on the north bank that is a justifiable splurge is Saiki Bekkan, a traditional Japanese building with tearooms and a lantern hanging out front to welcome guests.

FESTIVALS: If you don't like radium or the heat of summer try the Hanayu Festival on May 7 and 8. A central activity is tug-of-war contests among local farmers. The winners can expect a bountiful rice harvest, while the losers had better start training for the next year or plant cabbages.

27 Hawai

LOCATION: This spring is on Lake Tōgō, west of Tottori City, Tottori Prefecture. Take the Sanin Main Line to Matsuzaki Station and then ferry across the lake (10 minutes) to the spring. Or, get off at Kurayoshi Station and take a bus, a 15-minute ride, to the spring.

THE WATERS: The thermal water, which originates under the lake, emerges at twenty-eight different places. Ryokan at the lake's edge have built open-air baths on the lake front and a bathhouse on a pier extending out over the water. This means you can sit in warm comfort while taking in an expansive view or a spectacular sunset. Meanwhile, your body takes in all the good effects simple thermal water with calcium sulphate and sodium chloride can provide. Not a bad combination at all.

AROUND AND ABOUT: Although this spring is named after a nearby town, the local beach is probably named after the American Hawaii, no doubt a ploy to conjure up a bit of the exotica associated with tropical paradises. This spa town is therefore something of a summer playground for the rich and idle, with the requisite lavish night fare and deluxe high-rise hotels on the shore. Nevertheless, the scenery is superb, and the lights, lake, and sunsets are definitely romantic.

ACCOMMODATIONS: The modern hotel Hagoromo has a jungle bath. Asozuen is right on Lake Tōgō; you can practically fish from your bedroom window. All of the four baths at Asozuen look out on the lake.

28 Sekigane

LOCATION: This spring is southwest of Tottori City, near Misasa (26), in Tottori Prefecture. Take the Sanin Main Line to Kurayoshi Station. From the station, it's a 40-minute bus ride to the spring.

THE WATERS: This spring was discovered by the Buddhist monk Gyōki and then rediscovered by the monk Kōbō Daishi after it was buried in a landslide. Its spiritual beginnings are remembered in the annual thanksgiving ceremony held at the hot-spring temple, which was named after the Buddhist disciple Jizō (the patron saint of travelers, children, and pregnant women). You can see a Jizō statue in this temple, somewhat bigger than those that punctuate rural roadsides, as well as a statue of Yakushi Nyorai, the deity of medicine. The water, once called platinum water because of its rare benefits, contains radium and is good for skin, joints, and nervous complaints.

AROUND AND ABOUT: During the Edo period this town was a stopping place for travelers en route to Edo (Tōkyō) to pay their money and respects to the shogun. This past is recalled in the samurai parade held on October 7, when local folk dress in period costumes and swagger through the streets imitating their bold, warrior forebears. It is hard to believe these are the same people who devote a day, the third Saturday in April, to the azalea; the main activity during this azalea festival is the discreet discussion of the flowers' merits. Despite its rich history, this small town is most frequented by skiers in winter and mushroom lovers in autumn. The latter are after those *cordon bleu* mushrooms called *matsutake*—fragrant, tender, expensive delicacies.

ACCOMMODATIONS: Onseirō, a good ryokan, has a covered outdoor bath that can be used all year round. Kokuminshukusha Sekiganesō has an outdoor bath in a garden setting and camping facilities especially suited to summer weather. Campers can use the ryokan baths for a fee.

29 Kaike

LOCATION: This spring is just barely in Tottori Prefecture, west of Tottori City. Take the Sanin Main Line to Yonago Station. From there it's a 20-minute bus ride.

THE WATERS: The weak sodium-chloride water, originally located out to sea, was discovered by startled fishermen. In the early 1900s developers filled in this part of the sea so the spring is now on land. Like salty thermal waters, these waters are good for your digestion if imbibed and good for rheumatism and neuralgia if you soak in them.

AROUND AND ABOUT: Kaike is not so much a hot-spring town as a *bessō* area with ryokan. *Bessō* are holiday cottages built by affluent cityfolk. The natural beauty of the coastline and the proximity to Matsue City, Mount Daisen, and the Oki Islands have made Kaike a very popular destination of vacationers. In summer you can swim, fish, drive, walk, or just sit in the tub. When you get hungry, a short walk takes you to kiosks set up on the beach that serve shellfish taken straight from the brine. Lines of cool pines ward off the summer heat and complement the lavish ryokan gardens.

■ MOUNT DAISEN: This rugged, misty mountain of lush green that gives way to gray rock at higher altitudes is a 40-minute bus or car ride from Kaike. Worn stone and wooden steps lead up to Daisenji Temple. In spring the climb is edged in pink azaleas, in summer by fragrant green foliage, and in autumn by a cool chill in the air. The mountain is dotted with shrines, mute and silent like their surroundings. The peacefulness of Daisen is contagious and the scent of the trees, the gases they emit, are said to be beneficial to the health. ■ OKI ISLANDS: From the port of Sakai-minato, on Shimane Peninsula, you can take a boat to Dōgo, the largest of the Oki Islands. Besides Dōgo there are 3 other sizable islands and 180 smaller ones. Dōgo dates back a long way; its bull fights are a seven-hundred-year-old tradition and are now held on May 5, August 15, September 1, and October 13. Like Sado Island, also off this coast of Japan, Dōgo and several other islands served as a penal colony in centuries past. Now it's a wild, untamed land with roughly hewn coastlines and rugged mountainous inner reaches. You can hike or bicycle about or take buses to see a side to Japan you didn't think had survived the vending-machine revolution.

ACCOMMODATIONS: Inexpensive accommodations are hard to come by at Kaike, especially in summer when prices peak. But the ryokan are worth the money what with their spacious interiors, superb bathing facilities, and attractive gardens. Tōkōen is a modern ryokan with a Japanese garden, superb coastal views, and a restaurant with sea views for the romantics.

3 SHIKOKU ISLAND

Land of Writers and Fighters

The four prefectures of Shikoku (the name literally means "four provinces") are relatively ignored by both foreign and Japanese tourists, a surprising fact considering their natural beauty, religious importance, hot springs (one—Dōgo—is possibly the most famous spring in Japan), and dramatic past. Vestiges of its history remain in various forms, but Shikoku owes much of its fame to the work of writers and fighters.

Among the literary figures who lived in or visited Shikoku are the modern novelists Natsume Sōseki and Tamiya Torahiko and the famous haiku poet Masaoka Shiki, all of whom managed to capture the essence of life and thought on the island. Shikoku is also represented in Japanese folklore: the valiant exploits of Momotarō, a boy who fought mythical monsters, take place on Megijima, a small island off the coast of Takamatsu City.

The most illustrious man of letters of whom Shikoku can boast is undoubtedly Kōbō Daishi, founder of the Shingon sect of Buddhism. This scholar, priest, and saint was born in Tadotsu, Kagawa Prefecture, in A.D. 744. At the age of thirty-four, after a period of study in China, he returned to Japan to begin teaching Shingon (esoteric) Buddhism. He and his followers built eighty-eight temples, which make up the most famous pilgrimage in Japan today. Annually thousands of people walk through Shikoku, praying at the temples on the route. Many wear white coats or robes and carry a cane as their patron saint did. Some stick to a vegetarian diet as well. When it's hot or wet they shelter themselves under wide-brimmed, umbrella-like, woven grass hats. Following the complete course on foot can take two months or more, so some people undertake only segments of the pilgrimage and others go by bus. Quite a few of the "pilgrims" take the journey just out of curiosity. There is no end to the respect and admiration Kōbō Daishi evokes—he's like a Christ figure, surrounded by stories of miracles and piety. Among them are many related to the discovery of hot springs, although it's possible that quite a few are untrue.

Perhaps more like the men you imagine associated with Japan's past are the fighting men, the men of action and war. Shikoku produced a lot. It was the scene of twelfth-century clashes between the Minamoto and Taira clans and the hide-out of many a political exile. In the nineteenth century it saw the birth of Sakamoto Ryōma (1835–67), a stocky, stern warrior who opposed the rule of the shogunate and wanted a peaceful restoration of imperial court power. Despite his desire for a nonviolent transition, he was none-too-peacefully assassinated—ironically, just after the emperor had been restored to power. Of a later age is Yoshida Shigeru, the powerful postwar prime minister who, like the aforementioned men, wasn't known for doing things half measure. Seafarers and sailors have also contributed to the image of Shikoku as a land of spirited men. The one with the most exciting tale to tell must have been John Manjirō (1827–98). He was picked up by an American whaling boat after being shipwrecked off the southern coast of Shikoku and spent years in America. After a stint on the gold fields, he had saved up enough money to return to Japan, where he became an advisor to the shogun's government, which was keen to learn about the West. One of his contemporaries from Shikoku, Iwasaki Yatarō (1834–85), founded the Mitsubishi Group, one of the biggest financial concerns of modern-day Japan.

Why has Shikoku spawned so many men of passion and pursuit? Perhaps the difficulty of subduing the sea made the island inhabitants fight for survival. Possibly its separation from the mainland gave the men of Shikoku a certain amount of freedom and independence which, coupled with the knowledge gleaned by its wandering sons and imported with the exiles, gave its men vision and the will to act.

The past lingers on in Shikoku, accounting for some strange incongruities. On one hand you see people praying fervently at shrines or reflecting silently in gardens like Ritsurin Park (Takamatsu City). On the other hand, you come across spectators frenzily cheering on fighting bulls or dogs. Bull "sumo" (wrestling), as it is called, is a popular sport in Uwajima (Ehime Prefecture), and the names of the grips the bull is supposed to use to outwit his opposition resemble those of real sumo. The bull fights are held in January, April, July, August, October, and November. You could see one en route to

30
Matsuyama

EHIME PREF.

Uwajima

Kubokawa

NAKAMURA LINE
Tosa-Saga
Nakamura **32**

Cape Ashizuri

INLAND SEA

Shōdo Island

Tadotsu

Takamatsu

Yashima

34

KAGAWA PREF.

Ō-Naruto Bridge

Naruto

*KŌTOKU MAIN
LINE*

Awaikeda

Ikenotani

NARUTO LINE

DŌSAN MAIN LINE

33

TOKUSHIMA MAIN LINE

Tokushima

Naruto
Whirlpools

31

TOKUSHIMA PREF.

Kōchi

Tosa-Yamada

Ō Ōtochi

Ryūgadō Caves

KŌCHI PREF.

Tosa Bay

3 SHIKOKU ISLAND

30. Dōgo
31. Inosawa
32. Inomisaki
33. Iya
34. Aji

Cape Muroto

Inomisaki Hot Spring (32) or Dōgo Hot Spring (30). Dog fighting has always been popular in Shikoku, where the huge, powerful Tosa dog, of Kōchi Prefecture, is bred to fight.

These apparent incongruities, along with the slower pace of Shikoku, set it apart from much of the mainland. Whatever you read into its brand of frontier spirit and more peaceful pursuits, you'll feel the difference. But go soon, for the recently completed Ō-Naruto Bridge, the first connecting Shikoku with the mainland, promises to bring change to the island's special atmosphere.

30 Dōgo

LOCATION: Dōgo, on the eastern outskirts of Matsuyama City, Ehime Prefecture, is 20 minutes by bus or streetcar from the central station. Matsuyama is accessible from Hiroshima by hydrofoil (1 hour 10 minutes) or ferry (3 hours). Ferries from Ōsaka, Beppu, and Kōbe also stop at Matsuyama. By air it takes 1 hour 40 minutes to reach Matsuyama from Tōkyō.

THE WATERS: "If you went first class, for only eight *sen* they lent you a bathrobe, an attendant washed you, and a girl served you tea in one of those elegant, shallow cups that they use in the tea ceremony. I always went first class." So says Botchan, the hero of Natsume Sōseki's classic novel *Botchan*, of Dōgo. Botchan (and no doubt Sōseki himself) favored the public bathhouse Shinrokaku, of which it's still said "you haven't bathed until you've bathed here." The Momoyama-style building dates to the Meiji era (1868–1912). The outside presents a fascinating view of layered, tiled roofs with fluted, curved edges and big, paper-covered sliding doors leading onto fragile wooden balconies. At the very top is a pagoda-like turret, the resting place of a white heron wrought in metal. Legend cites a heron as the first bather at Dōgo, although the god Ōkuninushi no Mikoto is also counted among the early patrons of this spring. Shōtoku Taishi, a sixth-century prince, is the first human known to have definitely dipped at Dōgo, making it one of the oldest frequented springs in the country, sought out by the noble and the literary ever since its discovery. Several emperors have used it; to see how the other half bathes, visit the imperial bathhouse called Yūshinden in the Dōgo bathing complex. In the seventeenth century, the clan leader Matsudaira Sadayuki remodeled Dōgo, constructing all sorts of baths: one for samurai and monks so they wouldn't have to break soap with lesser folk like craftsmen and merchants, who had their own tubs, and even a tub for women only—a rather futuristic idea for the times. There were cheap tubs and medicinal tubs and a waiting yard for horses. Nowadays, the system at the public bath is a bit different; back-scrubbing is no longer a feature of first class. For first class (¥1,200) you get a yukata, towel, green tea, *kuri* *senbei* (chestnut cookies), and access to the "memorial" rooms on the upper floors. These are dedicated to illustrious literary dippers like Sōseki, Shiki, and others. Second class is a fraction less and you get less exotic cakes with your tea and aren't permitted rambles in the upper rooms. Both classes mean free access to the tubs on the second floor. For just a few hundred yen, third class, you get no frills, no yukata, no tea and goodies—just a plain, satisfying bath. But the alkaline simple thermal water, the atmosphere, and the other bathers from all over Japan make it a well-spent ¥200. The water aids stiff joints, soothes obstreperous digestive systems, and calms ruffled nerves.

AROUND AND ABOUT: Serious hot-spring aficionados should visit Dōgo Park, where an ancient tub heater is enshrined and shops sell a lot of hot-spring paraphernalia. If you prefer the sound of the waves, white sand, and steam, try the Iwaburo steam bath near Dōgo. It is on Sakurai Beach and open to the public for a fee, but only from July through September. Take the Yosan Main Line from Matsuyama to Imabari Station (1 hour 20 minutes), then take a bus to Magobesaku bus stop (20 minutes). When you get off the bus, Iwaburo steam bath is on the left. The steam baths are made using wet straw mats heated with burning ferns. ■ MATSUYAMA: It's hard to imagine this bustling city populated with topknotted samurai swaggering in and out of sliding wooden doors, but this was the case several centuries ago when Matsuyama was an important castle town. The castle, a good example of Edo architecture, still stands and is well cared for, as are the gardens and parks around it, which are peaceful and remote from the din of the city. But do put up with the din long enough to stop off at a fish restaurant and try some Inland Sea sashimi; Shikoku Island is said to serve the best sashimi in Japan. Matsuyama is also known for its *kamaboko* (pressed fish), its salty, gluey rice snacks (*shōyu mochi*), and its blue-and-white Tobe pottery.

ACCOMMODATIONS: The Funaya Ryokan has a large garden and specializes in sea-bream sashimi all year round. Breakfast is served at 6:00 A.M. so guests can go to the baths early. Tōuntei is a small, inexpensive ryokan situated near the public bath.

31 Inosawa

LOCATION: This spring is northeast of Kōchi City on the Monobe River. Take the Dosan Main Line (from Tadotsu in the north or Kochi in the south) and get off at Tosa-Yamada Station. Take a bus (a 1-hour ride) to Inosawa and the spring is a few minutes from there on foot. This direct bus runs only twice in the evening. So it might be quicker to take any bus for Ōtochi, get off at the terminus, and take a taxi (15 minutes) to the spring.

THE WATERS: Inosawa is a quiet, relatively unknown spring. As the bus approaches it, you'll be able to make out a sign brush-painted in red. From there you climb down to the spring, which sits on the riverbank. Shikoku women consider this a beautifying spring. If the beauty bit doesn't work for you, the hydrogen sulphide water should help rheumatism, skin diseases, and neuralgia. There are two tubs in the riverside annex that belongs to the ryokan Isuisō. One is heated and one is straight from the spring—a cool 17° C (63° F). The recommended routine consists of going back and forth between the two, sweltering and shivering alternately, an invigorating experience to say the least. The inn provides yukata and geta so that you can totter to and fro in comfort.

AROUND AND ABOUT: For a change of scenery, visit the Ryūgadō limestone caves, 20 minutes by bus from Tosa-Yamada Station, and on the way to or from Inosawa Hot Spring. These cold chambers of shiny, wet stalactites and dark recesses filled with icy water were once inhabited. A museum at the site provides information about the caves, and another museum is devoted to rare birds.

ACCOMMODATIONS: The above-mentioned inn, Isuisō, is the only place to stay. Like the thatched-roof annex where guests can stay, the dinner fare here is an integral part of the atmosphere. Dinner—river fish and mountain vegetables served in wondrous ways—is served in front of an open fire. This annex is very small, so reservations are necessary. After a typical meal and a drop of saké, you might find you understand why this cozy spot was so favored by the twentieth-century poet Yoshii Isamu, who named the annex (Keikisō, or "Gorge-Demon Cottage"). Outside, the sounds of the river, and the peaceful mountains and rice fields, are as calming as the mellow wood interior and glowing embers before you.

32 Inomisaki

LOCATION: This spring is located on the way to the large town of Nakamura, which is north of Cape Ashizuri, the southernmost point of Shikoku. Inomisaki is in Kōchi Prefecture. Take the Dosan Main Line from Kōchi to Kubokawa and then the connecting Nakamura Line to Tosa-Saga. The Inomisaki Onsen Hotel bus will collect you there, or you can take a taxi (20 minutes).

THE WATERS: The water contains sulphur for treating skin problems, especially dry skin, as well as rheumatism and general fatigue of body or soul. The hot-spring area is small, has a countrified air, and is near the sea.

AROUND AND ABOUT: Nakamura is about 20 minutes by train from Tosa-Saga Station. It tempts you with the best bonito (*katsuo*) sashimi in Japan. On November 23 to 26 it entertains you with three days of reveling when people parade through the streets in samurai garb sporting swords or carrying small portable shrines. On October 10 there is the Fuwahachiman Shrine festival, which features prayers for good harvests and a "marriage" of gods re-enacted on the riverbank. Nakamura also offers a hint of Kyōto. In the fifteenth century the court advisor Ichijō Norifusa fled from Kyōto to

Nakamura where he built houses and designed streets like those in his beloved city; which still remain. He is remembered in the Ichijō Taisha Festival in November. A unique offering is Nakamura's spider sumo tournament, staged on the first Sunday in August. During the event specially trained and fed spiders, called *jorō* spiders, fight it out until the bitter end—that is, until one gets a good grip on the other and devours him. ■ CAPE ASHIZURI: This landmark, about 2 hours by bus from Nakamura, is a good example of Shikoku's wild side. Its stone cliffs tower straight up and down and subtropical plant life abounds. The single bit of mankind, a white lighthouse, only serves to make the sea look a deeper, more dangerous blue. It was off this cape that John Manjirō (1827–98) was shipwrecked at the age of fourteen. He lived a Robinson Crusoe existence on an island to the south until he was picked up by an American whaling boat that took him off to America. After an invaluable education and a lucky stint in the gold fields there, this child of fortune returned to Japan and served the shogun as a diplomat, cartographer, and naval engineer. As a child he lived in Tosa-Shimizu near the cape, and upon returning from America he lived in Edo (Tōkyō). He was involved in translating the first U.S.-Japan treaty and was a member of the first official delegation to America. People say he had the fighting spirit typical of Shikoku men.

ACCOMMODATIONS: There is only one hotel here—Inomisaki Onsen Hotel. It serves live shellfish for you to cook at your table.

33 Iya

LOCATION: This spring is on the Iya River in northwestern Tokushima Prefecture. Take the Dosan Main Line or the Tokushima Main Line to Awaikeda Station. From there take the bus to Iya Onsenguchi, a 1-hour ride.

THE WATERS: Iya's communal, riverside, open-air bath is visited by bathers looking for an off-the-beaten-track hot spring. The jungle atmosphere of Iya, with its 450-odd steps (recently supplemented by a cable car) leading down to the pool in the gorge and the dense, impenetrable plant growth, makes it like an untouched Eden. This absence of bright lights combined with simple thermal healing power will surely ease any aches or pains.

AROUND AND ABOUT: For a bit of adventure worthy of the jungle, try crossing the Kazura Bridge farther along the Iya River. At your own risk and for ¥50 or so, you can sway and pray your way across the swirling waters below on this bridge made from woven vines. Take heart though, for the bridge is restrung every three years and so far no one has fallen, at least officially. Nor do you have to go back the way you came. There's a return path on solid earth. If it's any comfort, this bridge is based on historical precedent. After the battle at Yashima between the Minamoto and Taira clans in the late twelfth century, some of the defeated Taira fled to this area and built seven vine bridges, like the Kazura Bridge, that could be cut down if enemies approached. With such protection they were able to start a new life in their mountain hideaway. They changed their names and set themselves up as ordinary farmers. A house with a big thatched roof, called Asake, is the residence of the twenty-third generation of the Taira.

ACCOMMODATIONS: The closest inn to the bath is Hotel Iya Onsen, which is quite comfortable. A bit further away is Toshikosō, a minshuku.

34 Aji

LOCATION: Aji is northeast of Takamatsu City, Kagawa Prefecture, on the tip of the small peninsula near Yashima. From Takamatsu Station it's 45 minutes by bus to Aji.

THE WATERS: The water is hydrogen sulphide, ideal for aching limbs, nervous tension, rheumatism, and skin irritations. The slightly opaque, whitish water is good for healthy skins too, making them soft and creamy like the water.

AROUND AND ABOUT: Aji is near Yakuriji Temple, eighty-fifth in the famous Shikoku temple pilgrimage. The Buddhist priest Kōbō Daishi carved one of the Goddess of Mercy statues in the temple. A small spring in a fishing town, Aji borders one of the most scenic shorelines in Shikoku. The sea is the Inland Sea, with picturesque islets, bays, boats, and crinkled shorelines—all visible from Yashima Plateau. ▪ YASHIMA: This historic granite plateau, volcanically formed and separated by a narrow waterway from Shikoku Island, is where the Minamoto clan defeated the Taira clan in 1185. The hiking course around the plateau takes in all the sites associated with this famous battle, including the Pool of Blood, where the warriors washed their swords, and the place where the mythical Yashima badger—an animal capable of transforming himself into a human being—became disillusioned with life after his masters, the Taira clan, were defeated. This disillusionment led the metamorphosed badger to religion and he became a devout Buddhist. Also along the hiking course are a temple, a "snow garden" of white rocks, and excellent views of the Inland Sea. ▪ NARUTO WHIRLPOOLS: This natural phenomenon is caused by the changing tide and differing water levels in the straits separating Shikoku from Awaji Island. The resulting action is a like a washing machine gone wild. If you made your way to Shikoku by boat or ferry, chances are that you saw the whirlpools on your way across. If not, you might consider making the 2-hour journey from Takamatsu to Naruto. Take the Kōtoku Main Line from Takamatsu to Ikenotani (1 hour 20 minutes by express), then take the Naruto Line to Naruto (20 minutes).

ACCOMMODATIONS: The old Aji Onsen Aji Kankō Hotel, the only inn here, has a special fitness room for workouts after bathing. Dinner is a delightful assortment of seafood in all shapes and colors.

4 KINKI REGION
Seven Prefectures for the Lucky Traveler

Although seven isn't regarded as a particularly lucky number in Japan, the traveler to the seven prefectures of the Kinki Region will wonder why. The region is crammed with culture, tradition, and physical beauty, and as if to prevent you from getting too saturated with the arts it offers international ports and commercial expertise as well. From the seas on its boundaries— the Sea of Japan on the north and the Inland Sea on the south—to the lakes, mountains, and rivers in its heartlands, it can claim some of the more superior geographical possessions of Japan. Take the white sands of Shirahama (Wakayama Prefecture), for example, or Lake Biwa, the biggest lake in Japan (Shiga), or Ise-Shima National Park (Mie), Yoshino-Kumano National Park (southern Kii Peninsula), and Nachi Waterfall (Wakayama).

Kinki has more than its fair share of cultural possessions, too. Kyōto and Nara, between them, just about have it all sewn up. The Ise Shrine area is a close third in religious and historical importance, and for tradition of a different kind, the ports of Ōsaka and Kōbe are of equal stature. Throw in one of the most beautiful castles in Japan, Himeji Castle (Hyōgo); Bunraku, the puppet theater that is centered in Ōsaka; the internationally respected arts and crafts of Kyōto; the year-round, colorful festivals; and the exquisite cuisine, both Japanese and international, and you'll feel so overwhelmed that you'll want to head for the mountains of Hokkaidō. Better still, stay in the area and investigate one of the places introduced below, but take a break from it all at a quiet, out-of-the-limelight hot spring. But, again, choose

SANIN COAST

Hamasaka
Kinosaki
Tango Kizu
Oku-Tango Pen.

37
35
38

Amanohashidate
Toyo-oka
MIYATSU LINE

HYŌGO PREF.

Himeji Castle
○
Himeji
MT. ROKKŌ
36
Shin-Kōbe
TŌKAIDŌ-SANYŌ SHINKANSEN
Kōbe
Sannomiya
Ōsaka

Osaka Bay

Awajishima

Wakayama
WAKAYAMA LINE
Gojō
39
Kii Pen.
Minoshima
WAKAYAMA PREF.
40
44
43
Minabe
Kii Tanabe
Kii Katsuura
Shirahama
41
KISEI MAIN LINE
42

Cape Shionomisaki

35. Kinosaki
36. Arima
37. Yumura
38. Kizu
39. Arita
40. Ryūjin
41. Shirahama
42. Katsuura
43. Yunomine
44. Kawayu
45. Wataze
46. Yoshino
47. Tōsenji
48. Miyano
49. Yunoyama
50. Nagashima (Sunnyland Kurhaus)

4 KINKI REGION

Wakasa Bay

SHIGA PREF.

KYŌTO

HOKURIKU MAIN LINE

L. Biwa

SANIN MAIN LINE

Kyōto

Kusatsu

Otsu

TŌKAIDŌ MAIN LINE

KUSATSU LINE

Yunoyama

49

KINTETSU
YUNOYAMA LINE

Kōnan

48

Nagashima

Yokkaichi

KANSAI MAIN LINE

Nara

50

KINTETSU LINE

Tsu

Ise Bay

NARA PREF.

MIE PREF.

Yoshino

46

YOSHINO-KUMANO N. P.

Futamigaura

47

ISE-SHIMA N. P.

45

Nachi

Shingū

carefully: some of the thermal waters of Kinki are the most sought-after of their kind as well!

Kyōto: Don't waste your breath saying everyone goes there so you won't. You would bitterly regret missing Kyōto. Not only was it the capital of Japan from 794 to 1868 and the center of Buddhism, with more than sixteen hundred temples, Kyōto was, and still is, as any Kyōtoite will tell you, the cultural and artistic center of Japan. Besides visiting temples and shrines—magnificently somber and finely in tune with nature, or outspoken with gold leaf and bright red paint—you can treat your eyes to pottery, lacquerware, silk, bamboo crafts, and what look like dolls walking the streets, elaborately attired in what you expect Japanese women to wear in such an environment. Or treat several senses by sipping saké and nibbling delicacies too pretty to eat, in rooms overlooking the Kamo River. Nights mean traditional Kabuki or Noh drama or stage shows featuring _maiko_—girls trained in the traditional arts of music, dance, and song.

Any time of day is good for eating, a favorite pastime of the Japanese when they go to Kyōto. It's said that since Kyōto is inland and influenced by Buddhism, there are limits on what can be served at the table; fish and meat are not very important. Rather, the local cuisine is based on vegetables, bean curd, pickles, and lots of heart. The result is an exquisite art of presenting and arranging food. With a lot of care, a Kyōto woman will place before you small dishes of food that may contain minute morsels and may seem bland, but look again. If it's a grilled vegetable it will be steaming, but the green leaf placed beside it will be freshly sprinkled with water as, in nature, dewdrops collect on its surface. The choice of plate, the angle of food placement, the colors of both, and the cut of the morsel have all been carefully considered. You will be impressed. This is the level of art that sets Kyōto apart and makes the Kyōto woman the model for all, so delicate, feminine, and devoted is she. So even for those not enamored of temples, gardens, and museums, there's a wealth of social history to be experienced all about Kyōto.

Nara: According to legend, the first emperor of Japan was enthroned here in the seventh century B.C. Recorded history also shows Nara to be old: in the eighth century A.D. it became the first stable capital of Japan (prior to this the capital moved with the accession of each emperor). Japanese culture and spirit were molded in great part by Buddhism, which flourished in Nara at this time. Wandering among the sacred deer in Nara Park or through the city, you can feel the quiet, settled, muted air of antiquity—calming after the heady grandeur of Kyōto. The gilt on the Great Buddha seems faded, the wooden, stone, and bronze carvings in the shrines (Kasuga and Kasuga Wakamiya), temples (Tōdaiji and Kōfukuji), and gardens (Nara

Park) merge into the moss, trees, and tranquillity of their surroundings so well that you can't imagine them not being created all together at the dawn of civilization. In the mountains around Nara as you climb lonely paths you'll hear the gong of a temple bell being struck. The reverberation will drift across the valley, melting into the misty panorama, and you'll know you're close to the essence that is Japan.

Ōsaka: Although of a different kind, Ōsaka's history goes back even further than that of Kyōto and almost as far back as Nara's. Ōsaka is thought to have started its career as a commercial center in the fourth century A.D. Ōsaka never lacked energy or excitement. In the sixteenth century the great warlord Toyotomi Hideyoshi built a castle here and the town became a center of samurai activities. It all remains: the castle, the business acumen, and the samurai, who now wear navy suits and ties but are just as regimented and determined as ever. It's said that Ōsakans don't go much for cooking and like to eat out. Hence it is a city bursting with restaurants of all kinds, usually very good and inexpensive, that consume their share of the locals' salaries. A port, a hub of heavy industry, a town with a reputation for scandalous night life—all describe the inimitable Ōsaka.

Ise-Shima National Park: This park contains the most important Shinto buildings in Japan—the Naikū, or inner shrine, and the Gekū, or outer shrine, both part of the Ise Shrine complex. For centuries the imperial family has worshiped here, although formal links with the government have been discontinued since World War II. The buildings are fine examples of pure Shinto architecture—simple, wooden (cypress in some buildings), and unpainted. Most prized by connoisseurs is the sanctuary of the inner shrine and its thatched roof with logs and cross beams. The inner shrine belongs to Amaterasu Ōmikami, the Sun Goddess and most revered Shinto deity, and the outer shrine is dedicated to Toyouke no Ōkami, goddess of food, clothing, and shelter. Exploring the surroundings—a hill, river, gardens, shrine buildings (including stables of sacred horses for Amaterasu to ride), giant cedars and pines—can take up several pleasant hours.

Kōbe: For a change of pace or a bit of decadence after too much serious religious sightseeing, go to Kōbe. An international port with a visible cosmopolitan flavor, Kōbe is not just beef cut from the flanks of beer-guzzling cows massaged for endless hours by loving attendants. Granted, its beef is world famous, delicious, and expensive, but Kōbe has more—from traditional festivals to heavy industries to European confectioneries. If you take the overhead cable car to the top of Mount Rokkō, you can have good views of a bright, cluttered, booming harbor. Some parts of the city will surprise you with their European-style buildings, and the smells of Chinatown will transport you to Hongkong.

At this point our kaleidoscopic tour of Kinki must end. If you feel some places have been neglected, you are right. Some are touched on in the following pages, but many are not, so great is the wealth of information on Kinki that confronts writer and traveler alike. As a traveler you will at least be entertained by Kinki; at most you will go mad with frustration—how can anyone cram two thousand years of Japan into a seven-day holiday?

35 Kinosaki

LOCATION: Kinosaki is in northern Hyōgo Prefecture, almost on the Sanin Coast. From Kinosaki Station on the Sanin Main Line it's a short walk to the hot-spring area.

THE WATERS: Kinosaki is another eighth-century discovery, probably made by the monk Dōchi, who was spending a thousand days in penance in the area, fasting, praying, and chanting. While he was thus occupied a vision came to him, telling him of the existence of a hot spring nearby. The local people named it Mandarayu ("Mandala Waters") and a town grew up around it. From the beginning this town, Kinosaki, has been a destination of hot-spring fans. Particularly popular are the public tubs, which number seven including Mandarayu, Ichi-no-yu, Jizōyu (named after Jizō, guardian deity of children), and Kō-no-yu. Visitors make it a practice to tub hop, forsaking their ryokan tubs for the public baths. The water, sodium chloride, is the same throughout the area, but the decor and the shape and size of the public tubs vary. Some of the bathhouses also have family tubs (private baths for use by a single family at a time). The water should relax any stiff joints, but if it doesn't, a between-baths stroll under the willows surely will.

AROUND AND ABOUT: Kinosaki has a feeling of the past about it, aided no doubt by the picturesque Ōtani River that flows through town. Its banks are crowded with cherry trees (which bloom in April) and willows, and arched stone bridges span its waters. In the summer you can go swimming on the beautiful Sanin Coast, 10 minutes away by bus. In winter you can ski at Kinosaki very near the hot spring. For the more sedentary, there's an overhead cable car to the top of Mount Daishi with views of all that's around. This ascent also stops at Onsenji Temple, dedicated to the above-mentioned monk, Dōchi. A trail from the spa goes to the Genbudō caves, which have dark, marblelike pillars formed from solidified lava.

ACCOMMODATIONS: Kobayashiya is an old wooden ryokan situated in front of the public bathhouse Ichi-no-yu. It has a large, circular indoor bath. Another traditional ryokan is Tsutaya.

FOOD: The famous crabs with long, spindly legs found here are delicious, but beware, it's only the male crabs that taste good; there's little meat on the females.

36 Arima

LOCATION: Arima is north of Kōbe City in Hyōgo Prefecture on the slopes of Mount Rokkō. From Shin-Kōbe Station on the Shinkansen (bullet train) route from Tōkyō, the spring is 40 minutes by bus. From Sannomiya Station on the Tōkaidō Main Line it's 45 minutes. You can also approach Arima from other nearby cities like Kyōto and Ōsaka on private rail lines.

THE WATERS: All manner of stories relate to the discovery of this very old hot spring, which dates back to the eighth century. Gyōki, one of the three priests most active in the discovery of thermal springs, is said to have found and saved a sick man on Mount Rokkō, not far from here. Once cured, the "man" turned back into the deity Yakushi Nyorai, who had just been testing Gyōki. Gyōki then built a temple for the deity, which became the hot-spring temple. Another story relates how the monk Ninsei developed the town. He built twelve inns named after Yakushi Nyorai's followers; hence the proliferation of inns there with *bō* (priest) in their names. Arima owes its prosperity to *yuna*, women to attend the rich in the bathhouses. The attendants under twenty, called *koyuna*, had to take care of the tub and bathing utensils, while those over twenty, the *ōyuna*, performed the glamorous tasks of attending to clothes, beverages, back scrubbing, and anything their wealthy patrons desired at bathtime. Arima became very popular. People who bathed there tried to outdo one another in creating the reddest yukata. These light robes were worn in the Arima tubs, and because of the iron content of the water they changed color. The redder the robe, the richer the man, for only the wealthiest could afford to stay long at an expensive bathing resort. In addition to iron, Arima's water contains sodium chloride (in fact the water is twice as salty as brine) and is carbonated. The combination was thought to enhance fertility in the past; aristocratic women desiring sons came to visit from far and wide. You can try the water for this or just settle for treating anemia, skin irritations, muscular pain, or surface wounds. You can always try out the public bath, Shiei Onsen Kaikan, where you can soak all day for a few hundred yen.

AROUND AND ABOUT: Arima is a resort catering to visitors from Ōsaka, Kyōto, and Kōbe. In spite of this commercial bent, however, the surroundings are not unpleasant. Beyond the concrete and flashing neon the Rokkō Mountain Range stands unperturbed, beautifully tinted—like most of the area—with vivid colors in spring and autumn. To find quiet and seclusion, walk through the grounds of the hot-spring shrine or Zuihōjiato Park. In the park you can see a go board once used by the great warrior Toyotomi Hideyoshi himself. In all, the waters are good and so is the food. It's no wonder this is a top-ranked onsen.

ACCOMMODATIONS: Hashinoya is an Edo-style ryokan with lots of sliding doors and winding corridors. While you sit in the tub you can watch a garden waterfall in action. Another possibility is Goshobō Ryokan, one of the twelve built by Ninsei. It has been rebuilt in more recent times but retains enough atmosphere to be popular with writers today.

FESTIVALS: On January 2, statues of the hot spring's founders—Ōkuninushi no Mikoto, Ninsei, Gyōki, and Yakushi Nyorai—are carried in procession. They are then washed by women dressed as *yuna*. On November 2 and 3, Toyotomi Hideyoshi is remembered for another of his passions: drinking tea under red maples. Everyone joins in.

37 Yumura

LOCATION: This hot spring lies somewhat inland from the Sanin Coast in northwestern Hyōgo Prefecture. Take the Sanin Main Line to Hamasaka Station and then a bus to the hot springs—a 25-minute ride.

THE WATERS: This spring bubbles up in the center of town. Called Arayu, the source produces 490 liters of 98° C (208° F) water every minute. Much of it is used for bathing, cooking, heating, and washing, but a lot just runs down the Haruki River. The water is simple thermal and softens both skin and clothes (when used for doing laundry). It's also used to treat rheumatism. Near Arayu there are a series of small pools with wooden frames around them where you can cook your own vegetables, eggs, fish, or, if you want to be authentic, the local mineral-water delicacy—tofu and noodles cooked in simple thermal. The added flavor of the water is good, and the experience of cooking for yourself here is one you won't forget.

AROUND AND ABOUT: Strolling in yukata and chatting in the streets is highly recommended, for this is a real hot-spring town with lines of inns huddled together along the riverbank and crowding back toward the hills around. The inns compete for visitors with splendid tubs and table fare, the two main delights of spa towns. For the more energetic there are temples and shrines in the town to visit, like the temple dedicated to the spring's founder, the monk Jikaku Daishi. In winter you can ski at Nakayama, only 8 kilometers away, and in summer you can swim on the Sanin Coast, 30 minutes away by bus. Take advantage of the free bus service to the beach for guests of all the ryokan. Non-swimmers may prefer the boat tours leaving Hamasaka (the free bus service will drop you off here) that wind along this very beautiful stretch of coast.

ACCOMMODATIONS: Yumura Kankō Hotel, built to look like a castle, has an elaborate open-air bath complete with thatched-roof gate and stone lantern. Another inn where baths take pride of place is Izutsuya Ryokan, which has numerous tubs, including a huge *senninburo* ("thousand-person bath"). For après-bath fortification these inns offer such delicacies as crab, special beef dishes, and, of course, the local specialty, tofu and noodles.

FESTIVALS: The hot-spring festival is held on June 1.

38 Kizu

LOCATION: Kizu is on Oku Tango Peninsula, along the Sanin Coast, in northern Kyōto Prefecture. Take the Miyazu Line from Toyo oka (where it connects with the Sanin Main Line) and get off at Tango Kizu Station. From there it's a 5-minute walk.

THE WATERS: Kizu is another of Gyōki's eighth-century discoveries. It's the only natural spring in Kyōto Prefecture where the water is above 25° C (77° F) at the point of emission; the rest are cool mineral springs. The water is simple thermal and treats surface cuts and abrasions, skin irritations, and female disorders.

AROUND AND ABOUT: A small, quiet community with only a handful of ryokan, Kizu is a relaxing base for exploring the famous scenery all around. Most famous is Amanohashidate, on the other side of Oku Tango Peninsula. (Take the Miyazu Line to Amanohashidate Station, six stops from Tango Kizu.) This "Bridge to Heaven" is one of the, you guessed it, Three Most Beautiful Scenes in Japan. (The Japanese like to group things in threes.) Unless you know it's the spot where the gods stood and created Japan, you might think it was just another pine-clad sand bar extending out into Wakasa Bay. Try to feel the nostalgia and solemnity of it all. If you can't, lose yourself in the magnificent seascapes the gods made on either side. On the way back to Kizu, stop at Kotobikihama ("Koto-Playing Beach") and Taikohama ("Drum Beach") along the Kakezu Coast, on the northern side of Oku Tango Peninsula, and play some music on the sand. Toe wriggling at Kotobikihama produces a sound resembling the *koto* (Japanese harp) and some foot stamping at Taikohama produces a drum (*taiko*) beat. If it doesn't, don't despair—listen to the waves or watch the sun set instead. In about mid-April, depending on the weather, a tulip festival in Kizu turns the area into a vivid bright red and gold carpet, a welcome jolt to the senses after the white, cold, and gray of winter.

ACCOMMODATIONS: Ebisuya Ryokan, near the station, is close enough to the sea for a spot of brine dipping between thermal baths. This ryokan serves large platters of sashimi and "pine-needle" crabs (*matsuba-gani*), so-called because their legs are long and skinny like pine needles.

39 Arita

LOCATION: Arita lies on the coast a little south of Wakayama City, Wakayama Prefecture. From Minoshima on the Kisei Main Line it's 20 minutes by bus to the spring.

THE WATERS: Arita is known for its cable-car bath, called Apollo, which takes bathers from the main bathing area, across an inlet, and a little up the mountainside, providing scenic views while you soak. Apollo is only operated for groups requesting it but may be just the right change of pace for the jaded bather. If you suffer from motion sickness, stay on the ground and dabble in the milk bath or the *mikan* bath with its floating mandarin oranges, both designed to beautify complexions. As you may have gathered, the simple thermal water here has undergone some creative packaging, so if you're a hot-springs purist it may be better to leave Arita to the thrill seekers.

AROUND AND ABOUT: The Arita River, which runs through town, is one of several places in the area where you can observe cormorant fishing. These trained birds are put into the water to catch sweetfish (*ayu*) attracted by torchlight. The birds scoop up the fish whole but are prevented from swallowing them by a cord tied around their necks. The birds are pulled in by the long cords and forced to relinquish their sizable catch before being sent out for more.

ACCOMMODATIONS: A good place to stay is the Arita Kankō Hotel, the proud operator of Apollo.

40 Ryūjin

LOCATION: This hot spring is situated on the Hidaka River in eastern-central Wakayama Prefecture. From Kii Tanabe Station on the Kisei Main Line, it's 2¼ hours by bus. From Minabe Station, north of Kii Tanabe on the same line, it's about 2 hours by bus.

THE WATERS: Ryūjin was discovered by En no Ozuno, one of the three priests famous for hot-spring discoveries, and was rediscovered by another of the three, Kōbō Daishi, who developed it for religious bathing in the eighth century. Later Ryūjin underwent a drastic change in character—from quiet, reflective bath for the pious to country club for the Kishū clan officials and their entourages. Two mansionlike ryokan were built, Kamigoten for the elite and Shimogoten for their followers. Thereafter Ryūjin became quite fashionable, and many more ryokan were constructed during the Edo period (1603–1868). Today only four ryokan stand, including the reconstructed Kamigoten and Shimogoten—somewhat smaller, less costly, and more democratic than their precursors. The ryokan have their own baths, or try the public bathhouse near the bridge in the center of town, overlooking the river, that features segregated open-air baths. The water, sodium hydrogen-carbonate, has made Ryūjin one of the three most famous "beautifying" hot springs in Japan (the other two are Kawanaka in Gunma Prefecture and Yunokawa in Shimane Prefecture). The water here is also good for hysteria. If you have such a tendency try working yourself up a bit and then test the claim—it should provide some bathside entertainment for your bathing companions, if nothing else.

AROUND AND ABOUT: Compared with many hot springs in Wakayama, Ryūjin is relatively forlorn and forgotten. The trip there is time-consuming, but the bus ride is a pleasant one and Ryūjin is worth it. The town is in the mountains, which are havens of small temples and shrines such as Onsenji Temple, south of Ryūjin, which is dedicated to Kōbō Daishi and houses a statue of Yakushi Nyorai. The area is cool and green in summer and alive with color in autumn.

ACCOMMODATIONS: Shimogoten, first opened in 1639, sits on the bank of the Hidaka River. Its lantern out front is decorated with the original family crest. The similar Kamigoten is equally steeped in the past. A more modern alternative is Kokuminshukusha Ryūjin Onsen Lodge, which is near the public bath.

41 Shirahama

LOCATION: This hot spring is situated on the southwestern side of Kii Peninsula, in Wakayama Prefecture. From Shirahama Station on the Kisei Main Line the hot-spring areas are up to 30 minutes away by bus.

THE WATERS: In age Shirahama ranks with Dōgo (30) and Arima (36), and in popularity with Atami (51) and Beppu (1). This giant among thermal springs comprises six main spring areas. The oldest, Yuzaki, still has the best-positioned open-air pool. This pool, Saki-no-yu, is on the beach, ideally situated for viewing some of the best sunsets in Japan; Shirahama, say some, is synonymous with sunsets. Saki-no-yu is segregated and open to the public. The waters, sodium hydrogen-carbonate or sodium chloride, are good for backaches, women's complaints (anything from menstrual pain to menopausal tension), rheumatism, and, if imbibed, upset stomachs and constipation. Since the Taishō era (1912–26), Shirahama has blossomed as a resort area. Money from affluent travelers has poured into it, and developing transportation facilities have made it easily accessible to dwellers of such nearby cities as Wakayama, Ōsaka, and Nagoya. The increase in clientele has put little strain on the spring, however, since water flows abundantly from about a hundred sources. This, combined with the scenic countryside inland from Shirahama and the natural beauty of the immediate surroundings, makes it a very attractive spa destination, even with its concrete waterfront resort hotels. The white sandy beach adds the crowning touch to one of Japan's nicest imitation "Hawaiis."

AROUND AND ABOUT: Near the coast off Shirahama lies an unusual island known as Engetsujima, which is no more than an oblong rock with a hole through the center. If you're inclined to view this natural oddity you can take a cruise aboard one of the innumerable pleasure boats that ply the waters around here, especially in summer. The sea, sand, and sunset vistas from such a boat are not to be scoffed at, and in fact may be the source of Shirahama's popularity as a honeymoon resort.

ACCOMMODATIONS: Shirahama has numerous accommodations to choose from. For a bit of a splurge try Hotel Koganoi with its vast array of tubs: a rock bath, waterfall bath, thermal swimming pool, and so on. After dinner, honeymooners can take in the Polynesian floor show. For those on tighter budgets, there's Kokuminshukusha Meikō Shirahama Lodge.

42 Katsuura

LOCATION: Katsuura lies on the eastern coast of Kii Peninsula, just up from the tip, in Wakayama Prefecture. Take the Kisei Main Line, which runs along the edge of the peninsula, to Kii Katsuura Station. The closest ryokan are a few minutes' walk from there. You can also reach Katsuura by ferry from Tokyo, which operates on odd days of the month.

THE WATERS: This hot spring offers two very special baths: one at Hotel Nakanoshima on Nakanoshima Island in Katsuura Bay and a cave bath at Urashima Hotel. Take this opportunity to pamper yourself! A short, free boat trip from Kankō Sanbashi dock takes you to Hotel Nakanoshima and its top-class bathing and après-bath facilities. The split-level, segregated baths are practically part of the sea; just a natural rock wall separates brine and bath water. This tiny island boasts six thermal springs. The sulphur water will work on dilating your blood vessels, invigorating your heart, and removing toxins from your body. A mouthful will settle your stomach in preparation for the seafood extravaganza served at dinner time. The other special bath, called Bōkidō, is situated in a natural cave owned by Urashima Hotel. Bōkidō means "Forget-to-Go-Home Cave," named after what a nobleman of the Edo period did, so infatuated was he with this area. The cave opens out from a first-floor tunnel and its gaping mouth faces seaward. The silhouettes of rocks, people, and the cave entrance at dusk are the fabulous results of such a location. The water is sulphate and was once used by wounded warriors of the Taira clan after skirmishes with the Minamoto clan in the twelfth century. It's still good for any battle injuries you may have, as well as the usual skin, joint, and stress-caused ailments such water treats.

AROUND AND ABOUT: Katsuura is a resort town so if you feel like some quiet, it's best to go to one of the baths mentioned above or to Nakanoshima Island, which is rock-bound and densely covered with vegetation; you can push your way through it if you tire of the easy life. Or just sit back and let the spectacular sunset and view of boats shuttling people about the bay work magic on your spirits. Another way to escape the tourist activity in Katsuura is to take a boat to a ryokan on the tip of the peninsula, Cape Shionomisaki. Scenic cruises go out in all directions. The Kino Matsushima group of small islands off Katsuura provides particularly good views. Or travel inland (25 minutes by bus to Nachi on the Kisei Main Line) to see the famous Nachi Waterfall—133 meters of tumbling, frothing water. For a little adventure take the Kisei Main Line north to Shingū, the launching point for what amounts to shooting rapids in reverse. This several-hour boat trip up the Kumano River to Dorokyō Gorge is not exactly rapid or hair-raising, but the winding river, spectacular sights around bends, and occasional patch of fast current make it worthwhile. You can continue northward or return to Shingū by bus.

ACCOMMODATIONS: Hotel Nakanoshima and Urashima Hotel offer superb bathing experiences as well as fine food, accommodations, and service.

43 Yunomine

LOCATION: Yunomine is in southeastern Wakayama Prefecture, near the border with Nara Prefecture. Get off the Kisei Main Line at Shingū Station. The bus from there to the hot spring takes about 1½ hours.

THE WATERS: Don't leave Yunomine without trying out Tsuboyu, a small bath carved out of gray-brown rock that sits almost midstream, fighting off the Yunotani River tumbling about it on all sides. Behind it the riverbank is green and steep, supporting old, wooden ryokan. Tsuboyu is open to the public and segregated in shifts (certain hours are set aside for men and others for women). A partial enclosure provides some comfort for the modest. The sulphur water in the bath changes color seven times a day, mostly subtle shifts in opaqueness though at times it glows a definite orange-yellow. Don't let the color or the slimy feel to the water put you off, for it does wonders for complexions and aids an interminable list of aches and internal disorders. Beware its effects on jewelry, however. Two other public baths, Oguriyu and Kōmyōyu, are nice but not nearly as interesting as Tsuboyu. The thermal water at Yunomine is still used for cooking, and not just for tourist shows. Look for the big tubs of boiling water with bamboo baskets and ladles in front of Tōkōji Temple in the center of town almost under the bridge. This public cooking area is called Yuzutsu. By joining the local women, watching and listening to them, you should be able to put together a full course meal. The tofu made with spring water, as well as eggs, rice, and vegetables, are all available in the town. When you cook them here the rice emerges a pale saffron and the eggs, soup, and vegetables darker in color, but they all taste good.

AROUND AND ABOUT: Yunomine is a picturesque, typical hot-spring town, with a river flowing through the center, houses on the banks, and steep winding roads leading up the hillsides in all directions. Small, dark shops spill out onto these roads, selling anything you might want. At Tōkōji Temple you can see a statue of Yakushi Nyorai, the deity of medicine, carved out of sinter (hardened mineral sediment from the thermal water). A spring flows from his chest and this is the origin of the name Yunomine. Yunomune, an early name for the spring, literally means "chest of hot water"; somewhere along the line the name changed to the less arcane Yunomine, or "Hot-Water Peak." This story illustrates the religious connections bathing had with

Buddhism in the past. Yunomine has also long had connections with Shinto. Pilgrims en route from Tanabe in western Kii Peninsula to the famous Kumano Hongū Shrine near Dorokyō Gorge took a break from the arduous trek here. The mixture of Shinto and Buddhism in this area, while not being unique in Japan, may be a bit confusing for foreign visitors used to clearly defined religious philosophies.

ACCOMMODATIONS: The ryokan Azumaya has a wooden tub, as fragrant as a forest and quite a rarity these days. It also has a rock-enclosed outdoor pool. At Iseya you can choose a Japanese- or Western-style room. They will serve you meals or, if you prefer, you can cook your own at the public cooking facilities.

44 Kawayu

LOCATION: Kawayu is situated on the Totsu River in southern Wakayama Prefecture. Take the Kisei Main Line to Shingū Station. From there the bus inland to the hot spring takes an hour.

THE WATERS: This spring is a 500-meter stretch of gray pebbles on a riverbank that, with a bit of digging, will produce a thermal spring almost anywhere. Do you crave a large, warm pool surrounded by rocks, just barely separated from a river and opposite a dark green forest of pine? If you do, and if a misty, steamy atmosphere appeals, then Kawayu is for you. After you dig your own pool (bring your own spade or use one of the ones already there), be sure to add cold water by making a small channel from the river before you get in—the thermal water is a sizzling 70° C (158° F). The water is alkaline simple thermal—good for dull complexions, rheumatism, and convalescence. The setting itself should dispel fatigue and stress, replacing it with a euphoric calm.

AROUND AND ABOUT: Kawayu is a mountain-river area in one of the most beautiful parts of Wakayama. The recommended activity is to just sink into the pebbles for a bit, forget about museums, shrines, and castles, and let the river flow.

ACCOMMODATIONS: The ryokan Fujiya and Kameya both provide good accommodations and service. In addition to their own respective baths, there's a public open-air pool in front of the ryokan.

45 Wataze

LOCATION: Wataze lies 2 kilometers upstream from Kawayu (44) on the Totsu River. You can take a bus or, better still, walk from Kawayu. The bus from Shingū Station on the Kisei Main Line takes 1 hour 10 minutes.

THE WATERS: The style of bath here is like that at Kawayu (44)—wilderness and rock pools on the river banks. A new spring, which only opened a few years ago, Wataze is unspoiled, and the cliff faces, trees, and rocks visible from the pools make it as rugged and remote as a hot-spring bath could be. The water is sodium hydrogen-carbonate—good for unhappy stomachs, jarred nerves, and any aches incurred on the walk up from Kawayu. This beautiful setting is worth any number of muscle pains.

AROUND AND ABOUT: Wataze is a newly developed spa, surrounded by mountains, with only one hotel. So sit back and enjoy the relative solitude, or wander over to Kawayu for a change of thermal water.

ACCOMMODATIONS: Watarase Sansō is a modern, moderately priced inn with indoor and outdoor bathing facilities. Use the riverside facilities if you want to bathe out in the open.

46 Yoshino

LOCATION: Yoshino is south of Nara City, in central Nara Prefecture, on the Kintetsu Line. From Yoshino Station the hot spring is a 30-minute walk, or you can take a taxi or bus.

THE WATERS: This spring dates back to the eighth century, when it was a health retreat for monks living in the 120 temples in the area. Six hundred years later, Emperor Godaigo immortalized Yoshino in a poem he wrote about lying in a bed of cherry blossoms there. In the seventeenth century, Yoshino developed into a resort spa of great popularity, only to be closed in the mid-eighteenth century due to rife prostitution. Under a new name and with a new policy, it was rebuilt. Today it is known for its cherry blossoms. The water is carbon-dioxated and contains iron, lending it a reddish color. It's good for anemia, surface wounds, fatigue, and aching limbs.

AROUND AND ABOUT: You must visit Yoshino in spring: the whole area is virtually buried in pink cherry blossoms. The many temples and shrines just barely peeping out from under the petals make for an unforgettable sight. In fact so synonymous are Yoshino and *sakura* (cherry blossoms) that songs use the two words interchangeably. While many people travel to Mount Yoshino to see the blooms in late March or early April, few know Yoshino Hot Spring. Armed with small balls of pounded sticky rice wrapped in seaweed, a bit of nostalgia to cope with the concepts of transience and fleeting life (which the short-lived cherry blossoms symbolize), and a connoisseur's eye for the half-opened bud or the cherry-blossom "snow," you'll revel in spring the Japanese way. ■ NARA: As long as you're in the area, you should visit Nara, seat of the first imperial court in the eighth century when Buddhist and Chinese thought and culture were being introduced to Japan. The city, only 30 minutes from Yoshino Station by train, is a veritable treasure chest of traditional culture: temples, shrines, and pagodas, a Great Buddha and other statues, a museum, exquisite gardens, and even tame deer roaming Nara Park. See the introduction to the Kinki Region for more on Nara.

ACCOMMODATIONS: One old ryokan is Yoshino Onsen Motoyu, which requires reservations in spring. Formerly patronized by samurai, the inn has an outdoor pool and an attractive garden.

47 Tōsenji

LOCATION: Tōsenji lies on the Totsu River, south of Nara City, Nara Prefecture. Take the Wakayama Line from Wakayama City to Gojō Station. From there a bus will take you to the spring—3 hours of winding along cliff edges and around hair-raising curves.

THE WATERS: Tōsenji, consisting of four ryokan, hangs off the top of a cliff, and its simple thermal water flows from this same rocky front. The water contains sulphur, good for treating nagging back pain, stress (like that incurred on the journey here), problematic skin, allergies, and surface wounds. The last merit meant Tōsenji was a favorite with samurai, who dropped in over the centuries to heal their battle bruises. In those days it was known as a "hidden" spring, one known to few and thus safe for warriors on the mend.

AROUND AND ABOUT: This part of the Totsu River valley is remote and isolated. One of the more interesting activities is crossing the dam in front of the ryokan Yado Yunosato in a wooden box worked by ropes and pulleys. Local folk think the method of crossing the dam resembles that of wild monkeys crossing a ravine. This primitive cable car is called Yaen ("Wild Monkey"). You can visit the local folk and history museums or take a hike to Tamaki Shrine on Mount Tamaki. The atmosphere is like the area—old, rough, and quiet.

ACCOMMODATIONS: The oldest ryokan at Tōsenji—Yado Yunosato—is perched, like the spring, on top of the cliff face. In summer it is awash in breezes and the sounds of singing frogs.

48 Miyano

LOCATION: Miyano is in southern Shiga Prefecture, close to the border with Mie Prefecture. Take the Kusatsu Line from Kusatsu to Kōnan Station. From there you can walk about 30 minutes to the spring, or take a taxi.

THE WATERS: Two types of thermal water spring forth at Miyano: radioactive and sodium chloride. Both treat rheumatism, women's diseases, and neuralgia, and the radioactive water is good for skin problems. Miyano is a small settlement whose spring was discovered more than a thousand years ago, but there's little evidence of an old spa town about it now. This may be because Shiga Prefecture is not a prominent hot-spring area.

AROUND AND ABOUT: A trip to this sleepy hot spring may be the necessary antidote to the tourist-based activities that seem to dominate the Lake Biwa region. Although you can see mountains in the distance, Miyano is situated on a plateau that is not densely wooded or otherwise conducive to beautiful views. You can find quiet, however, and a leisurely country stroll will lead you to occasional shrines and temples, like Jōfukuji and Shōfukuji, and, best of all, to a deceptively ordinary-looking farmhouse that is now a museum dedicated to the ninja who once lived in the area.

ACCOMMODATIONS: The ryokan Miyano Onsen is, like the countryside around it, an unpretentious sort of place.

WHAT JAMES BOND DOESN'T KNOW: The Kōnan area was the home ground of some super sleuths even James Bond would be hard put to outperform. These well-known heroes, now beamed across the world in exciting Japanese TV drama series, were the ninja—black-cloaked glamour spies operating in the Edo period. Fleet of foot, they spent their nights speeding invisibly along cobbled streets or muddy tracks, throwing spiked wheels at trees or jumping castle walls like cats. They spent their days . . . well it's hard to say . . . which ones were they under those wide-brimmed, hide-it-all straw sun hats? They were master swordsmen, stickmen, and knife throwers and knew all there was to know about poisons, false ceilings, doors, and walls, and other such necessary aids. Feudal lords and shoguns employed them to spy on both friend and foe. The seventeenth-century general Tokugawa Ieyasu used ninja from the Kōnan area so good were they at patiently sitting between ceiling and roof. Did ninja bathe in hot springs? Nobody seems to know, for without the leggings and scarves, who would recognize them? Spike marks on the arms? To learn how to be a ninja, visit Kōga Ninjutsu Yashiki, a short walk from Miyano, to see it all. And, for good measure, eat a ninja cookie: sweet bean paste hiding in sponge cake!

49 Yunoyama

LOCATION: Yunoyama is on the eastern slope of Mount Gozaisho in northern Mie Prefecture, near the border with Shiga Prefecture. From Yokkaichi Station, on the Kansai Main Line, take the Kintetsu Yunoyama Line to Yunoyama Station. It is a 20-minute bus ride from Yunoyama Station to the hot spring.

THE WATERS: This radioactive water, artificially heated due to its low temperature, helps with skin problems, burns, cuts and abrasions, rheumatism, and beriberi. A Buddhist priest is credited with discovery, but the spring was used by deer in the area long before its formal beginning.

AROUND AND ABOUT: This is a medium-size hot spring—not too active, countrified, like a hot-spring town should be. In winter, the wooden ryokan lining the Mitaki River rise out of the snow creating a scenic composition of browns, grays, and whites. The riverbed holds massive rocks, some of which were used to carve Buddhist statues for nearby Dainichidō Temple. Other rocks have special names to fit their shapes or moods. Unusual for Mie Prefecture, skiing (on Mount Gozaisho) and skating (at Yunoyama Kōgen Kokusai Skate Center) are both possible in this area, making it a popular winter resort. Another possible outing is a trip, via the hot spring's cable car, up some 1,000 meters to the deer park on top of Mount Gozaisho.

ACCOMMODATIONS: Shin-Yunoyama Kankō Hotel boasts an open-air bath in a rock setting and pure Japanese-style architecture. Its indoor bathing facilities are superb, too.

FOOD: Various delicacies are available in Yunoyama. For starters try some edible mountain greens (*sansai*), followed by pheasant or guinea fowl, and top it off with scented tea made from tiny green marinated orchids.

50 Nagashima (Sunnyland Kurhaus)

LOCATION: Nagashima is on Ise Bay, Mie Prefecture. From Nagoya take the Kansai Main Line to Nagashima Station. From there it's 20 minutes by bus to the thermal waters.

THE WATERS: Nagashima Hot Spring is the site of Sunnyland, the only privately owned kurhaus in Japan; the rest are, for the most part, communally owned. Based on the German model, this complex has a gym, tennis courts, saunas, massage rooms, and, of course, a good selection of mineral tubs that vary in temperature and style—bubbles, cascades, swimming pool, hot, cool, and so on. For about ¥1,500 you can spend a day getting your body into shape one way or another. The water is simple thermal and treats just about anything from exhaustion to a poor complexion and tennis elbow. For further information, call Sunnyland Kurhaus (05944-5-1122).

ACCOMMODATIONS: As is the case with most kurhaus, it is not possible to stay on the premises of Sunnyland. But Nagashima is a large city where you can stay at anything from a super deluxe hotel to a minshuku, and commute to Sunnyland. Or you can stay at Nagashima Hot Spring. One possible choice is the Hotel Nagashima, a deluxe ryokan with a bath that can hold up to two thousand people. Just once you should try such a tub. You could find anything in it!

5 TŌKAI REGION

Romance and Tragedy

The Tōkai Region, protruding into the Pacific Ocean on the southern side of central Honshū, consists of three prefectures: Gifu, Aichi, and Shizuoka. The connecting link is the famous Tōkaidō Road. Once its stones were dislodged regularly by feudal lords and their retinues, journeying between Edo (Tōkyō) and Kyōto. Nowadays, it's a far less arduous undertaking, especially if you decide to travel on the sleek and speedy Shinkansen—the bullet train. Nevertheless, whether reclining in armchair comfort or trudging along on blistered feet, the wayside vistas, and in particular the first glimpses you catch of the incomparable Mount Fuji, near Shizuoka, will take your breath away, just as they did in the days of Edo.

The three prefectures of Tōkai may have this common route threading them together, but they also have many differences drawing them apart. Gifu is said to be the conservative one, stubborn and loyal to its rural traditions, which revolve around wood, water, and hot springs. The wood is the substance of its abodes: sturdy, somber structures, built to withstand the severity of the winter snows. These can be seen in the Hida area, once the name for Gifu's mountainous north. Water means sparkling, clean, melted snow, delicious to drink and pure enough for making exquisite paper. The southern half of Gifu, once called Mino, is still a production center for strong, multipurpose Mino paper. Hot springs, of course, mean Gifu has some very select little bathing spots, tucked away in deep valleys or out in the fields open to the sky.

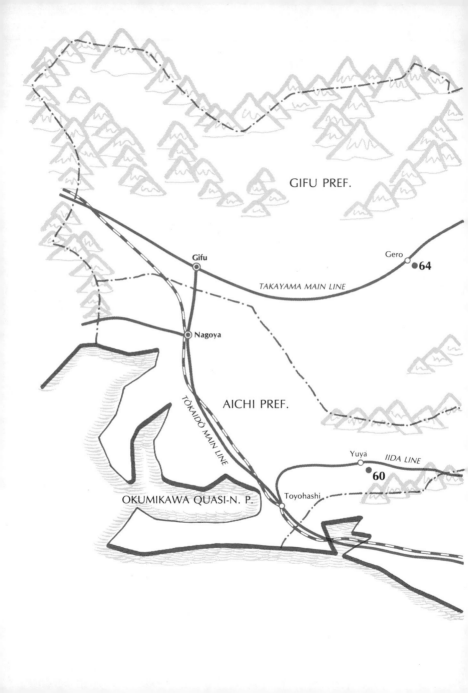

GIFU PREF.

Gifu

Gero

●64

TAKAYAMA MAIN LINE

Nagoya

AICHI PREF.

TŌKAIDŌ MAIN LINE

Yuya   IIDA LINE

●60

Toyohashi

OKUMIKAWA QUASI-N. P.

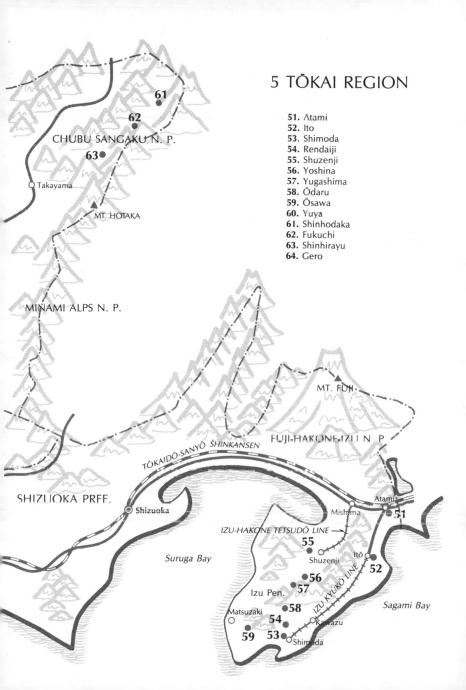

5 TŌKAI REGION

51. Atami
52. Ito
53. Shimoda
54. Rendaiji
55. Shuzenji
56. Yoshina
57. Yugashima
58. Ōdaru
59. Ōsawa
60. Yuya
61. Shinhodaka
62. Fukuchi
63. Shinhirayu
64. Gero

CHUBU SANGAKU N. P.

Takayama

MT. HOTAKA

MINAMI ALPS N. P.

MT. FUJI

TŌKAIDŌ-SANYŌ SHINKANSEN

FUJI-HAKONE-IZU N. P.

SHIZUOKA PREF.

Shizuoka

Atami

Mishima

IZU-HAKONE TETSUDŌ LINE →

Suruga Bay

Shuzenji

Itō

Izu Pen.

IZU KYŪKŌ LINE

Matsuzaki

Sagami Bay

Kawazu

Shimoda

Further confirmation of Gifu Prefecture's leanings toward nature is the small section of the Japan Alps (Chūbu Sangaku National Park) in its northeastern corner. This is a beautiful, sweet-smelling area where alpine flora climb up the lower reaches of rugged mountains, and where ponds rimmed with tangled undergrowth can make you feel like the first intruder. You can see the Alps up close as a climber willing to take on some of the toughest slopes, in some of the most indecisive weather, or you can view them from behind the glass windows of a bus or a train.

Unlike Gifu, Aichi Prefecture has had to forgo a lot of its rustic inheritance. Ever since the shogun Tokugawa Ieyasu decided to build Nagoya Castle in 1610, the area has been caught up in successive waves of frenzied progress. Nagoya City, and consequently Aichi, is usually associated with massive production lines that churn out everything from cars and buses to clocks, dinner plates, plastic bowls, and cookies. However, there are also places where exquisite cloisonné, fine china, and tie-dyed cloth are made by hand.

If Gifu, then, is the country cousin, and Aichi, the city industrialist, Shizuoka Prefecture must be the fun-loving son devoted to the good life. This is very obvious when you look at Izu Peninsula, which extends into the Pacific Ocean between Suruga and Sagami bays. The rest of the prefecture can challenge the charms of Izu only with tea plants—rows and rows of closely clipped hedges from which some of Japan's finest tea is brewed.

Izu is an epicurean's playground, although it does have some drawbacks. Because its superb vistas, sumptuous fish platters, and excellent mineral waters are desired by the millions of Japanese who live only 100 kilometers away in Tōkyō, you can be sure you'll never be sampling its delights alone. In fact, when you leave the Tōkaidō at Atami and head south, you will be one of the thousands who continually stomp through. The mild climate here means there is no off-season, and this in turn means it's always hard on your pocketbook. All this notwithstanding, a stint of some length at Izu's hot springs is a must for anyone who considers himself or herself a true hot-spring connoisseur. The volcanic activity of the region has endowed the peninsula with all of the best in hot-spring repertoires. Unhappily this means that the ground may shake under your feet from time to time. Some say that should the next Great Earthquake strike here, the whole peninsula would disappear into the ocean!

Izu's moods don't end here; it has a colorful past that can excite even the most passive observer. A lot of this color is associated with romance. For example, the besotted student in Kawabata Yasunari's story *Izu no Odoriko* ("The Izu Dancer") found Izu's interior very suited to a young man suffering from unrequited love. In Edward G. Seidensticker's translation: "A heavy rain began to fall about sunset. The mountains, gray and white, flattened to two dimensions, and the river grew yellower and muddier by the minute. I felt sure the dancers would not be out on a night like this, and yet I could not sit still." Today, those in love are usually jubilant honeymooners enchanted by the steamy valleys and misty mountains, although distraught lovers, like the student above, still find the sea off Izu's jutting coastlines consoling—there are several Lovers' Leaps along the eastern coast.

This combination of romance and tragedy in Izu's past is also part of its present-day allure for many Japanese visitors. At Shuzenji Hot Spring, in central Izu, people like to read about or see the reenactment of the tragic death of Minamoto Yoriie. He was stabbed to death in one of the bathhouses during a power struggle in the twelfth century. His very own mother planned his assassination. In a similar way, the tale of Tōjin Okichi, the reputed mistress of the first American consul to Japan, Townsend Harris, is a part of Shimoda's past that many like to contemplate on visits to the cliff Okichigafuchi, where the distraught woman threw herself into the sea. These episodes linger on; Japanese travelers see the intense emotions involved as an integral part of Izu's lush, wanton terrain. Foreign visitors may be hard put to feel the same way. Their eyes may see the fleeting rain showers as merely soggy and wet, and they may not find romance in the shrill song of the cicadas in summer. But even so, the brilliance of the autumn moon reflected on the sea, the freshness of the inland waterfalls, and the sun setting over the village bays on the western coast must give some inkling of why Kawabata had his young man pursue his gypsy dancer through Izu.

51 Atami

LOCATION: Atami is about 100 kilometers southwest of Tōkyō on the northeastern coast of Izu Peninsula, Shizuoka Prefecture. By Shinkansen (bullet train) from Tōkyō Station the trip takes less than an hour, and it's not much longer on the Tōkaidō Main Line. You can also use the private Odakyū Line from Shinjuku in Tōkyō, changing to the Tōkaidō Main Line at Odawara. From Atami Station the ryokan are within walking distance; taxis and buses are also available.

THE WATERS: Atami, contracted from atsuumi, or "hot sea," is a large and bustling resort visited by countless thousands every year, and rates with Beppu, Kyūshū, as the most popular hot spring in Japan, its proximity to Tōkyō making it an especially prime target for charter-bus companies, travel agents, innkeepers, and geisha. Hundreds of springs gush forth into hundreds of tubs in a circular bay area, closely ringed by steep, luxuriously green mountains. The inns, some wooden and creaky, many concrete and quiet, climb up the lower slopes of these mountains, from whose peaks Atami appears not unlike a Mediterranean city with its blue sea, white buildings, and bay of lazy boats going nowhere in particular. The city retains something of the old hot-spring town up and away from its cluttered piers, but in general it's a maze of souvenir shops in covered arcades, flanked by night clubs, bars, amusement halls, and convenience stores. Actually, there's no need to stir at all from what are some of the best bathing facilities in Japan, for Atami's inns and hotels offer just about every kind of decor and variety of bathing comfort. Your only problem may be in trying to balance your desires with your bank account. Remember that the Izu Peninsula is an expensive hot-spring area, especially along the eastern seaboard and at New Year's and in the summer. Inland, on the west coast, and at minshuku, prices will be lower. For the low-budget crowd there are public baths. The Atami waters were discovered in A.D. 749 when hot water suddenly emerged from the sea bottom, frightening some fishermen out in their boats in the bay and, worse still, boiling their livelihood alive. They called in Mankan, a monk famous for subduing natural nuisances, who "moved" the spring inland to its present location. Things in Atami then got so good that, during the Edo period, water was even carried from here to the castle in what is now Tōkyō so the shogun could have a decent bath, and masters of Atami bathhouses were made honorary samurai. These magic waters, simple thermal with salt and calcium sulphate, calm nerves and irritated skin and invigorate tired blood.

AROUND AND ABOUT: As you might imagine, there's a lot to do when you get sick of the tub. Besides the night life and sports facilities (golf, tennis, swimming, boating, and bowling), there are scenic drives down a jutted, rocky coast or inland through tiny villages with terraced fields and groves of bent-over bamboo. At the MOA Museum, a modern complex making superb use of its views of Atami Bay, the offshore islands, and the surrounding mountains, pottery, paintings, screens, and other examples of priceless Japanese art transport you away from the modern sprawl around the station below. From Atami you can also reach the spectacular Izu Skyline highway for forays into Hakone and the lake district of Fuji-Hakone-Izu National Park.

ACCOMMODATIONS: Some possibilities are Atami Tsuruya Hotel, a deluxe ryokan with an equally deluxe Versailles Bath (ornate columns, marble, the works). The quiet, Japanese-style Hanamura Ryokan is in the hills. Tōrikyō in Izusan, a hot-spring area in northern Atami, has exquisitely designed Japanese-style rooms, a magnificent garden overlooking the sea, and a non-thermal pool for summer swimming.

52 Itō

LOCATION: Itō is one-third of the way down the eastern coast of Izu Peninsula in Shizuoka Prefecture. A local train on the Tōkaidō Main Line from Tōkyō Station takes nearly 3 hours, while an express train takes only 1½ hours. The ryokan are clustered near the station.

THE WATERS: The hot spring at Itō is listed in historical records as far back as the ninth and eleventh centuries A.D. Its water, like Atami's, was ordered by the shogun's castle in Edo and carried there in barrels on the backs of servants in procession. The modern city of Itō, situated on the Matsu River, which empties into the sea at one end and disappears abruptly into the mountains behind, boasts more than eight hundred springs. Originally it was known as a *me-no-yu* (hot spring good for eye problems), while today current techniques in rehabilitation from a variety of illnesses are used at the National Health Resort hospital. The water, simple thermal with sodium sulphate, treats rheumatism, gastroenteric problems, and stress.

AROUND AND ABOUT: The ryokan are built along the river, with the more expensive ones being near the mountains. Although Itō is a thriving resort spring, its position down the coast, surrounded by mountains and with a river through its center, makes the commercial aspects a little less visible, as do the many old wooden inns and people clomping about in geta, yukata, and *tanzen* (clogs, a light kimono, and top coat). Itō's seafaring past may also be obvious enough to distract the visitor from the modern trappings, especially after James Clavell and his novel *Shogun*, for it was in Itō that the Englishman William Adams, upon whose life Clavell's story was based, attempted to build a ship for the shogun. Was he really distracted by the beautiful Mariko? Or did he just spend too much time in the bath? Like all Izu hot springs, Itō is a good place to go all year round; you'll never be cut off by snowdrifts or baked in scorching summer heat. But it does have its fair share of typhoons and earthquakes, and more than its fair share of traffic jams, the latter being so bad you'd best travel by train or in the wee hours of morning by car. The city is alive with cactus gardens and tropical parks. The Ikeda Museum—30 minutes from the station by bus—exhibits both Japanese and Western art.

ACCOMMODATIONS: There's a lot available, so where you stay really depends on your budget. Hatoya Hotel has an aquarium bath where you and a lot of exotic fish can stare each other down from your respective adjoining tubs. Another place with an exotic touch is Itōen Hotel, whose hanging ferns and small statues in its indoor Angel Bath, and similarly lush surroundings bordering the outdoor pool, are designed for quiet dipping in a junglelike garden setting. Also having a pleasant naturalistic outdoor bath is the ryokan Oyado Ryūseki. Finally, Tōkaikan, with more tradition and less panache, is on the river.

FOOD: Itō is fish. Wooden serving boats hold sashimi so fresh it watches as you pick up your chopsticks and dares you to attack it. For those who lose heart, there's a wide variety of dried fish. In fact, all over Izu you will see fish drying on racks on the beaches and even in vacant parking lots. You may see them again at the breakfast table, since dried fish is usually included in a traditional Japanese-style breakfast. If you take an early morning bath you'll probably smell them grilling in the kitchen as you walk past. Called *himono*, they are a rich source of calcium—if you can get your teeth through the bones. A squeeze of lemon helps mitigate their salty taste. Nowadays *himono* are disappearing from the beaches and are dried in specially designed ovens. It's a sad loss.

FESTIVALS: William Adams was known in Japan as Anjin-san (''Mr. Pilot'') and on August 8 to 9 there is a festival in his honor, called the Itō Anjinsai, that involves floating paper lanterns on the river. At the beginning of July (the first Sunday) wooden tubs race down the river in the Tarainori Festival, while in August, fireworks light the bay at night for summer holiday makers. The brightest display is on August 9.

53 Shimoda and 54 Rendaiji

LOCATION: Shimoda is nearly on the tip of Izu Peninsula, most of the way down the eastern coast. An express train from Tōkyō Station along the Tōkaidō Main Line takes less than 3 hours. (Since sections of the train separate along the way, make sure you board the section headed for Shimoda—if you don't you might end up in a town without a hot spring!) If you are already on Izu's eastern coast use the Izu Kyūkō Line. Rendaiji, 4 kilometers to the northwest, is a 10-minute bus ride from Shimoda Station.

THE WATERS: Shimoda gets its water from a thermal spring at Rendaiji that is thought to have been discovered by the monk Gyōki, some twelve hundred years ago. Rendaiji Temple was constructed near the hot spring and gave the spring its name. The water, simple thermal, is good for rheumatism, skin problems, and neuralgia. While Rendaiji ryokan go in for jungle baths— large pools surrounded by unruly masses of dank greenery—Shimoda favors more deluxe baths with tiles and statues, befitting its reputation as the place with the finest accommodations in Izu.

AROUND AND ABOUT: Although Shimoda and Rendaiji are close together, each has its own distinct atmosphere and offerings. ■ SHIMODA: This port is very popular with foreign tourists, especially Americans, and it's not difficult to see why. Commodore Matthew C. Perry and his American fleet dared to drop anchor here in 1853, a time when Japan was closed to barbaric foreigners. Perry was asking for trading agreements, which took five years to draw up and were to a great extent responsible for the fall of the shogunate and ultimately Japan's emergence as a world industrial power. On May 16 to 18, Japanese and American military personnel gather in Shimoda for the Kurofune Matsuri (''Black Ship Festival''), which includes a street parade of men in naval attire marching to the beat of brass bands. The festival commemorates the landing of Perry's fleet. Another reminder of this period is the Gyokusenji Temple's collection of personal belongings used by Townsend Harris, the first American consul to Japan, who arrived soon after Perry and set up residence in this temple. In the temple grounds you can see the tree under which the consul first had a cow slaughtered, much to the worry of non-meat-eating local farmers who feared their beasts of burden would end up under a mound of vegetables and the equivalent of ketchup on foreigners' Sunday luncheon tables. Shimoda has some attractive old buildings with black-and-white tiled walls. The scenic shoreline includes swimming beaches, and there are many parks. ■ RENDAIJI: Rendaiji stands apart from Shimoda and is quieter, though still a large hot-spring town with some fascinating characters in its history. There is Tōjin Okichi, for example, who threw herself off Okichigafuchi Cliff, apparently unable to live in the town after her affair with Townsend Harris, who by then had returned to America. Okichi's beauty and whether she actually had a liaison with Harris have long been a source of controversy, but so profitable has the tale become for the tourist companies and the movie industry that most people don't want to know what really happened. Rendaiji is also where the patriot Yoshida Shōin, who advocated the emperor's return to power, hid from the shogunate while waiting to escape on a ship bound for America. Holed up in the attic of a house belonging to the Murakami family, Yoshida seems to have lived a kind of Anne Frank existence. He never made it to America. Rendaiji, being somewhat inland, offers more mountain vistas than Shimoda, and the rivers and inns have the feeling of an old hot-spring town about them.

ACCOMMODATIONS: In Shimoda there are many deluxe resort hotels offering both Western and Japanese accommodations. You can choose futons or beds and cuisine to match. One such is Kurofune ("Black Ship") Hotel overlooking the sea. Another, not as centrally located as the Kurofune, is Shimoda Yamatokan, which is also on the coast and close to a beach for those interested in brine as well as mineral waters. Both hotels specialize in fish—raw, marinated, or grilled, and in keeping with Shimoda's famous culinary traditions. In Rendaiji there is Seiryūsō, a deluxe ryokan with a traditional Japanese-style garden. Former U.S. President Jimmy Carter once stayed there. Also in Rendaiji is Yubatakan, which has a jungle bath with lots of hanging foliage—a shady green nook meant to remind you of an untouched jungle pool.

55 Shuzenji

LOCATION: Shuzenji is in north-central Izu Peninsula, inland from Itō. The Tōkaidō Main Line's Odoriko-gō, a direct express train named after Kawabata's Izu dancer, takes 2¼ hours from Tōkyō. If you use one of the more frequent regular expresses on this line, you will have to change to the Izu-Hakone Tetsudō Line at Mishima, 1½ hours from Tōkyō. From Mishima to Shuzenji takes 35 minutes.

THE WATERS: The crystal-clear water of the Katsura River flows through the center of Shuzenji, where wooden inns with glass-enclosed sun porches overhang the rocky banks in the quaint and attractive manner of a mountain hot spring. Several bright red bridges straddle the river. Pale green willow branches dangle down toward the water's edge. According to legend, Shuzenji began as a hot-spring town after Kōbō Daishi, seeing a boy washing his sick father in a hot pool in the riverbed, founded a temple here. This temple, Shuzenji Temple, is on the river in the center of town. The simple thermal springs that flow into the riverbed contain sodium chloride and help cure many kinds of aches, pains, skin problems, and nervous tension as well as speed recovery from illnesses, operations, and accidents. There are four public baths, among them Tokko-no-yu, which is located in the riverbed and surrounded by a circular, wooden-slat fence.

AROUND AND ABOUT: Even though Shuzenji is a popular hot-spring town not lacking in garish souvenir shops, the riverside walkways and red bridges, the mountains all around, and the twisting back streets make it very appealing. It's always been associated with literary figures like Natsume Sōseki, Kawabata Yasunari, and Okamoto Kidō, and with the themes of their writings. Especially in spring and autumn does Shuzenji evoke this romantic nostalgia. Sōseki wrote about his stay in Shuzenji, where he was treated for stomach ulcers, in *Shuzenji Nikki* ("Shuzenji Diary"). Kawabata evoked views of Shuzenji in his story *Izu no Odoriko*. Okamoto, the playwright, dramatized what is probably the most popular local story—that recounting the death of Minamoto Yoriie, who was blinded and brutally murdered in the bath. The plot was instigated by his own mother, Hōjō Masako, in A.D. 1204. Played out on the stages of Shuzenji theaters, the story clearly shows how treacherous political waters, and sometimes bathhouse waters, can be. The mother repented, however, and the monument, Shigetsuden, that she erected to comfort her son's soul still stands today near Shuzenji Temple.

ACCOMMODATIONS: Asaba Ryokan has a beautiful garden where the haunting tales so appropriate to this romantic, tragic place are acted out on a Noh stage. Reservations are required for the performance. Another classy place is Arai Ryokan, which has a Roman bath complete with decorative columns. The literati among you will be interested to know that Natsume Sōseki, the writer, stayed at Kikuya Ryokan, which is a good, traditional inn.

56 Yoshina

LOCATION: Yoshina, on the river of the same name at the western foot of

Mount Amagi, can be reached in 20 minutes by car or bus going south from Shuzenji.

THE WATERS: One of the oldest hot springs in Izu, Yoshina was supposedly discovered by the monk Gyōki some twelve hundred years ago. Later, as a temple hot spring, it was associated with fertility as it was visited by a mistress of the shogun Tokugawa Ieyasu who wanted to conceive a child and who later succeeded. The simple thermal water with sodium sulphate also revives tired limbs and helps in curing diseases of the nervous system.

AROUND AND ABOUT: The area around Yoshina is cut off by mountains that rise in continuous layers throughout this central Izu region. The peaks are cloaked in mist, and what with deep green valleys, clumps of shiny bamboo, and watery terraced rice fields all around, it's as Japanese as you could want, just the kind of hot spring to repair to when you tire of Izu's seascapes and fish diet. Just as spectacular as the coastal regions, but much quieter, the peninsula's inland areas offer a more varied cuisine of wild boar, mountain plants, and mandarin oranges.

ACCOMMODATIONS: Tōfuya Ryokan is a traditional inn with an outdoor bath. The menu—featuring pheasant and wild-boar stew in winter—matches the surroundings; both are first class.

57 Yugashima

LOCATION: Situated at the junction of the Kano and Nekko rivers in central Izu, Yugashima is very near Yoshina (56) and 30 minutes by bus from Shuzenji Station.

THE WATERS: Despite its tranquil location, Yugashima has abundant hot water and ryokan with mammoth baths designed to cope with a thousand or more bodies. The town is divided into four areas: Nishibira, Arajuku, Sekonotaki, and Kidachi. Kajika-no-yu, the more standard-sized public bath in Nishibira, offers simple thermal water with magnesium hydrogen-carbonate, very good for those with skin, muscle, and creaking joint problems. They say it's also good for tennis elbow. (The only mystery here is the lack of tennis courts in the vicinity.)

AROUND AND ABOUT: The mountain air wafts down into this valley, clean and fresh, while the ever-present sound of running water is typical of this part of Izu. People who want to honeymoon or just bathe and sleep come here, as do hikers. If you want to appear more energetic than most, take a walk through Namezawa Gorge on the Kano River, a compact rendition of the mountains and valleys all around, or throw a line into the river and wait for something to swim by. At night there's the moon, the same one Kawabata's lovelorn student gazed at as he pursued the little Izu dancer through this area: "I closed the shutters and got into bed. My chest was painfully tight. I went down to the bath again and splashed about violently.

The rain stopped, the moon came out; the autumn sky, washed by the rain, shone crystalline into the distance."

ACCOMMODATIONS: Yumotokan, where Kawabata wrote *Izu no Odoriko*, is next to the public bath, Kajika-no-yu. Another traditional inn is Ochiairō, whose name means "Meeting Tower" in reference to the junction or meeting of the Kano and Nekko rivers. You'll be served delicate dishes featuring local vegetables and river fish at both of these ryokan.

58 Ōdaru

LOCATION: Ōdaru, due south of Shuzenji and two-thirds of the way down the Izu Peninsula, is on the Kawazu River. From Itō take the Izu Kyūkō Line to Kawazu Station and then the bus for Kawazu Nanadaru; get off at Honnashimoto (a 30-minute ride) and walk 10 minutes. Infrequent buses from Kawazu run all the way to Ōdaru and will deposit you at the ryokan Amagisō. The bus to Shimoda from Shuzenji, which lets you off at the same stop, takes a little more than an hour.

THE WATERS: Ōdaru's well-known riverside ryokan, Amagisō, has seemingly countless outdoor baths, including seven small iron tubs, each named after one of the seven waterfalls (Nanadaru) nearby. The thermal water comes from springs in the Kawazu River and is a weak sodium chloride solution good for cuts and bruises. More magically therapeutic, however, are the settings of the baths themselves, which are all owned by the ryokan Amagisō and which are yours to enjoy for a small fee even if you are not staying at their inn. The outdoor bath is a clear blue-green pool edged in rough-shaped rocks, completely natural, and very near the spillway of a steep, frothy white waterfall. As you sit here and watch the water falling down, splashing green leaves on its way, you wonder why it took you so long to find such a bathing Eden. If you prefer a darker bathing mood, one with a bit of the unknown about it, try Amagisō's cave bath: another natural setting but this time 20 meters into solid rock—you can wander in as far as you dare. In its dimly lit recesses watch out for embarrassed bathers waiting for you to leave before they emerge. The separate men's and women's entrances, you see, lead to a single communal chamber. There is also a women-only outdoor bath, a pleasant pool in natural sculpted stone overlooking scraggly trees and bushes. In all, Ōdaru has some twenty baths for you to while away the day in, each in its own way exploiting the natural bounty of this gorgeous area.

AROUND AND ABOUT: Ōdaru is for relaxed, indulgent dipping, and without even stirring from your bath you can take in the physical beauty of the countryside. But if you are feeling a bit waterlogged, other small hot springs like Nanadaru and Yugano are within walking distance—20 minutes—and are pleasing examples of Izu mountain towns moving slowly along at their own pace. For a lovely brush with nature, follow the well-kept riverside trail upstream and see the seven, mostly modest waterfalls.

ACCOMMODATIONS: Amagisō has superb bathing facilities and wonderful meals of river fish, mountain greens, eel, wild boar, and saké. If you want to bathe here but stay more economically, try the minshuku Urushiya, next to Amagisō.

59 Ōsawa

LOCATION: Ōsawa is in southwestern Izu Peninsula, near Mount Basara, a short distance inland from Matsuzaki City. From Shimoda on the Izu Kyūkō Line, take the Izu Kyūkō bus bound for Matsuzaki for 45 minutes, get off at the Ōsawa Onsen Iriguchi stop, and walk the 10 minutes to your ryokan. Another way to go is to take the Izu-Hakone Tetsudō Line from Mishima to Shuzenji, take a bus from the station to Matsuzaki—a 40-minute ride— and then catch the bus bound for Shimoda, getting off at the stop noted above, a 10-minute ride.

THE WATERS: This small hot spring in the mountains is one place you'll never need make-up, because the bath here will do for your appearance what make-up does, or in some cases can't do. The water is simple thermal with calcium sulphate, and as well as beautifying your skin, it will dispel nervous tension and creaks in your joints and make you feel physically rejuvenated. On the Naka River, very close to the hot-spring complex, is a public outdoor bathing pool where for a small fee (around ¥1,000) you can bask in the water and sunshine behind bamboo partitions while the river tumbles by.

AROUND AND ABOUT: The Ōsawa area, including the calm and quiet city of Matsuzaki, offers the perfect balance between relaxation and culture— the opportunity to see arts and crafts that preserve the traditions of the past. Iwashina Kyōdokan in southern Matsuzaki houses two floors of implements once used in farming and everyday life, as well as plaster friezes by the Edo-period artisan Chōhachi. The nearby temple Jōkanji boasts a plaster relief ceiling, also the work of Chōhachi, and carved lattice transoms between the ceiling and the upper parts of the interior walls. Jōkanji is within a 10-minute walk of Matsuzaki bus terminal. The gaps between "civilizations" are wider and there are fewer signs of tourism at work on this, the western side of Izu.

ACCOMMODATIONS: The ryokan Ōsawasō has a large outdoor bath edged by rocks and bushes so naturalistic you'll think you're intruding in some wilderness preserve. Ōsawa Onsen Hotel is a combined hotel-ryokan with an outdoorsy tub made of cypress wood, an object of worship among true connoisseurs of bathing, and for that reason alone worth sampling. The hotel, more than three hundred years old, is noted for its criss-crossing wall designs of white on gray, carved out by the famous plasterer named Chōhachi in the Edo period. Chōhachi's walls combine with the tiled roofing to make an unusual and impressive sight. Ryokan Nakagawa is a small Japanese-style inn with attached cottages.

60 Yuya

LOCATION: Yuya is on the Ure River at the foot of Mount Hōraiji, southeast of Nagoya in Oku Mikawa Quasi-National Park, Aichi Prefecture. Take the Iida Line from Toyohashi Station, a major station on the Tōkaidō Main Line. Get off at Yuya Station and walk 5 minutes to the ryokan.

THE WATERS: The source of the hot spring is in one of the gorges winding into Mount Hōraiji, but since its temperature is a low 30° C (97° F) the water must be heated before it reaches the bathing areas. Legend says that the Yuya waters became famous after local folk sighted a flying hermit-sage hovering over the hot spring, playing a kind of flute. This man, Rishū, lived in the mountains and often came down to bathe, and everyone imagined it was miracle water from the springs that enabled him to take to the skies. Soon many people came seeking help, and while some were cured, it seems only Rishū learned how to fly here. Despite this wondrous event, the water contains not much more than sodium chloride and today does only mundane things like heat the body to relieve aches and pains and various nervous twinges.

AROUND AND ABOUT: This is a beautiful area. About fifteen hundred stone steps carved into the mountainside take you to Hōraiji Temple, founded by Rishū, the floating sage. The path, winding up between ancient cypress trees, pines, and dark green moss-covered rocks, evokes a primitive mood in keeping with this peaceful, religious place. Hōraiji has been rebuilt several times—the gate, however, is very old and in an excellent state of preservation. At one time Hōraiji was lauded for the blessings it bestowed upon women wishing to become pregnant. A very noteworthy example of legend is Tokugawa Ieyasu's mother, who is said to have conceived this mighty man after praying here . . . no mean feat. A less joyous event in Yuya's past was the defeat of the Takeda family at nearby Nagashino Castle. The victors were the combined forces of the above-mentioned Tokugawa and Oda Nobunaga, who aimed to destroy the Takedas at this Battle of Nagashino during the Edo period. To see the ruins of the castle, take the Iida Line from Yuya Station two stops to Nagashinojō. The castle remains are in front of the station.

ACCOMMODATIONS: Near the public swimming pool is Grand Hotel Hōyō, a four-story building with mountain views from all its windows, a family bath, and special activities for children, such as insect collecting, a favorite summer pastime of Japanese boys and girls. A smaller traditional place is Miyako, where winter brings forth wild boar stewpots.

61 Shinhodaka

LOCATION: Part of the Oku Hida hot-spring group, Shinhodaka is in the Hida Mountains, within Chūbu Sangaku National Park, northeastern Gifu Prefecture. Take the Takayama Main Line, which runs from Toyama in the north to Gifu in the south, get off at Takayama Station, and take a bus to Shinhodaka Onsen (1 hour 50 minutes), the last stop.

THE WATERS: This area is known as "*rotenburo* (outdoor pool) heaven." It's not hard to see why, for here is bathing on a grand scale and in a glorious natural setting. Each ryokan has its own rocked-off section of the Gamata River that creates a huge natural tub as big as all outdoors, with steep mountainsides for walls (covered in that wispy, spindly growth you associate with the snow country) and a wide, high ceiling in celestial blue and white. In spring white and pink blossoms decorate the "room," while in autumn there are maple leaves in three shades of red. Winter is white with sparkling arrangements in ice; summer is bright, abundant green. The sulphur water here will cure anything, and, when imbibed, will clean out your digestive system, replenish your iron supply, and make you slim—providing you don't eat too much at dinner, that is. There is a public bath near the bus terminal, but it can't compete with the ryokan bathing facilities.

AROUND AND ABOUT: Owing to its location in the Japan Alps, this area is fabulously scenic and popular in summer for hiking. While there are numerous trekking routes from Shinhodaka, there is also the Shinhodaka overhead cable car—at 3.2 kilometers, the second longest in the world—that whisks you up and away over the western part of Mount Hotaka for spectacular views of beautiful landscapes. So far, the area has been able to absorb all the nature lovers, climbers, skiers, and bathers who flock here without losing any of its serenity or expansive mood.

ACCOMMODATIONS: The ryokan Shinzansō is set into the mountains and has a huge outdoor bath in the river that flows quickly past its front door. You reach the bath by crossing a bridge. Imadakan is an old traditional ryokan with cooking pots suspended over open fires (*irori*) and a bath room and tub in Japanese cypress, a richly aromatic wood that in these days of tile and stainless steel will make your bath seem as luxuriant as the natural tub set in the river outside.

62 Fukuchi

LOCATION: Also part of the Oku Hida hot-spring group in the Hida Mountains, Fukuchi is south of Shinhodaka (61) on the Takahara River in northeastern Gifu Prefecture. From Takayama on the Takayama Main Line catch the bus bound for Shinhodaka. Get off at Fukuchi—the bus ride takes 1 hour 20 minutes.

THE WATERS: The carbonated simple thermal waters that are piped into outdoor pools here will do wonders for stomach aches, work worries, and stress. Like Shinhodaka, Fukuchi is a small hot spring lost in the grandeur of physical beauty that surrounds it. What with the mountains and the nearby river as a background and the spacious tubs bordered by wild shrubs and trees and rocky cliff walls, you'll never know where nature ends and the man-made begins.

AROUND AND ABOUT: For nature lovers there is Shizenkan, a museum displaying plants, rocks, insects, flowers, and some fossils from the area. For history buffs there is a folk museum, the Hida Shūkokan, with some two thousand exhibits covering the whole span of Japanese culture, from gardening tools used in the Edo period to Jōmon pottery dating as far back as 5,000 B.C. Several temples and shrines are nearby, and of particular interest is Jōganji Temple and its bell inscribed with the names of 110 prostitutes from the famous Yoshiwara red-light district in Edo. These women got together the money to buy the bell after the original amount of money intended for the bell was given away in Yoshiwara by a man whose inability to resist their charms had driven him into hopeless debt. Ironically this temple also houses the three good monkeys who see, hear, and speak no evil.

ACCOMMODATIONS: The ryokan here have retained some aspects of the Hida architecture (see Shinhirayu Hot Spring, which follows), so commonly seen in this northern region of Gifu Prefecture. They have done away with thatched roofs, but the sliding doors and windows still display the heavy, wooden grating of Hida-style buildings. The interiors have been modernized as well, but many still feature stews cooked in pots suspended above open fires. The ryokan Magokurō is in the typical Hida style and boasts a wooden tub. Another traditional ryokan is Yumoto Chōza, with its naturalistic outdoor bath, dinner cooked in a hanging pot over a fire, and mellow atmosphere.

TASTY TIDBITS: This area is famous for its unique serving dishes, fragrant *hō* (*Magnolia hypoleuca*) leaves. These large, dried leaves are smeared with red miso and then placed on a grill over a flame. Sliced fish, meat, and vegetables are then arranged on the leaf and cooked. The mixed aromas of the food and the smoke-tinged *hō* leaf are said to enliven even the most listless of appetites. The leaf itself is not eaten; it is cleaned off in preparation for the next feast.

63 Shinhirayu

LOCATION: Shinhirayu, east of Takayama in the southern part of Chūbu Sangaku National Park, is the largest hot spring in the Oku Hida group. From Takayama Station on the Takayama Main Line the spring is 1½ hours by bus.
THE WATERS: When a retainer of the great sixteenth-century military leader

Takeda Shingen saw a monkey curing itself in the water here, he and several other wounded samurai doffed their armor and jumped in. The hot spring subsequently became one of the secret spots used by battle-scarred warriors to recuperate without having to worry about an enemy attack. The carbon-dioxated or sodium hydrogen-carbonate water will heal your cuts, too, and soothe your embattled nerves. It's also good for unsettled stomachs and rheumatism—maybe samurai suffered from these as well.

AROUND AND ABOUT: Shinhirayu is more commercially developed than the other hot-spring areas in this group, but nature still holds sway and many of the buildings are in the traditional Hida style. Again there's an odd assortment of things to look at when you stir from your garden bath, such as a bear farm where all the bears have moon-shaped collars of white fur around their necks, a small museum of stones from all over the globe (the South Pole, the top of Mount Everest, and the like), and a naturalist's museum of plants, mounted insects, and dried wild flowers. On April 14 and 15 and October 9 and 10 (in the Takayama Festival), a special dance called Tōkei is performed by young men wearing headdresses made from chicken feathers. This elaborate costume, coupled with the intricacy of the dance, is offered as a tribute to the gods of the shrine here. The dance is a thousand years old, and can be seen during shrine rituals in many parts of northern Gifu, or the Hida region. While you're roaming about, you'll get hungry, and then it's time for some river fish, pickled mountain greens, or the excellent, fat noodles (*udon*), a local specialty. ■ HIDA FOLKLORE VILLAGE: Hida is the old name for the mountainous north of what is now Gifu Prefecture. Perhaps what calls it to mind most vividly is the local style of architecture. Known as Hida architecture, this style of constructing houses began in the sixteenth century and is still visible in many parts of Hida. To see it in a folk-village setting or in the form of refurbished houses still in use, you could try a few hours of walking in Takayama City on your way to or from Shinhirayu Hot Spring. This city is very popular with tourists and it disappoints very few. Twenty minutes by bus from Takayama Station you can wander through Hida Folklore Village (Hida Minzoku Mura), an authentic collection of Hida houses, workshops, barns, and storehouses. The houses are huge places, with very steep roofs making them look like thatched tents for giants. The ground floor can be divided up by screens or left open for eating and socializing around hanging pots, blackened and well-seasoned by many winter stews. The warmth from the open fireplace, which is set in a hole in the wooden floor, rises up and is trapped in the ceiling or filters between mezzanines of two or more levels built below the roof. These higher levels were sometimes used for sleeping, but generally they were dark, dry, and terribly smoky—fit only for the rearing of silkworms in winter. Inside the houses and outer buildings, you will see the trappings of country life in Hida in bygone eras: cultivating tools, snowshoes for men and horses, cooking and grain-grinding utensils, storage caskets and water containers, and even a creaky water wheel still churning out energy for the village. In the workshops old folk sit and embroider or fashion things from the exquisite paper made in southern Gifu, which was once known as Mino. Potting, weaving, lacquer art, toy making, and other crafts are also nurtured in Takayama. A walk through Takayama proper will lead you to any number of museums or craft centers of interest. You really don't have to work hard at cultural studies here; the rows of Hida buildings will help you pass the time effortlessly. The atmosphere is tranquil, as if the age of the surroundings and the somberness of the dark brown wood and thatching don't allow too much frivolity. Many people say Takayama is how they imagine old, rural Japan to be.

ACCOMMODATIONS: The ryokan Shirakabasō has a water wheel, a beautiful garden, alpine views, and an outdoor bath. The traditional Gizan Ryokan serves bear stew, trout on bamboo leaves, and other delicacies.

64 Gero

LOCATION: Gero, the best-known hot spring in Gifu Prefecture, is northeast of Gifu City, halfway to the Hida Mountains. The bathing areas and ryokan are in front of Gero Station on the Takayama Main Line.

THE WATERS: Since its discovery in the tenth century, Gero has had its share of ups and downs. When it was not buried in flood waters, it was one of the most popular hot springs in Japan, although the thermal water did have a disturbing tendency to suddenly disappear—it was not until this century that the source was secured and a constant supply harnessed. The hot-spring town, on both sides of the Mashita River, features two public baths, Shirasugi-no-yu and Yakushi-no-yu. The latter is an open-air pool on the riverbank at the end of a street lined with Buddhist banners bearing prayers written in Chinese characters. These scroll-like banners are usually displayed only during festivals or on special occasions. That is why this line of banners, flapping in the breeze, is a rare sight. The water, alkaline simple thermal, is good for aching limbs, fatigue, and neuralgia. Public fountains supply water for drinking that will aid your digestion and calm your stomach.

AROUND AND ABOUT: Gero has the concrete hotels and souvenir shops you expect in a hot-spring resort, but the river is wide and clear and the mountains around tower far above any deluxe hotel complexes. At the Gasshō Mura museum, 5 minutes by taxi or 20 minutes by bus from Gero Station, you can see paper being made and wide-brimmed all-weather hats, dolls, and toys being woven from straw. This section of town offers close-up views of the traditional Hida-style houses so abundant and well preserved throughout this part of Gifu. When you tire of wandering about, stop in at a restaurant and enjoy the taste of trout and rice wrapped in fragrant *hō* leaves, a Gifu specialty.

ACCOMMODATIONS: Suimeikan, a deluxe ryokan in traditional hot-spring style, has a women-only outdoor bath, a thermal swimming pool, and a garden. Another possibility is the minshuku Moriyama, a two-story, wooden structure built in the Hida style.

6 KŌSHINETSU REGION

Wine, Women, and Song

Imagine an ornate, smoky, gray-tiled roof sitting above brown wooden shutters. The shutters are almost invisible behind lines of bamboo poles hung with strings of round, peeled, orange persimmons drying in the winter sun like gaudy, dangling baubles. The sky is the brilliant deep blue of a Japanese country winter. Wind ruffles the pines, barely separating the thick, dull green needles, but allowing the sweet fragrance to escape. Such pastoral scenes are the stuff of dreams and of the Kōshinetsu Region. Here, in three prefectures—Yamanashi, Nagano, and Niigata—is enough rustic beauty and quaint charm to stir even the most jaded of tourists.

Yamanashi Prefecture: In Shōsenkyō Gorge and Chichibu-Tama National Park, the autumn mountainsides shout vibrant color at each other across the ravines. Flashes of scarlet break up the blends of orange and gold in tiers upon tiers until the eye tires and you run out of superlatives. In the vineyards around Kōfu City, the wine capital of Japan, dusty, purple winegrapes hang heavy, waiting for the cityfolk to spread their tarpaulins beneath and begin their bacchanalian feasts. (In other fields, in earlier months, these same revelers have picked apples, pears, or peaches, often before retiring to a quiet, out-of-the-way hot spring for the night.) The urban vacationer might drop into one or two wineries on his way back to the city, just to make his weekend complete. The modern-day traveler may find it hard to imagine that Kōfu was also the stronghold of one of Japan's greatest warriors and that Yamanashi was the site of many ferocious battles. The rivers ran blood red, not wine red, in the days of yore.

The majestic Mount Fuji, on Yamanashi's southern border, needs little introduction. Fuji is the most visited, snapped, and revered mountain in, and probably out of, Japan. Adorning woodblock prints, paintings, postcards, screens, even bathhouse walls, the mountain has captured more limelight than instant noodles and Walkman ever will. From long ago revered as a fire goddess, Mount Fuji has commanded imperiously, using a combination of extreme beauty and grandeur, along with the occasional eruption, when respect dwindled. Annually she lures thousands up her five ascent routes, even during the wee hours so that the sunrise can be viewed from her loftiest point. At her feet are five guardian lakes around which the faithful camp, fish, relax, and wait, hoping to catch a glimpse of her face blushing or her icy blue mood or her morning visage tinged with the gray light of early dawn. Who can dare to visit Japan and not pay homage to this enigmatic, powerful lady?

Nagano Prefecture: Way up on the mountainous "roof" of Japan in Nagano, when skiing or retracing the old salt routes of this land-bound prefecture, you'll find it very easy to look down on the rest of Japan, so magnificent is the scenery here. Consider Nagano's rugged, towering slopes, twisting valleys, and crystal streams. In winter add bracing air and sunlight sparkling on snow-capped thatched roofs. In summer you will be enchanted by damp, mossy shrines and women in baggy pants and floppy hats bent over in the fields, tilling the earth. Perhaps it's these women who appreciate most the hot springs of the Japanese countryside.

They work long hours both out-of-doors and in their homes. They leave the fields in the evening. When time allows, they drop by a local hot-spring bath to talk with friends and revitalize their hardworking bodies. In the tub, singing and laughing, no one cares about wrinkled, browned skin that has seen too much harsh weather, or bent backs that have tended too many rice seedlings and vegetables, or heavy thighs that have climbed too many slopes carrying too many heavy baskets. The water is soothing and invites anyone in regardless of her shape or size.

There is another, quite different kind of woman who often visits Nagano. She is the woman who escapes the summer heat by fleeing to her luxury hideaway in famous summer retreats like Karuizawa. The town of Karuizawa boomed starting in the Meiji era. It was a place where a crown prince could meet a gracious lady on a tennis court and make her his wife. The present crown prince met his wife, Princess Michiko, here about thirty years ago. Today the remnants of this atmosphere linger among the stately pines, but for the most part it is a resort of fashionable youth and name-brand shops, mock European restaurants and fast fooderies.

Niigata Prefecture: They move forward slowly in formation, knees bending

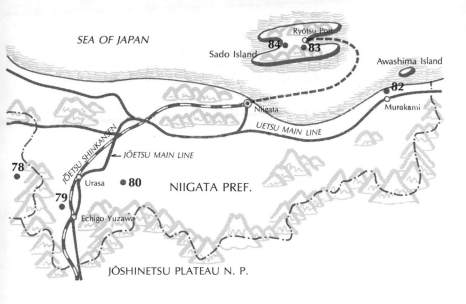

SEA OF JAPAN

Ryōtsu Port

Sado Island

84 • ● 83

Awashima Island

● 82

Niigata

Murakami

UETSU MAIN LINE

JŌETSU SHINKANSEN

— *JŌETSU MAIN LINE*

78

Urasa ● 80

NIIGATA PREF.

79

Echigo Yuzawa

JŌSHINETSU PLATEAU N. P.

6 KŌSHINETSU REGION

one way, hands pointing the other, heads hidden under tent-shaped bonnets tilted ever so slightly. They wear indigo-and-white yukata highlighted by splashes of red at the neck and waist. The dancers' hands are nimble, but the song is sad. For it's the "Okesa Ballad" of Sado Island, a former penal colony in Niigata Prefecture. Originally the ballad was a work song sung by the criminals sent to Sado to work off their sentences, often lifetimes, in the gold and silver mines there. One version of the song tells the story of a poor noodlemaker who longed for a woman to love. His cat turned into a beautiful woman one day and she danced and sang away his loneliness. The men of Sado put all their suffering and longing into the ballad; they had little hope of being happy like the noodlemaker. The women who dance today have fair skin and fine features, typical of the northern Japanese beauty. In fact, it is said that the most attractive women in Japan come from Sado Island. It's certainly possible that the severity of the winter here keeps her indoors, out of the sun, a lot of the time, contributing to her smooth, clear complexion. More in keeping with the fierce winters of Sado is the exciting drum beating performed here. The drummers wear devil masks and beat furiously—quite a rousing and even frightening sight. But this contrast between gentle dancing and stirring drum music typifies the extremes of the island's climate and terrain.

65 Shimobe

LOCATION: Shimobe is about 3 hours west of Tōkyō by train, in Yamanashi Prefecture. Take the Chūō Main Line from Shinjuku Station, Tōkyō, to Kōfu City. Transfer to the Minobu Line and continue on to Shimobe Station. From there it's less than 10 minutes by bus to the hot spring. If you're traveling toward Tōkyō on the Tōkaidō Main Line, you can transfer to the Minobu Line at Fuji Station.

THE WATERS: This is one of the famous "secret springs" known as *Shingen no kakushiyu*, or Shingen's hidden baths. Takeda Shingen was a sixteenth-century daimyo who thrived on hot springs. After battle he sought out thermal waters that would restore his body and ready him for the next attack. So convinced was he of the benefits of the hot springs in Kai (now Yamanashi Prefecture), he urged his men to follow his example. Hence a choice group of springs just outside Kōfu became the secret bathing places of Shingen and his followers. They were kept secret, not because the samurai were ashamed of their spare tires, but because an attack by the enemy, always on the lookout for unarmed opposition, would be devastating in such circumstances and because the samurai didn't like to bathe with the local riff-raff. The simple thermal water at Shimobe is still good for cuts, broken bones, bruises, and sword wounds. Today the water is favored by victims of car accidents, and, in keeping with its "warrior status," Shimobe now caters to professional athletes, sumo wrestlers, and baseball players who find soaking in a quiet setting to be suitable preparation for their next battles. The temperature of the water is a low 28° C (82° F) so some baths are heated. Others are reserved for long periods of soaking at room temperature. In addition to the private baths at the ryokan, there are a communal public bath, used mainly by campers and guests at the minshuku, and a mineral swimming pool at the Onsen Kaikan Center, which is open to the public. You can also get a massage at this center, if the water doesn't work. But the efficacy of Shimobe's mineral water is legendary. During World War II it filled the canteens of Japanese soldiers. Today it is bottled under the name Mineraru Uōta Shingen ("Mineral Water Shingen"), and sold at department stores and at the Rokumeikan pub near the south exit of Ikebukuro Station in Tōkyō.

AROUND AND ABOUT: This hot-spring town consists of ryokan lining both sides of the Shimobe River, with mountains close behind. In autumn Shimobe is a crimson and gold extravaganza. In summer it's a leafy, green bower, offering an ideal respite from city heat and crowded beaches. If the mineral water and the scenery don't lull you into a stupor, try one of the many good hiking trails in the region or, simpler yet, get your exercise at the shrine in the center of town. The entrance to this shrine—a flight of 280 stone steps—is on the route of early-morning joggers; it's not unusual to see disguised baseball players, sumo wrestlers, and elderly men and women running up and down them. In the shrine precincts is the evidence: abandoned crutches and canes, presumably discarded by present-day runners, testimony to the good effects of the waters—and the stairs. Just don your shoes and follow the joggers.

ACCOMMODATIONS: The ryokan Gensenkan has two large communal baths set in rocks in the building's basement. One is heated, one is not; patrons are encouraged to follow a bathing routine suited to their illness. Visitors passing through may also use these baths for a minimal fee.

FESTIVALS: May 14 and 15 are put aside to celebrate Takeda Shingen and this hidden bath. Donning samurai and geisha dress, local folk re-create the atmosphere of the past.

66 Masutomi

LOCATION: Masutomi is north of Kōfu City on the western edge of Chichibu Tama National Park in Yamanashi Prefecture. Take the Chūō Main Line from Shinjuku Station in Tōkyō and go through Kōfu to Nirasaki. From Nirasaki Station it's about 1¹/₂ hours by bus to the hot spring.

THE WATERS: Another of Shingen's hidden baths, Masutomi was originally developed as a gold mining area by the daimyo Takeda Shingen. But as war intensified and wounded soldiers multiplied, he decided to make it an off-the-beaten-track stop for rest and recuperation. The water contains radium—in the highest concentration in Japan. The inns encourage patrons to make the most of the water by following prescribed hot and cold tub routines, tailored to their ailments. People recovering from major surgery, broken bones, wounds, skin diseases, and burns soak in the water, while those with digestive, liver, and kidney problems drink it. You can use the mineral water for cooking, too, but be advised that the taste requires some getting used to. There are plenty of public fountains and baths that are open to the public.

AROUND AND ABOUT: Hiking is a popular activity here especially in summer and autumn, but Masutomi is primarily a serious bathing spot. People in the region, and bathing buffs up on mineral waters and cures, like this hot spring. Although often crowded, it's far enough away from the scenic routes to be always quiet. There are few ryokan, and after eight at night there's nothing to do but listen to the river pounding the rocks and the occasional person clacking by in geta. Masutomi is typical of the kinds of villages found throughout Chichibu-Tama National Park. This haven, so close to Tōkyō, is a maze of unspoiled walking trails that lead to thatched-roof farmhouses or small shrines covered in moss. The rivers flow swiftly, the source of delicious river fish that are often served at dinner time with mountain vegetables and noodles—all specialties of the area.

ACCOMMODATIONS: The ryokan Furōkaku has a cool—25° C (77° F)—mineral-water pool set in natural rock. The reddish water bubbles up from the bottom and sets you a-tingling. At dinner you will probably be served tofu made from the spring water, called *Masutomi-dōfu*. Another old, well-appointed ryokan is Kinsentō.

67 Yumura

LOCATION: Yumura is on the northern outskirts of Kōfu City. From this city, accessible via the Chūō Main Line from Shinjuku Station in Tōkyō, it is a 10-minute bus ride to the hot spring.

THE WATERS: Yumura (literally, "Village of Hot Water") is a well-patronized resort spring where you can do traditional things like cook food in thermal water or modern things like *karaoke* (singing into a microphone along to taped instrumental music) and downing whiskey-and-waters in local "snack" bars. This was once one of Shingen's hidden baths, although the spring was actually discovered by Kōbō Daishi, a Buddhist monk, who is said to have seen a white heron dabbling here, and read it as a sign of good things to come. This was so; Yumura boasts very hot, sodium chloride water that sends white steam swirling about the ryokan on the riverbanks. The water is cooled off before you get in, and treats those suffering from anemia and neuralgia in particular, and stomach disorders if imbibed. Local folk also use the water for heating their homes in winter. At the source (Arayu) there is a pool for boiling eggs and vegetables. The food is placed in a basket, which is lowered into 98° C (208° F) water. Don't confuse this pool with the one used for laundry—98° C probably doesn't do a lot for designer jeans. If you fancy just a soak or a boiled egg, you can drop in and bathe in the public bath and then continue on.

AROUND AND ABOUT: Although Yumura is near the city of Kōfu, there's a lot of countryside visible as well as picturesque touches like the red bridges spanning the river. Three national parks are close by—Chichibu-Tama, the Minami Alps, and Fuji-Hakone-Izu. Although the city of Kōfu isn't a photographer's dream come true, the surroundings are beautiful. In these parks you can walk, boat, hike, visit temples, eat corn on the cob and ice cream, or get away from it all by yourself in some spectacular, lonely spots. Nearer to Kōfu you can watch autumn leaves fall, pick fruit, and eat grapes under trellises. In Kōfu there's a lot of Takeda Shingen to see: monuments, a shrine, castle ruins, and old battle sites. The millions of tourists who come to this area tend to descend all at once in autumn. They come to see the brilliant reds, golds, and purples (grapes) the region is famous for. You can avoid some of the rush by choosing weekdays, but the autumn foliage is well worth braving even the weekend crowds. ■ WINERIES: Kōfu is in Japan's wine country, an area that produces nine hundred kiloliters of wine annually. The grape-wine industry was born in the late nineteenth century, and new local brands as well as blends with foreign wines are still produced. Wine, however, poses no serious challenge to the domestic beer or saké industries. Wineries near Kōfu include Suntory, Mercian, and Sainte Neige. Since there are no arranged wine tours as such, it might be best for the traveler interested in sampling or buying local wines to visit the Budōgaoka Center, a short walk from Katsunuma Station between Ōtsuki and Kōfu on the Chūō Main Line. There, for an admission fee of ¥1,000, you can sample as much of as many wines as you can take in an afternoon, or a day. Otherwise, if you have a car, you can drive to the above-mentioned wineries where you will be welcomed and permitted to sample and, of course, buy the wine. ■ SHŌ-SENKYŌ GORGE: Some say this is the most beautiful gorge in Japan. There is a bus to Shōsenkyo Gorge from Yumura (30 minutes). Go on a weekday, preferably, when you don't have to fight for steppingstones across the river. The winding ravine provides all the cliff, stone, rapids, and waterfall shots a photographer could desire. Add to this a "guess the name of the rock" game, which you play as you walk past strangely shaped rock formations. You should see a goblin's nose, a cat, a reclining camel, a person, a mushroom, a rising dragon, and so on. If you don't, you may have the wrong rock or you might not be familiar enough with Japanese goblins. Shōsenkyō is very much worth a visit.

ACCOMMODATIONS: Hotel Yuden is a modern concrete structure with an attractive adjoining garden. The thermal water used there comes from a spring source originally discovered by Takeda Shingen. Old harnesses and a palanquin are displayed inside the hotel. For a centrally located, inexpensive, traditional inn, try Tsuruya Ryokan.

FESTIVALS: On the weekend closest to April 12, local men dress in full battle regalia—helmets, armor, swords—and stage battle scenes in Kōfu. On horseback, they spar with each other, and on foot, they stalk around bonfires, wielding swords. The color, noise, and general fun of this event is infectious; onlookers can't help shouting out encouragement to the players.

68 Oshino

LOCATION: Oshino is near Mount Fuji, in southern Yamanashi Prefecture. Take the Chūō Main Line from Shinjuku Station in Tōkyō to Ōtsuki; transfer to the Fuji Kyūkō Line and proceed to Fuji Yoshida Station. The bus from there to the hot spring takes 20 minutes. Or, you can make the entire trip by bus. At Shinjuku Station in Tōkyō board the bus bound for Lake Yamanaka. Get off at Oshino Iriguchi (after 2 hours of travel) and from there take another bus to Oshino Fujikyū Hotel Mae or Oshino Onsen Mae (10–20 minutes).

THE WATERS: Hot springs are surprisingly scarce around here. Even though Oshino is near the volcanic area around Mount Fuji, it is in fact a tepid spring whose waters must be heated. The water is 28° C (82° F) and classified as simple thermal, although it does not contain a large quantity of minerals. It treats tired bodies, tired blood, and aching limbs and joints. Its mildness makes complexions glow; and they say that no soap is necessary in Oshino water.

AROUND AND ABOUT: The pure water of Oshino's ponds—meltwater from Mount Fuji—has attracted potters and glassblowers, who have given the town a new lease on life; tourists come to look at and purchase their works. Oshino is also a favorite haunt for photographers determined to get a good shot of one of the world's most famous mountains. ■ MOUNT FUJI: People from all over Japan come to Oshino to pay homage to Mount Fuji (*Fuji-san*)— also known as the "wealthy warrior," the "mountain that never dies," and the "fire goddess." Energetic folk will climb this illustrious cone to see the sun rise; lazy folk will view it from the tub in one of the strategically placed baths Oshino offers. Sometimes the mountain is icy blue, sometimes fiery red. To ascend Fuji is to make a pilgrimage—definitely in the physically arduous sense of the word. The shrine at the top is reached after 8 hours of climbing, give or take a couple of hours depending on your level of fitness. A Japanese saying goes: He who has not climbed Fuji even once is a fool. He who has climbed it more than once is an even bigger fool. To get to Mount Fuji from Oshino first take a bus to nearby Lake Kawaguchi; then transfer to another bus for a 1-hour ride to the fifth station on Mount Fuji's slope. From there you can start climbing if the weather is right, or just admire the views. For good reason (treacherous and unpredictable weather conditions), climbing further is only permitted from July through August.

ACCOMMODATIONS: The Oshino Fujikyū Hotel also has cottages, a huge garden, and a special Shingen stew (*Shingen nabe*) named after the great warrior himself. The ryokan Oshino Onsen is situated on the river, providing fabulous sunrise views of Mount Fuji.

FESTIVALS: The Hakkai Festival on August 8 is dedicated to the eight dragon kings who protect the eight Oshino ponds. A fire burns in the shape of the Chinese character "eight" on the slope of Mount Kōza near Oshino. The local people dress in yukata and perform Bon dances. On August 26 the Yoshida Fire Festival is held in Fuji Yoshida, 20 minutes by bus from Oshino. At night a line of bonfires starting at the Sengen Shrine is lit, making the route brighter than in the daytime. Men in happi coats, short pants, and headbands carry portable shrines through the streets, and everyone thanks the gods for the safety of climbers.

WATER FROM THE GODS: Once when Mount Fuji erupted and the people were calling out for water, a voice from the heavens promised to deliver water in exchange for a bit of respect. The people agreed to the condition and the god formed a pond—one of the eight Oshino ponds. This pond is still filled with water that seeps down into it from the top of Mount Fuji, and the myth lives on. The sacred shrine carried during festivals here is washed in this water from the heavens.

69 Bessho

LOCATION: Bessho is south of Nagano City, Nagano Prefecture. Take the Shinetsu Main Line to Ueda City. From there it's a 30-minute bus ride to the hot spring, get off at either of two bus stops—Hanaya-mae or Ishiyu-mae. You can also take a train (the Ueda Kōtsū Bessho Line) from Ueda to Bessho Onsen.

THE WATERS: This town is totally devoted to its thermal waters. The many sources are at least a thousand years old; one of their claims to fame is mention in the tenth-century classic *The Pillow Book*. Sei Shonagon, the author and a refined lady of the court, considered Bessho one of the three best springs in Japan. Even before this, in A.D. 825, the Goddess of Mercy is said to have appeared here in a puff of smoke to inform the monk Enjin of the thermal waters. Even the mythical gods of Japan bathed here. A white-haired seer told one, Yamatotakeru no Mikoto, that a bath at Bessho would protect him from the seven diseases that attack the flesh if he bathed in all seven springs. Four of those springs are now public baths: Ishiyu, Daishi-no-yu, Ōyu, and Genzaiyu. The water is simple thermal with sulphur—good for sallow complexions, rheumatism, uterine diseases, jarred nerves, and fatigue.

AROUND AND ABOUT: There's a lot to see here. For serious sightseers there are many temples, shrines, old buildings, and even venerable trees. Among the highlights are a three-tiered wooden pagoda at Anrakuji Temple and, within the grounds of Kannondō Temple, a special place to tie a prayer paper (*omikuji*) if you are looking for a mate and haven't had much luck so far. Along the roadsides you can also see the small stone Dōsojin carvings of couples (sometimes embracing) that protect travelers. An area that once belonged to the Hōjō family, rulers of Japan in the thirteenth century, Bessho is known as the Little Kamakura of Nagano because of its rich historical past and the historical relics that can still be viewed today. For those not into serious sightseeing, there's eating, picnicking, or browsing in souvenir shops. Local delicacies range from the succulent, fragrant *matsutake* mushroom to sticky rice cakes covered with chestnut sauce. In between there are mountain greens, apples, handmade noodles, dried persimmons, and ginseng. In Ueda you can see the rough-surfaced silk known as *Ueda tsumugi*, which used to be for everyday wear and is still not worn on formal occasions, despite its price tag.

ACCOMMODATIONS: Kashiwaya Bessō is an old, classy ryokan with a big garden and two open-air baths. On a smaller scale there is Katsurasō, which takes pride in its traditional cuisine. Another possibility is Hanaya Hotel, traditional in service and appearance—it's shaped like a Japanese castle. The marble bath within is large.

70 Kakeyu

LOCATION: Kakeyu is 3 kilometers southwest of Bessho. From Ueda Station on the Shinetsu Main Line, it takes 1 hour 20 minutes to reach the hot spring by bus.

THE WATERS: The name Kakeyu, written with the Chinese characters for deer, teach, and hot water, refers to the spring's discovery by a deer. Situated on the Uchimura River, it is a typical Nagano hot spring—mountains on most sides, a lot of fast-flowing rivers, and good bathing facilities of which the townspeople are proud. The water here is very effective, suiting the spring's status as a National Health Resort. The town has several hospitals with rehabilitation facilities as well as research centers and a kurhaus. The simple thermal water is particularly good for those who've had brain hemorrhages, but its high reputation derives from the local programs designed to aid people suffering from palsy. In fact there's a slope, Chūkizaka ("Palsy Slope"), that is part of a climbing route to a public bath particularly beneficial to those who come for palsy treatment. Patients lodge prayer papers between the rocks of the wall that edges the route. People with high blood pressure are also drawn to Kakeyu—by some of the most advanced treatment programs in Japan. Social or spare-time activities could include hiking courses (such as the "Twenty-one Scenic Spots Tour," 8 kilometers long), which are part of a stay in Kakeyu. ■ KURHAUS KAKEYU: From the minute you walk in onto the geothermally heated carpet, you know you're in for some good bathing and exercising. At the reception desk you fill out a health chart which, if answered honestly, will send you off to Kakeyu Hospital or into the gym to follow a program suited to your aches, pains, obesity, lethargy, or whatever. This program and a towel and gym suit will cost you about ¥1,000 a day. The kurhaus is well equipped with sports facilities, sauna, and a variety of baths.

AROUND AND ABOUT: For those healthy travelers who just want to bathe, eat, sleep in the countryside quiet, and perhaps do some hiking, Kakeyu is an ideal destination, for it is located at the gateway to Utsukushigahara Plateau, a very beautiful, suitably challenging hiking area (in spring and summer). One of your walks might take in Kasa Iwa ("Umbrella Rock"), rather polite nomenclature for what everyone agrees resembles a giant penis, and in fact women go there to pray for conception.

ACCOMMODATIONS: Kakeyu Sansō is a traditional ryokan with lovely marble baths. On the less elite side there is Shikanoya, a traditional down-home inn.

FESTIVALS: There are many in Kakeyu. The Monjudō festival is held on April 25. The Sasara Summer Festival is on the third Sunday in July, and the Shimenawa Shrine festival is on October 4.

71 Shirahone

LOCATION: Shirahone, 1,400 meters above sea level, lies at the foot of Mount Norikura in Chūbu Sangaku National Park. It is just inside Nagano Prefecture. Take the Matsumoto Dentetsu Line from Matsumoto City and get off at Shinshimashima Station. From there it's about an hour by bus to Shirahone, the terminal stop on the bus route.

THE WATERS: This hot spring was originally called Shirafune—"White Ship"—after a limestone bath here that was shaped like a ship. Over time the name evolved into Shirahone, "White Bone," for reasons still apparent. The water ranges in color from slightly murky to thick calcium white. Its softness may remind you of a milk bath. The "milk" contains hydrogen sulphide and is good for the complexion, of course, as well as the stomach, nerves, and iron-poor blood. There are seven open-air baths.

AROUND AND ABOUT: Shirahone is set in Yugawa Gorge and doesn't demand anything more strenuous of you than looking for reindeer, collecting edible plants from the slopes, wallowing in the clear air scented with pine, or listening for the nightingales. Shirahone was formerly a medicinal spring, but the coming of the Kamikōchi Superhighway meant the coming also of walkers, climbers, skiers, and nature lovers. The surrounding Kamikōchi area is a beautiful venue for everyone from the vacationing tourist to the serious outdoorsman.

ACCOMMODATIONS: Awanoyu Ryokan has a leafy outdoor bath and good indoor baths as well. The deluxe Shirafunesō Shintaku Ryokan also has an open-air bath. Yumoto Saitō Ryokan is an older, traditional wooden inn.

72 Nakabusa

LOCATION: Nakabusa is in the Japan Alps in western Nagano Prefecture, near the point where Nagano, Gifu, and Toyama prefectures meet. Take the Ōito Line to Ariake from Matsumoto City. From there it's 1 hour by bus to the hot spring. This bus doesn't run from November through April.

THE WATERS: Set deep in the mountains at the source of the Nakabusa River, Nakabusa Hot Spring is a quiet one-ryokan hideaway. Not many people find their way here. The ryokan, built in 1822, is still managed by descendants of the original owners. The several open-air pools along the river are a popular gathering place for local folk in spring when the warm weather and the cherry blossoms make it an idyllic place to be. In summer it's also pleasant—green and cool—as the monkeys who chatter in the trees above seem to agree. Hardy folk brave the snow and hike to the pools in winter when it's a cozy place surrounded by soft, white snowbanks. This year-round bathing venue draws on two sources of water; one is hydrogen sulphide and the other is simple thermal. Together they treat rheumatism, broken bones, skin problems, burns, respiratory ailments, and, when imbibed, digestive disorders. In addition to the outdoor pools there is a steam bath behind a small wooden door where you lie on straw mats and soak in the hot mist that wafts up and over you.

AROUND AND ABOUT: This lonely, mountain haunt is known to few men and many monkeys. Although the area is volcanic—potatoes and even whole chickens can be cooked in the hot soil near the hill called Myōban-yama—it's not all gray ash. There are waterfalls, fields of *wasabi* (Japanese horseradish), unmatched spring vistas, and nightingales, which can be heard, if not seen, in the trees.

ACCOMMODATIONS: The ryokan Nakabusa Onsen is comfortable and simple and suits its surroundings. It is closed in winter.

73 Shimosuwa

LOCATION: Shimosuwa is on the northern shore of Lake Suwa, in central Nagano Prefecture. Take the Chūō Main Line from Shinjuku Station in Tōkyō to Shimosuwa Station. From there walk 10 minutes to the spring.

THE WATERS: This hot spring was at the crossroads of three old major highways—Nakasendō, Kōshūkaidō, and Inakaidō—so everybody stayed here at one time or another. The legacy is a multitude of public baths to choose from. You simply buy a ticket and dip in the bath or baths that capture your fancy. The oldest is Wata-no-yu, and even though the name means "Cotton Water," it is in fact as smooth as silk and should leave your body in a similar condition. The waters are simple thermal and sodium chloride, recommended for rheumatism, neuralgia, high blood pressure, and diabetes.

AROUND AND ABOUT: There's still something of the old junction town about Shimosuwa—the ryokan clustered around Wata-no-yu, the stone guideposts giving scratched, worn, and almost illegible directions to the main routes out of town, and the townspeople's interest in travelers, although this could be due equally to their long winters of isolation. Anyone with an inclination to step into the past can do it easily here; rickety, wooden houses, sturdy *kura* (storehouses), and barns and sheds from a bygone era abound. Also pleasant to visit are several shrines; Raigōji Temple, where an invocation bestows beauty on the supplicant; and a Buddhist statue with a difference—a round rock topped by a smaller rock with a face carved in it, somewhat resembling a sumo wrestler. The statue, called Manji no Sekibutsu, was unearthed by the famous contemporary artist Okamoto Tarō, whose designs often include sun symbols.

ACCOMMODATIONS: The ryokan Minatoya has an outdoor garden bath, and serves homemade fruit wine and horse-meat dishes for dinner. Another inn offering good service is Kameya Hotel, which also boasts a nice garden. For the budget-minded, there is Kokuminshukusha Sannōkaku.

A STORY FROM LAKE SUWA: In the mythical age of the gods, there was quite a falling out between Ōkuninushi no Mikoto's son and another god, which resulted in the son's moving to Suwa Shrine from the main shrine area. As luck would have it, a beautiful goddess lived in Suwa, and, of course, the two fell in love. But the course of true love never runs smoothly and the two could only visit each other in winter when the ice on Lake Suwa made a natural pathway from his shrine at the top of the lake to hers at the bottom. They endured a bit and then got married. But the course of marriage never runs smoothly either, and being stubborn gods, they fell to squabbling and arguing about domestic trivia. She moved out and back to her old shrine (Shimosha). This is why shrines in Suwa come in pairs—Kamisha and Shimosha, Akimiya ("Autumn Shrine") and Harumiya ("Spring Shrine"). This is also why, so one story goes, the ice on the lake cracks on cold winter nights; it's the two lovers walking to meet each other during their courtship. Another result of their courtship—a bonus for the hot-spring buff—is the spring that appeared where the goddess dropped her face lotion. The spring is now known as a beautifying bath (*bijin-ni-naru yu*).

74 Kamisuwa

Visitors to Shimosuwa may want to take in Kamisuwa Hot Spring as long as they're in the area. To get there from Shimosuwa, take the Chūō Main Line to Kamisuwa and then walk 5 to 10 minutes. The water is simple thermal like Shimosuwa's, and there is a very unique public bath (Katakurakan) that used to be a stocking factory. The building, unusual for a bathhouse, features a stained-glass window and tower. Inside the spacious, barnlike structure are many tubs. Visitors can drop in for a dip and pass on. Other local curiosities include the toilets on the Kamisuwa Station platform, which use spring water, and a bathhouse in the big department store Marukō, the only department store in Japan that offers a bath between purchases.

75 Goshiki

LOCATION: Goshiki lies 30 kilometers east of Nagano City. From Nagano take the Nagano Dentetsu Line to Suzaka Station. From there take the bus headed for Yamada Bokujō and get off at the stop called Goshiki Onsen—a 1-hour ride.

THE WATERS: As the name Goshiki (literally, "Five Colors") suggests, the water here has five shades that come and go according to the weather and the sunlight. It's almost impossible to stay long enough to witness this phenomenon, so you will have to take it on trust. The colors are milky white, creamy white, green, cobalt blue, and black. The minerals are hydrogen sulphide and calcium sulphate, and the benefits are cures for those suffering from diabetes, high blood pressure, women's ailments, and infertility. Another novel and very pleasant bathing experience offered at Goshiki is a moonlight bath in the open-air pool near the river. The ryokan proprietor provides you with a lamp to help you find your way to the pool. There you moon-gaze to the accompaniment of nightingales and singing frogs—something everyone should do at least once in his hot-spring journeys.

AROUND AND ABOUT: The lone white ryokan here stands on the rocky riverbank in front of densely covered green slopes. The owner, Mr. Mizuno, is a haiku poet who encourages his guests to add to his collection of visitors' efforts. In such an environment, it's not difficult to wax lyrical. One of his haiku, carved into a rock, greets you at the entrance. His message is about eating miniature crabs, which are specially prepared here. In fact, food is the pride of this ryokan. Besides the crunchy, tasty crabs (*sawa-gani*), other gourmet dishes of myriad colors and textures are laid out on your dinner table: things like autumn leaves covered on one side with tempura batter, mountain mushrooms cooked with bean curd, or grilled river fish served with green vegetables and lemon. This is what awaits you after an outdoor dip or a bath in the cypress (*hinoki*) tub inside. If the food, the haiku, and the baths are not enough, you can hire a rod and go fishing, go walking by the river, or drop by the nearby dairy, Yamada Bokujō, for a drink of fresh milk.

ACCOMMODATIONS: The only ryokan is Goshiki-no-yu, which serves a very nice wild-grape Juice, made on the premises, in addition to the delicacies noted above.

76 Jigokudani

LOCATION: Jigokudani is in Shiga Heights, Jōshinetsu Plateau National Park, in northeastern Nagano Prefecture. From Nagano City take the Nagano Dentetsu Line to Yudanaka Station. From the station take a bus (15 minutes) to the bus stop Kanbayashi Onsen. Get off and walk for 30 minutes along the Yokoyu River to the solitary ryokan called Kōrakukan.

THE WATERS: In 1557, with a sudden mighty whoosh, steam and boiling water spouted from the river. Although eruptions like that of Mount Asama in 1783 have caused the flow to temporarily disappear, it is going strong today and is famous as a protected natural wonder. The monk Gyōki blessed this hot spring, dedicating it to longevity and tradition and, of course, to its most famous inhabitants, the once wild, now tame mountain monkeys that come to bathe in their own pool after the first snow falls in winter. The very hot, sodium chloride bath, besides extending your life, is good for upset stomachs, fatigue (like after the hike to the ryokan), and hemorrhoids.

AROUND AND ABOUT: Jigokudani is surrounded by spectacular scenery and quiet punctuated only by the sounds of the whooshing steam and chattering monkeys and birds. You can hike in spring and summer, and ski in winter. Shiga Heights (Shiga Kōgen) is one of the choicest skiing spots in Japan, what with its fine facilities, the number and variety of slopes, and the breathtaking vistas of the Japan Alps in all directions.

ACCOMMODATIONS: Kōrakukan is an old, wooden ryokan whose name means "Later-Pleasure Inn," perhaps a reference to the fact that the long walk to the establishment must precede the pleasures of bathing. Its two open-air baths are segregated in winter—one for guests and one for monkeys. The innkeeper, a descendant in the family line that has managed the ryokan for a hundred years, serves river fish, mountain vegetables, and *chimaki*—sweet, gluey rice rolled in a bamboo leaf, a dish that originated in China. Steaming the rice over mineral water, the innkeeper makes this symbolic rice sweet to give to the spirit of the dragon-snake, a wretched creature that used to live in the river.

THE LADY AND THE DRAGON-SNAKE: There once was a very beautiful girl who liked moon gazing. One chilly night, while walking along the river, she saw the form of a man rise out of the water and drift toward her. He was young, handsome, and everything she had been looking for in a man. The love affair went along nicely, night after night, but her parents didn't approve of her evening walks, and worse still they were very worried about her appearance. She was thin, pale, and forlorn, no longer the village belle. They called in a fortuneteller who told them she was possessed by the dragon-snake who lived in the river and that if they couldn't break the two up, she would die. Her father went to the shrine to get some sacred objects to ward off evil and her mother locked the girl indoors. Fortunately they had an ally, for the dragon-snake was so angry he planned to kill the whole family. This ally, the god of a nearby mountain, turned the river into hot vapor, causing the dragon-snake to suffocate. Thus the bubbling, belching volcanic area called Jigokudani ("Hell Valley") was formed. Anyone who feels the dragon got an unfair deal can throw *chimaki* into the river to console him.

MONKEY CHATTER: Although the monkeys are cute, it's been proven that they don't like eye contact. Those unable to resist trying to outstare one should make sure it's from behind a camera lens or through dark glasses.

---

77 Yudanaka

When you've had enough of Jigokudani's solitude, retrace your steps to the Kanbayashi Onsen bus stop, and take the bus to Yudanaka Station. It could be a day trip, or a more extended stay if you crave the bright lights of resorts like this. The sodium chloride water is good for rheumatism, skin problems, and neuralgia. Yudanaka is another good base for exploring Shiga Heights. As with many thriving resorts, thermal water, coffee shops, and restaurants abound.

---

78 Hoppo

LOCATION: Hoppo is in Jōshinetsu Plateau National Park in northeastern Nagano Prefecture. From Yudanaka Station on the Nagano Dentetsu Line it's an hour by bus to Hasuike and then 10 minutes by overhead cable car to the hot spring. From Yudanaka you can also take a direct bus to Hoppo (a 50-minute trip).

THE WATERS: Hoppo (pronounced "hope-oh") was discovered about two hundred years ago. The oldest ryokan here, Tengu-no-yu, was built by a man named Shinsaku, who was led to the thermal water's source by a long-nosed goblin (*tengu*). Masks commemorating this discovery, in the form of rather fierce-looking goblins with improper noses, decorate the foyer of the ryokan-hotel. The water is simple thermal, just what you need after a day's skiing or hiking in the panoramic surroundings to get your muscles back in shape for the next day.

AROUND AND ABOUT: The ryokan that constitute this hot-spring community, set on the side of Mount Higashitate, are cut off from each other by snow in winter and dense foliage in summer, so wherever you stay it's quiet and scenic with white or green slopes stretching down to the bottom of the gorge. If you're in the habit of mountain climbing in spiked heels you'll appreciate Mount Higashitate. From the top of the Hoppo overhead cable car you take a chairlift and then a bus to Takamagahara and then a chair lift to the top of the mountain—all without stumbling on one rock. The views are superb and it couldn't be an easier "climb." In August a snake festival, possibly related to the Jigokudani dragon-snake incident, is held near Lake Biwa. The activities include selection of a new "Miss Shiga Kogen."

ACCOMMODATIONS: Most of the ryokan here, about ten in all, are modern structures with Japanese- and Western-style facilities. The ryokan Tengu-no-yu specializes in good food and will serve *kumazasa* tempura—lightly battered, fried bamboo leaves—if you order in advance. In winter, fondue is served, a dish that, in combination with the sparkling slopes, will evoke images of Switzerland in the Japanese mind.

79 Echigo Yuzawa

LOCATION: Echigo Yuzawa is in the Mikuni mountain range, in southern Niigata Prefecture. Take the Jōetsu Shinkansen (bullet train) or the Jōetsu Line from Ueno Station in Tōkyō to Echigo Yuzawa Station.

THE WATERS: This resort hot spring, popular in the region for more than eight hundred years, became known throughout the nation with the publication in the 1930s and 1940s of Kawabata Yasunari's novel *Snow Country* (*Yukiguni*), which was set at Echigo Yuzawa. The water is simple thermal, and you are encouraged to bathe in between snow gazing (*yukimi*) and saké drinking. Combining the latter two activities is known as *yukimi-zaké*; both are favorite pastimes around here in winter, and the tub adds the third and final dimension to a perfect experience. The water will take away the chill and settle your stomach if the other activities prove hard going. The water is also good for blood circulation. There are many tubs in town. You will find the biggest open-air pool at Yuzawa Tōei Hotel.

AROUND AND ABOUT: Around and about is snow, snow, and more snow, which makes Echigo Yuzawa perfect for thermal bathing and skiing. Nearby Naeba ski slopes are said to be some of the best in the world. Whether you like snow or not, you'll be impressed by the mounds of it packed around the houses and towering above you on the sides of paths. Summer here is fun, too. You can play tennis or wander in the fields looking for *wasabi* (Japanese horseradish) to grace your table with. For a pleasant scenic hike, follow the trail through Kiyotsukyō Gorge to Kiyotsukyō Hot Spring. It takes time—about 6 hours—but it's well worth it, and besides, think of all the *wasabi* you might find along the way.

ACCOMMODATIONS: The deluxe Yuzawa Tōei Hotel has a huge outdoor bath capable of holding a thousand people. For something a little more traditional, try Ikariya Ryokan.

FESTIVALS: The hot-spring festival is held from August 14 to 16. A ski carnival is held on the first Saturday and Sunday in March. This European-style carnival includes skiing races, games, and acrobatics performed by experts and amateurs alike.

80 Tochiomata

LOCATION: Tochiomata is south of Niigata City, Niigata Prefecture. Take the Jōetsu Shinkansen (bullet train) from Ueno Station in Tōkyō to Urasa Station. From there it's a 1-hour bus ride to the hot spring.

THE WATERS: This is a medicinal spring where people come to bathe over several days, often cooking for themselves and socializing in the manner of the olden days. Tochiomata opened its doors in the eighth century, boomed during the Silver Rush of the seventeenth century, and now offers an inexpensive holiday centered around bathing. The water in the most popular public bath, used by both ryokan guests and local folk, is not very hot—39° C (102° F)—so some people sit in it for many hours. In fact, it is a *yozume* (all-night) bath, with the purest water supposed to flow in at about 1:00 A.M. During the all-night stints many bathers sing. For others, who might doze off and drown, there are special ropes to hold one above water. If you can deliver a spirited rendition of a national song from your own land, you'll probably win the singing contest. Besides treating insomnia, neuralgia, burns, skin irritations, and rheumatism, Tochiomata's radioactive water is said to be the most effective infertility-curing water in Japan. As a result, grandmothers and grandfathers come to this hot spring, bathe, and hang dolls in plastic bags on the walls near the statue of the hot-spring deity in the hope that their daughters will conceive!

AROUND AND ABOUT: Tochiomata is a snowy, mountainous, unpretentious place where life revolves about the bath. If you decide to cook for yourself, buy your vegetables and other ingredients from the farmers' wives who come to the ryokan each morning, selling their wares packed in huge panniers on their backs. During the day, when you're not cooking or eating cakes with tea served by the older people staying here, you can go to Ōyu Hot Spring. Ōyu is across the Sanashi River from Tochiomata. You can walk there in 10 minutes or you can take the bus (5 minutes). Ōyu offers skiing facilities and simple thermal water. Alternating this water with that of Tochiomata is the perfect routine for your body, your soul, and your daughter's fertility. Ōyu is in a valley amid rugged peaks with tall strong cedars and pines protecting the wooden buildings. As in Tochiomata, the ryokan baths are open through the winter, which some say is the best time to come since you'll appreciate the bath and the warm bonhomie inside all the more.

ACCOMMODATIONS: The three ryokan—Jizaikan, Jinpūkan, and Hōgandō—are very inexpensive if you cook for yourself and pay for accommodation only. This kind of arrangement, although difficult for foreigners in the beginning, is the best way to get to know people who know all about hot springs and the customs associated with them. But if you like comfort, Western-style food, and privacy, then this style of communal cooking and bathing may not be for you. The above mentioned ryokan do offer facilities for city folk (meals prepared for you).

81 Renge

LOCATION: Renge is near the Hime River in western Niigata Prefecture. Take the Ōito Line from Itoigawa to Hiraiwa Station. From there the bus to the spring takes 1½ hours. The single ryokan at Renge is open from the end of March to mid-October, but the bus there runs from June through October. Before June you have to have your own transportation, or hike in.

THE WATERS: This unique hot spring has seven outdoor pools within walking distance of the single ryokan. Each contains slightly different water, so in one stop you can cure anemia, athlete's foot, backache, stress, rheumatism, fatigue, cuts and bruises, and probably any other afflictions. The water ranges from simple thermal to acidic, from sodium chloride to hydrogen carbonate. The baths, all communal, are simple wooden structures—no more than wooden planks to hold the water in. You'll feel as if you're sitting in a pond in a grassy field, surrounded by green, scraggly mountains (part of the Shirouma Mountain Range) in four directions. Outside the pools are wooden benches, especially arranged for moon gazing. Renge was discovered in the mid-fifteenth century by a doctor looking for medicinal herbs.

AROUND AND ABOUT: This area has always been popular with alpinists, who use the hot springs in the area as "refreshment" stops to get tired bodies back into working order and ready to attack the next incline. Two other such springs, Himekawa Hot Spring and Shirouma Yari Hot Spring, are hikes away from Renge. The Renge baths seem to have changed little from their earliest days as pools for quiet, no-fuss dipping on the way up or down the mountain. Those staying at Renge and wanting a bit more than tubs and treks can go to Shirouma Sanroku Prefectural Park and see the jade stones in the Hime River bed. This jade used to be fashioned into comma-shaped beads (*magatama*), but is now a protected national monument. To get there, take the Ōito Line from Hiraiwa Station to Kotaki Station; from there it's a short walk.

ACCOMMODATIONS: The ryokan Renge Onsen is a simple three-story mountain lodge with few frills and a feeling of rustic Niigata about it. From your windows you can see the steam rising from the tubs and out of the ground.

The hot pools suitable for dipping are marked with wooden stakes driven into the ground. The name of the pool is scratched onto the stake. Just follow the path toward the group of people standing in the middle of nowhere in their long white undies!

82 Senami

LOCATION: Senami is on the Sea of Japan coast, north of Murakami City, northern Niigata Prefecture. Take the Uetsu Main Line from Niigata City and get off at Murakami Station. The bus to the hot spring takes 15 minutes.
THE WATERS: Senami dates back to the turn of the century when oil drillers found a different type of liquid—water laced with sodium chloride. The derrick that first tapped the mineral water remains today for those interested in strokes of fate. The water settles stomachs, smoothes skin, gets rid of sleepless nights, and helps women who have given up on their gynecologists.
AROUND AND ABOUT: Senami is a resort spa—modern and comfortable, with sports and after-dark entertainment facilities for when you tire of mountain and frontier lands. One of the few hot springs on the coast of Niigata, Senami is also a good place for viewing storms over the sea. These come thundering in with a vengeance in winter, churning up the blue-gray sea and sending the sea birds scuttling. Take a long walk on the beach to watch the bruised blue clouds come in with the rain or, in summer, to soak up some sun and do a bit of paddling. Further afield, in Murakami, are the ruins of Murakami Castle, once the fortress of the northern daimyo during the Edo period. In Murakami there are also two old, weather-beaten temples, Jōnenji and Shōjōji, and a folk museum, Iwafune Bunka Hakubutsukan, that displays local folk crafts and arts. ■ AWASHIMA: If you want a quiet place for hiking or fishing, consider a trip to Awashima. This tiny island, about 2 hours by boat off Murakami, is nearly uninhabited. You arrive at an old-fashioned fishing village, the only town on the island. In summer you can camp out, but in winter ryokan or minshuku beds are advisable. Experts say this island is headed for a boom, so don't put off going there too long unless you like a lot of company.
ACCOMMODATIONS: The ryokan Senami Garden Miharashi features sea views from all windows. The inn Taikansō has an open-air bath where the water laps around oddly shaped, sooty-black rocks.
FOOD: Senami is heaven for shellfish lovers. For something without a shell try cod (*tara*), baby sardines (*shirasu*), or sea bream (*tai*).

83 Katakami

LOCATION: Katakami is on Sado Island, off the coast of Niigata Prefecture. Take a ferry (2 hours) or hydrofoil (1 hour) from Niigata City. Both vessels dock at Ryōtsu, the main port on the island. From there take the Minami bus to Tennōshita, a 10-minute ride, and then walk 10 minutes through the rice fields to reach the hot spring. Ferries to Sado leave from other ports on the mainland as well.

THE WATERS: This very old, isolated hot spring has just one quaint, two-story ryokan, still a favorite meeting spot with the local people, who come to use the ryokan bath. The reddish, relatively cool water contains sulphur—good for treating skin problems, neuralgia, and rheumatism. Legend attributes the spring's discovery about 750 years ago to a white heron, but the townsfolk prefer to think it was a crested ibis (*toki*), an endangered species that is greatly revered on the island.

AROUND AND ABOUT: The crested ibis is found only on Sado Island. The few of them that remain are now being cared for in captivity, in the hope that this salmon pink, long-necked, graceful creature will not abandon the earth forever. They are not on public view. While ibis once roamed the area freely, now only the heron can be seen wading in the rice fields. Sado is separated from the island of Honshū by a temperamental stretch of water that made Sado a perfect prison. From as far back as Emperor Juntoku in the thirteenth century, felons and political nuisances were banished to Sado to rot in the gold and silver mines, prey to loneliness, winter storms, and harsh treatment from equally unhappy guards. Tales of those times are captured in the "Okesa Ballad" sung by women on Sado, although the dance and rhythm of the song don't seem particularly forlorn. On a winter's day you can experience the bleakness of Sado for yourself, but in summer, which is when most people visit, it's hard to imagine the island as a penal colony.

ACCOMMODATIONS: Hōsenkan is a small two-story wooden inn where you can choose dining and bedding arrangements to suit your wallet. While you're on Sado, take a moment to admire the local ceramics. This pottery is made from red clay found in the gold mines. The bowls age beautifully, turning a shiny red with time and loving care.

FOOD: Sado is another source of excellent shellfish, not to mention crab, oysters, prawns, and plebeian fish as well.

---

84 Yawata

For a change of scenery and water type, catch a bus around to Yawata Hot Spring on the other side of Sado Island. The water is simple thermal and the signs of human hands, including the comfortable ryokan Yawatakan (closed for renovation until spring 1988), are all but obscured by giant pines. A visit to this hot spring would be a good way to see the extremes of Sado's terrain, and since it's on the opposite side of the island from Ryōtsu Port, it's quieter and less touristy.

7 KANTŌ REGION

Tōkyō's Playground

In 1456, a feudal lord named Ōta Dōkan built a castle in an inconspicuous, swampy place on the Kantō Plain called Edo. One hundred and fifty years later, in 1590, Tokugawa Ieyasu, the greatest shogun Japan has known, decided to make it his headquarters. Then, in 1868, the restored Emperor Meiji also moved to Edo, and the castle town, complete with the new name of Tōkyō, became the capital city and center of Japan.

Despite various attempts by fires, earthquakes, and bombers to dampen its spirits in subsequent years, today Tōkyō remains the stalwart, bold, and unchallenged hub of the archipelago. Its vitality, changing facades, and mixture of old and new make it a mecca, not just for its native followers, but also for Japan's many foreign residents and tourists. Like their hosts, these visitors are fascinated by the lingering spirit of Edo and, simultaneously, by the spirit of modern-day Tōkyō. They like to watch the people of old Tōkyō (Shitamachi) parading through the streets during the shrine festivals—bouncing shrines on their shoulders, their eyes bright, their voices hoarse, and their feet shod in straw sandals. Afterward, the visitors join the locals over saké and sushi or grilled chicken pieces (*yakitori*) liberally splashed with soy sauce—the way the Shitamachi people like it. It is these Edokko, natives of old Tōkyō, who embody the spirit of the past. You can see it in their keen business sense, rough speech, and warm hearts.

The visitor can get to know the modern Tōkyōite across town in Shibuya, Roppongi, or Shinjuku. You will meet over imported coffee and expensive cake in an elegant tea parlor above a chic boutique. An evening rendez-vous may take place in an exotic discothèque, jazz club, deluxe hotel lounge. Modern Tōkyō has virtually everything; the visitor need never stir.

But that would be a mistake. The surrounding Kantō Region competes readily with Tōkyō, and will reward you for taking the time to explore it. The following are a few very good reasons why the tourist or resident should extend his playground beyond the boundaries of Tōkyō.

Kanagawa Prefecture: South of Tōkyō, bordering Tōkyō Bay, this prefecture is known primarily for its heavy industry and its bed-town—a residential area where Tōkyō workers spend the precious few hours between stints on the train and in the office. But Kanagawa can also claim the spectacular Hakone area 2 hours southwest of Tōkyō, made up of lofty, luxurious peaks, deep, twisting valleys, swift, clean streams, and some of the finest hot springs in Japan. The springs are found near Lake Ashi, a caldera lake, which is the scenic center of the area. Hot springs near the lake compete with neon lights, popcorn, and boat rides, but the hot springs a little further back in the mountains are nestled deep in the valleys, secluded and away from the bustle.

If you start to miss the bustle, but aren't yet ready to return to Tōkyō, you might travel to Kamakura, south of Tōkyō on Miura Peninsula. This old city was the political center of Japan from 1185 until 1333, an era named after the city. It is admired for its countless temples and shrines and its great bronze Buddha (Daibutsu) in the grounds of Kōtokuin Temple. During the Kamakura period, feudalism and the samurai way of life were firmly established, and Buddhism, especially the Zen sects, spread beyond the nobility to the lower classes. This accounts for the profusion of temples and religious festivals. The architecture and art of the period are known for their understated, simple style, evident in the local places of worship.

Not far from somber Kamakura is the gay port city of Yokohama. The harbor is never dull, and you can be sure that Yokohama's Chinatown, with its authentic cuisine, noisy sidewalks, and bright, brassy knickknacks, will greatly divert you.

Saitama Prefecture: This landlocked prefecture to the north of Tōkyō is another bed-town with a fair share of industrial skyline. But Saitama, too, has its attractions, and is perfectly situated for a day trip from Tōkyō. This day could be spent very pleasurably in Chichibu-Tama National Park, 2 hours from the city. The park is known for the Chichibu Pilgrimage, which encompasses thirty-four temples (see Araki Hot Spring, 99). The region is densely wooded, with rivers running through valleys where old farmhouses squat undisturbed. Here, in dark, fragrant arcades of pine and cedar, you'll wonder what the dazzle of Tōkyō's arcades is all about.

Chiba Prefecture: Chiba Prefecture consists of Bōsō Peninsula and a spur

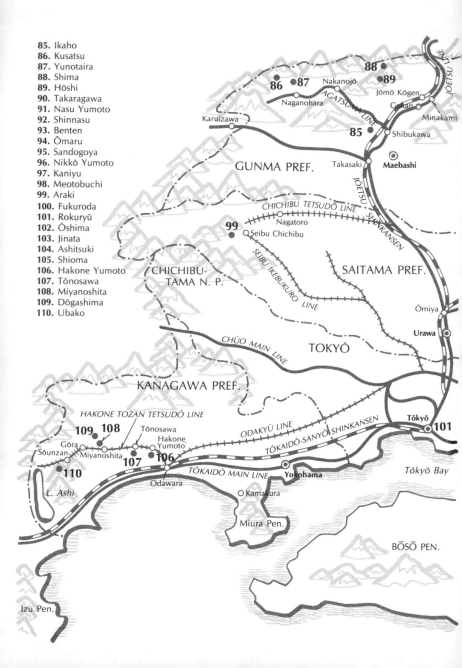

7 KANTŌ REGION

MT. ASAHI

●90

●96

●97

●98

L. Chūzenji

Nikkō

TŌBU NIKKŌ LINE

TŌBU KINUGAWA LINE

Kinugawa Onsen

TOCHIGI PREF.

NIKKŌ LINE

●95

MT. NASU

●94

●93

●91

●92

TŌBU LINE

Utsunomiya

Nasu-Shiobara

TŌHOKU MAIN LINE

TŌHOKU SHINKANSEN

Kuroiso

○ Mashiko

IBARAKI PREF.

Fukuroda

●100

SUIGUN LINE

JŌBAN MAIN LINE

Mito

Chiba

Tōkyō

CHIBA PREF.

○ Narita

Ōshima Island
102

103
104

Shikinejima Island

Hachijō Island

105

that separates Saitama and Ibaraki prefectures. Yet another bed-town for Tōkyō's office workers, Chiba too has some long industrial scars on its face. But it has equally long stretches of fishing villages and harbors, some large vegetable fields, and, of course, beaches, if you can find them under the oiled bodies crammed between surf and sea wall. A traveler escaping from Tōkyō in search of peace and quiet may want to save Chiba for the cooler months, when the fish tastes better, the villages are deserted, and the beaches belong to the birds and scattered diehards. For a change of pace, you might visit Disneyland in northern Chiba, extremely popular among the Japanese.

Unfortunately, Chiba Prefecture has no hot springs to speak of. The water doesn't contain enough minerals to qualify, and springs that once existed, for various reasons, have for the most part been closed. Travelers in search of mineral springs should continue on to another part of the Kantō Region or return to Tōkyō for a dip in a mineral bath like Rokuryū (101).

Ibaraki Prefecture: Like Saitama, Chiba, and Kanagawa, Ibaraki is in effect a vassal of Tōkyō; its fields produce vegetables, rice, peanuts, and tobacco for the city, and its coastline is dotted with oil refineries catering to urban needs. But its temperate climate and flat riverlands and canals attract sportsmen—water skiers, fishermen, boatmen—in droves, and recently tennis courts have begun springing up on the riverbanks. Another regional attraction is Naritasan Shinshōji Temple in Narita City. The original structure was built nearby in 940 and moved to the present site in 1705. The complex includes modern concrete buildings that reflect the austerity practiced by the Shingon sect of Buddhism that owns the temple. Millions of pilgrims visit this very sacred temple annually to pray for everything from long and healthy lives to success in finding a marriage partner. While you're in town, you might wander down some of the meandering streets in the old quarters of Narita.

Tochigi Prefecture: Tochigi Prefecture, to the north, competes handily with the attractions of Tōkyō. Not only does it have some superb hot springs, remote and drenched in natural beauty and tradition, but it also boasts its own seats of art and culture—Nikkō City and Mashiko, the pottery town. Mashiko ware, glazed in earthy browns, black, and white, is the folk pottery made famous by the great potter Hamada Shōji. Check with the Tourist Information Center for the dates of the biannual discount sales.

Nikkō, one of Japan's most treasured cities, is famous for its blazing autumnal colors and temples covered in snow. In fact, the Japanese say you don't know the meaning of "magnificent" until you've seen Nikkō, with its extravagant Tōshōgū Shrine and its splendid surroundings, which include Lake Chūzenji. The city has enjoyed various golden ages since the thirteenth century, so that cultural and religious history are welded into its architecture, festivals, and even into the cedars lining the avenue to Tōshōgū Shrine—they were donated by a lord unable to afford anything finer. After visiting Nikkō, you can snuggle down into a nearby hot-spring bath and reflect upon the skill of the city's creators.

Gunma Prefecture: Like its eastern neighbor, Tochigi Prefecture, Gunma offers the traveler in Japan many reasons to leave Tōkyō. Some very alluring hot springs lie nestled in the mountainous regions of its interior, and can be reached in about 2 hours via the bullet train from Tōkyō. Gunma's interior is an old world of country hospitality, where strong, wiry women serve delicious concoctions of mountain vegetables, fowl, and wild boar, so famous in this area. You will find riverside hot pools, scented wooden tubs, in short, the best kinds of thermal baths. In between soakings, you can don your skis or hiking boots, depending on the season, and explore Gunma's other delights.

The pleasures of the Kantō Region are manifold. Escape, if you can, from Tōkyō's charms, for even a short distance away lie thermal and cultural delights unlike any in the metropolis.

85 Ikaho

LOCATION: Ikaho is in central Gunma Prefecture, on the eastern slope of Mount Haruna. Take the Jōetsu Shinkansen (bullet train) from Ueno Station in Tōkyō to Takasaki Station. From there take the Jōetsu Line to Shibukawa Station and then a bus—a 30-minute ride—to the hot spring.

THE WATERS: The first inn opened for business in Ikaho in the sixteenth century after the innkeeper received the land from the famous warrior and hot spring devotee Takeda Shingen. But even before that local people were using the hot spring. The water, calcium sulphate, is good for infertility among other ailments. Drinking it is recommended for anemia and stomach disorders. The reddish color of the water—and your towel after bathing—is due to the carbonated iron in the water. At a new public bath, Ishidan-no-yu, located near the steps in the center of town, you can soak all day for a few hundred yen. The fee includes access to a hot-spring museum above the bath for between-bath diversion, or you can walk through Ikaho Shrine to the public open-air bath, where you can bathe for a small fee. There is a small thermal-water fountain for drinking near the open-air bath.

AROUND AND ABOUT: Ikaho has been a popular hot-spring town for many years, especially since the novel *Hototogisu* was published in 1900. *Hototogisu* is a sad, romantic tale of love, and people climbing the 311 stone steps leading to Ikaho Shrine in the center of town are wont to reminisce over their own past loves and losses. In fact, this is the perfect town for after-bath strolling in yukata and geta. Because the town consists of stairways with narrow lanes winding off them, you can clomp about carefree and carfree, stopping off in tiny bars and restaurants and generally feeling like a hot-spring buff, even if your yukata barely hits your knees. The next day could be spent hung over or in pursuit of culture. The Roka Kinenkan, a room in a ryokan, kept in its original state, containing books, pencils, paper, and one rattan chair, is where *Hototogisu* was created. The Takehisa Yumeji Kinenkan museum exhibits the watercolor and brush paintings and etchings of this early twentieth-century artist. For the energetic there's the dark, old Ikaho Shrine at the top of the steps and picturesque Lake Haruna 15 to 20 minutes away by bus from the hot spring.

ACCOMMODATIONS: Chigira Jinsentei, a traditional ryokan on a hill, is where Tokutomi Roka wrote the novel *Hototogisu*. It has a cascade bath. Another deluxe possibility is Matsumotorō, a first-class ryokan.

FOOD: The local sweet bean confection is called *yunohana* (sinter) cake and is brown, sticky, and covered in flour. The powdery flour seems to be the connection with sinter.

FESTIVALS: The hot-spring festival, held September 19 to 20, is a good one. The geisha who work here carry a saké barrel full of thermal water on their shoulders in procession just like the small portable shrines usually featured in festivals.

86 Kusatsu

LOCATION: Kusatsu is in northwestern Gunma Prefecture on the slopes of Mount Shirane. To get there take the Jōetsu Line from Ueno Station in Tōkyō to Shibukawa Station. From there take the Agatsuma Line to Naganohara Kusatsuguchi Station. From Naganohara it's 25 minutes by bus to the hot spring. There is also a bus from Karuizawa (on the Shinetsu Main Line) that takes 2 hours.

THE WATERS: Kusatsu's reputation rests on its scalding hot "time baths" (*jikan-yu*), dating back to the Meiji era, and its very abundant water. Only fifteen percent of the spring water is used, the rest flowing away down the river. Those deemed qualified by the bath master (*yuchō*) are awarded three dips of three minutes each in water hovering around 52°C (125°F). The bath master will ask about your medical history and your current ailment and then judge you as earnest and in need, or as just a thrill seeker to be dismissed. The needy bathers first undergo medical checks and bathing in water not quite as hot as the *jikan-yu*. Before plunging in, you and the other patients stir the water with long sticks to cool it. After the bath master measures the temperature, the victims lower themselves gently into the tub, trying not to ripple the water and thereby increase the agony. As the bath master counts off the minutes, no one moves even a little finger and no one gets out. This process is repeated three times. Women usually endure it better than men do, although everyone swears by it afterward. Chiyo-no-yu is the name of one such time bath. The acidic water contains iron, acid-aluminum sulphate, and hydrogen sulphide. The time baths are great for getting sluggish blood whipping around the body. They are also good for all skin diseases and over a period of time are said to cure baldness (who could take it long enough to disprove the theory?). For tourists to Kusatsu there is a time-bath show at the bath called Netsu-no-yu where women in kimono stir the waters rhythmically and sing the special Kusatsu bath songs. The less adventurous may prefer trying one of the ordinary baths like the open-air pool at Sainokawara Park, a picnic bathing spot swathed in steam. Don't worry about stumbling into a *jikan-yu* by mistake; it hasn't happened . . . yet.

AROUND AND ABOUT: Kusatsu is a genuine hot spring—from the steam and sulphurous smell to the fields where sinter is collected (*yubatake*) and then sold so visitors can make their own time baths at home. The new public bath, Otakinoyu, offers restrooms and tea; people come to make a day of it. After bathing you can walk in the woods and absorb the sweet, clean air, which is good for humans as well as trees. Or you can take the dangling cable car to the top of Mount Shirane and get a view of the emerald green crater lake, Shiranesan Yugama. In winter Kusatsu is a good base for skiing. In August (the date varies) there is a classical music festival.

ACCOMMODATIONS: Kirishimaya Ryokan, modern and comfortable, welcomes foreign guests. Yamamotokan has the atmosphere of a hot-spring ryokan and views of the sinter fields. There are minshuku and cook-for-yourself inns for those on a budget.

87 Yunotaira

LOCATION: Yunotaira is near Kusatsu in the northwestern corner of Gunma Prefecture. To get there take the Jōetsu Line from Ueno Station in Tōkyō as far as Shibukawa Station. Take the Agatsuma Line from Shibukawa to Naganohara Station. Then take the bus bound for Hanashiki Onsen, getting off at Yunotaira—a 40-minute ride. Once off the bus, follow the path along the river for 15 minutes to the suspension bridge connecting the solitary inn with civilization.

THE WATERS: The water here contains sulphur, which is especially good for women with premenstrual or menopausal complaints. For men the water is relaxing and for both sexes it's recommended for skin problems. The outdoor bath is in a delightful bower of shady green where you can sit and listen to the river pounding by.

AROUND AND ABOUT: If you find all this sitting around in the same place too much to take, get back on the bus bound for Hanashiki Onsen and travel

20 minutes to Shiriyaki Hot Spring. Shiriyaki literally means "Bottom Burning," so called because you sit in the bed of the Shirasuna River and heat your bottom in small hot pools. This means it's good for hemorrhoids, to say nothing of the fun of digging your own hole.

ACCOMMODATIONS: Upon arrival at Yunotaira you may think you've stumbled upon the last hot spring holding out against tourism, but be forewarned: if it's spring or summer the sole inn, Shōsenkaku, will be heavily booked. Quite a few others have also stumbled upon this lone outpost recently. Nevertheless, it's a small traditional inn (sleeps sixty guests) and the nook it rests in is remote and quiet. The very special specialty of Shōsenkaku is tempura made with loquats (*akashia*), which are in season from mid-May until the end of June. Flower lovers can have ordinary vegetables if they prefer.

88 Shima

LOCATION: The Shima Hot Spring area is a 3-kilometer-long stretch of gorge on the Shima River, in northeastern Gunma Prefecture. Take the Jōetsu Line from Ueno Station in Tōkyō to Shibukawa. From there take the Agatsuma Line to Nakanojō and then a bus to the hot spring. The bus takes 50 minutes.

THE WATERS: This hot spring dates back to the tenth century when one of Minamoto Yorimitsu's retainers discovered it. Today Shima is a National Health Resort and many people come to stay awhile to take advantage of the good water, baths, and company. The water, sodium chloride, is good for rheumatism, stomach problems, skin diseases, and neuralgia. The town is divided into four districts, each of which has an open-air bath that looks out on the Jōetsu Mountains, which almost encircle the town.

AROUND AND ABOUT: Sitting astride the Shima River, Shima presents a picture of the small country spa: ryokan built to the edge of the river, bridges crossing a river that rushes by in some places and barely trickles in others, beautiful scenery, and travelers wandering around taking in the serenity. The houses and inns are old and laundry hangs from the balconies over the river. Shima is a medicinal spring with few signs of touristy commercialism and is one of the quietest near Tōkyō.

ACCOMMODATIONS: Tamura Ryokan has a large, steamy bath—the steam rises through lattice mats—which is meant to make you feel like you are in heaven; it is named the Paradise Bath. The ryokan has smaller tubs as well. The ryokan Sekizenkan is an old, wooden building with cook-for-yourself facilities and an unusual European-style bath with sculptured recesses in the walls, high ceilings, and rounded glass windows, all of which is elegant but has seen better days. Many Japanese come to such cook-for-yourself inns carrying their own rice and chopsticks and set up camp for several days.

FESTIVALS: The hot-spring festival, held on October 7 and 8, features parading floats and street dancing performed by revelers wearing kimono.

89 Hōshi

LOCATION: Hōshi is in the northwestern corner of Gunma Prefecture near the Naeba ski area. From Ueno Station in Tōkyō take the Jōetsu Shinkansen (bullet train) to Jōmō Kōgen Station and, from there, the bus bound for Sarugakyō Onsen. Get off at the terminal stop—a 35-minute ride—and transfer to the bus for Hōshi Onsen, which takes 25 minutes. You can also take the Jōetsu Line from Ueno to Gokan Station and take a bus for 1 hour.

THE WATERS: Hōshi, one of the Mikuni group of hot springs, used to be a wayside stop for travelers crossing the Mikuni Mountains by way of the Mikunikaidō Road. The name Hōshi is derived from *Kōbō Daishi*, although it's not certain what part this priest played in the spring's discovery, if any. The baths in the single ryokan here were built on the riverbed so that the thermal water bubbles up through the pebbles, naturally. The water contains calcium and magnesium sulphate and treats cuts, burns, pimples, hiccups, and hysteria, as well as nervous disorders and hardening of the arteries. In the mixed tubs wooden logs float on the water for use as headrests; such are the inducements to soak leisurely at Hōshi. Evening bathers will hear voices raised in song; the high ceiling lends itself to singing contests.

AROUND AND ABOUT: Hōshi consists of one ryokan in the middle of the woods. In front flows the Nishi River and around are the Mikuni Mountains. Beyond the inn there are places to hike or walk when the weather lets you out of the tub. From one point in the Mikuni Pass near here you can look down over Gunma, Nagano, and Niigata prefectures. The three gods representing them—Akagi (Gunma), Suwa (Nagano), and Yahiko (Niigata)—are said to be present at the entrance to Mikuni Tunnel in Mikuni Pass, the point where the three prefectures meet. The spot is called Mikuni Gongen. One pleasant walk, possible only in summer, is to Shima Hot Spring (88)—a 5-hour hike along a path that winds parallel to the prefectural border. From the highest point you can see the temple-strewn town of Nikkō on a clear day. The going is not hard, but ill-fitting shoes will make you wish you'd stayed in the tub at Hōshi. When the sun sets at Hōshi in winter, you'll hear two sticks being beaten together. This is the fire-prevention reminder heard throughout Japan in the evening.

ACCOMMODATIONS: Chōjukan is the solitary, superb inn at Hōshi. The proprietor believes in the past and doesn't use anything plastic on the premises. Hence this old, wooden building, with its covered walkway over the river and its hanging cooking pots, is as much of an experience as the tubs are. After your innumerable baths you'll sit down to spiced and sauced mountain greens, mushrooms of all sorts, and calorie-free *konnyaku* (gelatin made from devil's-tongue root) cooked in a high-calorie sweet sauce. Some rooms have a pot hanging from the ceiling over a fireplace where a stew of vegetables and meat will be cooked. For fish lovers there is carp.

90 Takaragawa

LOCATION: Takaragawa is in northern Gunma Prefecture, near Hōshi Hot Spring (89). Take the Jōetsu Line from Ueno Station in Tōkyō to Minakami Station and then a bus—a 50-minute ride—to the hot spring. You can also take the Jōetsu Shinkansen (bullet train) from Ueno Station in Tōkyō to Jō-mō Kōgen Station and then take a bus for 1 hour and 10 minutes.

THE WATERS: Takaragawa is said to have the best outdoor pools in Japan. On most of the many sumo-style charts ranking outdoor baths in travel magazines, it rates at the top as grand champion (*yokozuna*). And certainly for those who go for riverside baths set deep in the mountains, it's a winner. There are four baths open to the public for an entry fee of around ¥2,000. One bath is just for women and the others are communal. You can choose a spot near the foaming river or under the small thermal waterfall. If you like things a little gentler you can sit among the rocks or in the middle of the pool proper. People sit and chat or just watch leaves or blossoms falling in autumn and spring. In summer you can sunbathe on the rocks and in winter you can stay snug and warm with just your head poking out to take in the white snowbanks all around. The alkaline simple thermal water treats stiff joints and skin irritations and, if imbibed, stomachs. The spring's discovery is attributed to a wandering god with an eye for picturesque open-air pools—Yamatotakeru no Mikoto—who was led here by a white heron.

AROUND AND ABOUT: There's not much going on in Takaragawa, but in such an outdoor-pool heaven you don't need much more. If you wish to try some meditation (*zazen*), your innkeeper at Ōsenkaku can arrange for you to be instructed in the art (in Japanese) at Zazendō, the small temple above the baths that honors the hot-spring god Yakushidō.

ACCOMMODATIONS: Ōsenkaku is a huge ryokan complex that includes an old thatched-roof building. The menu includes river fish, mountain vegetables, and thick handmade noodles.

BEARS ONLY: A long time ago, some cold bears happened to come across Takaragawa Hot Spring. It was so warm and such fun that they came back every winter to bathe. The current proprietor of Ōsenkaku has a soft spot for shivering bears and has installed a "bears only" bath, but if you would like to try this pool, the two bears occupying it almost all year round probably won't object to some bare company.

LADIES ONLY: Takaragawa has another claim to outdoor bath fame: it was the first in Japan to designate a "ladies only" outdoor pool. The pool isn't as large as the men's, but it's definitely bigger than the bears'!

91 Nasu Yumoto

LOCATION: Nasu Yumoto, one of the eleven springs in the Nasu group of hot springs, is in northeastern Tochigi Prefecture. Take the Tōhoku Main Line from Ueno Station in Tōkyō to Kuroiso Station. From there it's a 40-minute bus ride to the hot spring. Or, take the Tōhoku Shinkansen (bullet train) to Nasu-Shiobara Station and proceed by bus—a 50-minute ride—to Nasu Yumoto.

THE WATERS: Nasu Yumoto was discovered by a hunter pursuing a deer that took refuge in the mountains and finally in the hot spring itself. The hunter found the water as warm and healing as the deer did, and so began human use of the spring. One of the public baths in Nasu Yumoto recalls this history in its name—Shika-no-yu ("Deer Bath"). During the Edo period, Nasu Yumoto was well patronized; there were at least a hundred ryokan and six public baths. Well-known dippers like the poet Bashō and Minamoto Yoritomo liked this spring. Today it still thrives as a resort onsen. The water is simple thermal, which is good for women's disorders, rheumatism, and stomach problems.

AROUND AND ABOUT: The high altitude of Nasu makes it the perfect place to beat the summer heat or to see autumn at its most spectacular. If you tire of watching the leaves change color, you can visit Minamigaoka Farm, 20 minutes by bus from Nasu Yumoto, which caters to tourists looking for something different. There you'll find fishing ponds, leafy walks, tired horses that won't mind if you don't ride them, souvenir counters selling cheese, walnuts, homemade cookies, and jam, and, for fortification, an indoor or outdoor "Genghis Khan" (all-you-can-eat) barbeque. The grilled meat and vegetables are served in rustic surroundings enhanced by old farm implements, straw hats, snowshoes, and cloaks hung on the wall. With the meal you can sample local wine. In all, most visitors pass a very mellow afternoon here. For something even more different, go see the stone called Sesshōseki, which emits deadly fumes capable of gassing insects that come too close. This true-life phenomenon can be observed at the "hell" place Sainokawara—a gray, rocky, smelly, desolate expanse on the way up Mount Nasu. Sainokawara is a 10-minute walk from Nasu Yumoto Hot Spring.

ACCOMMODATIONS: Shimizuya Ryokan is nestled among the inns that crowd each other up the main street. Hanaya is another large comfortable ryokan.

FESTIVALS: On September 18 and 19, hot water is served to the shrine gods at Nasu Yumoto. Travelers passing through can see how important a part these spirits played in the development of hot springs and take part in the local shrine festival. The local people encourage participants by presenting them with packed goodies like mountain vegetables, noodles, and fresh flowers. On September 19 there is a lively fireworks display.

THE STORY OF A STONE: A long time ago, in 1155 to be exact, there lived a beautiful lady. The wife of the lord of Nasu Castle, this lady was very fond of parties. One night as the musicians entertained her guests, a strange light began to waft around her. Her husband called in the local expert on such things and he commenced an exorcism. Something went wrong, however, and the lady turned into a golden fox with nine tails that began screaming abuse at the guests. Horrified and embarrassed, the guests stormed out. The fox-lady slunk off and the men got together to plan her capture. They plotted and trained and wrote haiku. Finally they were ready and set off after her. Naturally, they weren't successful—Japanese foxes know lots of tricks. She just turned into a stone and started emitting poisonous fumes. No one could go near her. Today this stone is called Sesshōseki and continues to emit what scientists have identified as sulphur dioxide, deadly to insects but harmless to human beings. You can see the stone at Sainokawara on the slopes of Mount Nasu. Sesshōseki means "Creature-killing Rock."

92 Shinnasu

Five minutes on foot from Nasu Yumoto is this newer spring, first developed in the Taishō era (1912–26). Shinnasu Hot Spring also falls in the Nasu group of hot springs, along with Benten (93), Ōmaru (94), and Sandogoya (95). The waters, simple thermal, treat the same disorders as those of Nasu Yumoto. Situated near the Japanese emperor's summer house, Shinnasu is considered a dignified area devoid of excessive neon. To experience a bit of extravagance yourself, stay at the ryokan Sanraku. Its inviting bath—an outdoor pool surrounded by flowers in a forest nook—and carefully cultivated garden, perfect for after-bath strolling, make this a likely spot for one of those once-in-a-lifetime hot-spring experiences.

93 Benten

LOCATION: Benten is one of the Nasu group of hot springs in northeastern Tochigi Prefecture. From Kuroiso on the Tōhoku Main Line take a bus bound for Nasudake (Mount Nasu), getting off at the stop Benten Onsen. The bus ride takes 50 minutes. In winter (November through April), you have to transfer at Nasu Yumoto to a bus bound for Ōmaru Onsen. Get off 20 minutes later at Benten Onsen.

THE WATERS: In addition to the usual indoor baths, Benten features an outdoor thermal pool that in winter is a cool dash from the ryokan and in autumn is afloat with fallen leaves. The water, with a little iron and dissolved carbon dioxide, is good for premenstrual and menopausal discomfort and for chilblains. In former times it was used as an antidote to Nasu Yumoto water, which somehow caused pain in some bathers' private parts. The afflicted dashed on up to Benten for relief, or so it's said.

AROUND AND ABOUT: The road up toward Mount Nasu is quite wild with spindly snow-country growth covering the mountain slopes and cliff drops.

Of course there are the occasional shops and lookout turn-offs for tourists. When you walk away from this road and down into the hidden elbow that holds Benten, however, you can see only natural landscapes. The ryokan, white buildings with green roofs, sits on a river. The rambling parts of this complex seem designed for quiet corridor strolls after bathing. In autumn the area is spectacular—reservations should be made in advance. Although there is nothing other than the ryokan in the immediate vicinity, the region offers good hiking in spring and summer.

ACCOMMODATIONS: Benten Onsen Ryokan was named, as the hot spring was, after Benzaiten, the Buddhist god of fortune. It is comfortable and has good bathing facilities, including a tepid mineral swimming pool for when it's warm enough to don a swimsuit. Five minutes on foot from this hot spring there is a complex called Nasu Kokumin Kyūka Mura, a modern Western-style hotel and campground where you can stay and bathe in mineral water. Campers can use the Benten Onsen Ryokan baths for a small fee.

FOOD: You'll be served fresh river fish as well as green ferns, bracken, and butterburs transformed into delicate, nutritious dishes. Food sources are limited in the mountains, so much creativity is needed in the preparation of your meals.

94 Ōmaru

LOCATION: Ōmaru is 5 minutes by bus from Benten (93). The bus from Kuroiso Station on the Tōhoku Main Line takes about an hour to get to Ōmaru.

THE WATERS: The main attraction of Ōmaru is its outdoor bath set right in the Shirato River. The natural pool is separated by rocks from the main stream. The water, simple thermal, will invigorate your stiff limbs, massage your aching back, and calm your nerves. This spring was favored by Nogi Maresuke, a military leader during the Meiji era. His mother, it is said, used to pour cold water over him in the garden as a form of punishment, and so he grew up to be highly disciplined and partial to physical hardship. It's not that Ōmaru is primitive, but it's definitely not your deluxe, five-star spa just off the main highway.

AROUND AND ABOUT: Ōmaru lies on the Shirato River in a valley, but even so it's at one of the highest elevations (1,250 meters) in Nasu Heights (Nasu Kōgen). The surrounding mountains sport an odd assortment of scraggly bushes and trees among patches of rocks. The vegetation increases in density as you get closer to Mount Nasu. You can hike in the area, although scenic spots are few and far between. Probably it's best to go to Mount Nasu by bus and take the elevated cable car most of the way up to see the views around. The mountain itself is unappealing in the sense that it's rocky, dusty, and brownish gray—like a volcano should be.

ACCOMMODATIONS: Ōmaru Onsen Ryokan, the only place to stay, is large, but you still need reservations in autumn. It has a new building as well as older quarters that will carry you back to old Japan.

95 Sandogoya

LOCATION: Sandogoya, situated on the side of the Nasu Mountains near Mount Nasu, is the most remote of the Nasu group of hot springs. From Kuroiso Station on the Tōhoku Main Line take the bus bound for Nasudake (Mount Nasu). Get off at the terminal stop, a 70-minute ride, take the overhead cable car to the top of the mountain, and then put on your climbing boots. Walk along the top of the ridge and down Mount Asahi—a 2-hour trek—to reach the hot spring. You can also reach Kuroiso Station by taking the Tōhoku Shinkansen (bullet train) to Nasu-Shiobara Station where you can transfer to the Tōhoku Main Line.

THE WATERS: Sandogoya commenced business in a big way early in the twelfth century when it was a wayside station for travelers on the Aizukaidō Road who stopped to bathe and "play." Fortunately for them the water is good for syphilis. After the Edo period, when daimyo no longer had to travel back and forth to Tōkyō to pay their dues to the shogun, Sandogoya, like many other such inn towns, fell into decline. Out of more than fifty inns, only two remain. Both have outdoor baths. The water contains sulphur and is good for skin problems, anemia, stomach ailments, rheumatism, and, still, syphilis.

AROUND AND ABOUT: The route to Sandogoya prepares you well for the kind of place it is. The final leg of the walk is pleasant but the stretch near Mount Nasu is spooky—the white steam, scant vegetation, and slatelike rocks underfoot leave a desolate impression not easily erased by the green immediate surroundings of Sandogoya. Needless to say, perhaps, the primary pastimes here are bathing and hiking. The spring is also known for its near lack of electricity. After nine at night, both inns use Meiji-style lamps in their corridors and candles in the bedrooms. Before nine they generate their own electricity. It's this aspect of the past that attracts many people here; they come to see things as they were, authentically reproduced. But for those who like modern gadgets and are not used to traveling in climbing boots, this hot spring would be a disastrous choice. The inns have no frills and even the rare combination of snow and cherry blossoms in May might not be enough to compensate for the frugal, rustic way of life. All seasons are beautiful.

ACCOMMODATIONS: Daikokuya Ryokan and Tabakoya Ryokan are the two inns of yesteryear that provide basic accommodations in this lovely environment.

96 Nikkō Yumoto

LOCATION: Nikkō Yumoto is a little west of the center of Tochigi Prefecture. From Asakusa Station in Tōkyō take the Tōbu Nikkō Line to Nikkō and then a bus—for 1 hour 20 minutes—to Nikkō Yumoto.

THE WATERS: Nikkō Yumoto dates back twelve hundred years at least. It was blessed by Kōbō Daishi, the monk famous for finding and blessing hot springs. In the fourteenth century, this was an important spring, with government officials appointed to run it and keep the baths clean for the higher officials who had their own private tubs here. Its pleasant summer climate made it an attractive place for the elite to get war and politics out of their systems for a while. Women were not allowed to bathe here until the Meiji era—for religious not political reasons (women were considered unclean). The water, from a spring under the lake bottom, is a mixture of sodium sulphate and hydrogen sulphide—recommended for rheumatism and diabetes. There are also public baths here.

AROUND AND ABOUT: The bus from Nikkō Station takes you up to Nikkō Yumoto. This spectacular, curvy ride alone makes a visit here worthwhile. En route you pass Lake Chūzenji, which also boasts thermal waters, but the water is from Nikkō Yumoto and it's much busier, particularly in summer when people who own summer cottages come to fish and wind surf on this beautiful expanse of water. If you enjoy walking, follow the trail from Nikkō Yumoto down through meadows, swamps, and mountain forests to Lake Chūzenji or vice versa. It takes about 2 hours. Nikkō Yumoto itself is situated on Lake Yuno in a small hollow in the mountains—closed off and peaceful, especially in winter. The lake freezes over and you can skate or just sit and listen to the pattering snowflakes. ■ KEGON WATERFALL: This waterfall, near Lake Chūzenji, is a photographer's dream of rainbows come true. After a lengthy elevator ride you arrive at a platform from which you can watch, listen to, and feel spray from the thundering water. It's delightfully framed in red and gold foliage in autumn. To get there take a bus from Nikkō Yumoto bus stop bound for Chūzenji Onsen Station and get off after 30 minutes, at Kegon no Taki, the waterfall. From the bus stop it's a few minutes to the elevator. ■ NIKKŌ: This city, set in beautiful Nikkō National Park, inspires love-hate reactions from sightseers. Citing the magnificent artistry in Nikkō's temples and shrines, some say Nikkō is the best tourist stop in Japan. Others bemoan the gaudiness and flamboyance of the Chinese-inspired architecture. The most remarkable example is the Tōshōgū Shrine, where the stout, cunning womanizer Tokugawa Ieyasu is buried. For the construction of the original mausoleum and shrine, there seems to have been no limit placed on the expense. Under avenues of tall cedars, the complex of buildings— ornately carved and painted gold, red, yellow, and green—staggers the senses. Thirteen years of work by the most skilled men in the country went into the gates, sanctuaries, storehouses, bells, towers, and stables. So perfect and exquisite was the workmanship in the shrine that a column in the Yōmei Gate was deliberately carved upside down so that the gods would not become jealous of talents rivaling their own. Carved elephants, monkeys, a cat, guards, ceilings, walls, and oratories compete for your attention. Even color-sensitive eyes must be impressed by the craftsmanship. Nikkō is lush in summer and snowy in winter, but it's at its most splendid in autumn when the leaves compete with the buildings in taking away your breath. Further information on Nikkō is endlessly and readily available; check out any guidebook on all of Japan.

ACCOMMODATIONS: Kamaya Ryokan commands good views from its elevated location, and serves home-grown vegetables. If you reserve them in advance, you can rent rowboats in summer and skis in winter. Ryokan here serve a tasty dish called *Nikkō yuba*—the skin off the top of boiled tofu milk that is filled with meat and vegetables and then fried. For dessert you can try *shio yōkan*, a slightly salty, sweet-bean gelatin.

97 Kaniyu

LOCATION: Kaniyu is in the Oku Kinu group of hot springs in northern Tochigi Prefecture. From Asakusa Station in Tōkyō take the Tōbu Kinugawa Line to Kinugawa Onsen Station and then a bus to Meotobuchi Onsen—a 2 hour ride. From there Kaniyu is 1 hour 40 minutes on foot.

THE WATERS: The milky white water contains hydrogen sulphide and calcium sulphate. Drinking it is good for intestinal troubles and diabetes, and bathing in it is good treatment for skin, neuralgia, and metal poisoning. There is a riverside open-air bath and thermal-water swimming pool.

AROUND AND ABOUT: Kaniyu is deep in the wilds on the Kinu River, surrounded by mountains that glow with color in autumn. There is just one ryokan, which has done little to introduce modern trappings; here natural wood tables and tree-trunk stools suffice. Hikers, fishermen, and city escapists find Kaniyu a perfect place to visit. If you're not a hiker or fisherman, you'll spend your time bathing, eating, and taking photographs of the magnificent scenery all around. This spring is a gem, very much worth the trouble of reaching it in any season.

ACCOMMODATIONS: The inn Kaniyu Onsen is the solitary place to lay down your head. Wooden and rustic, it specializes in mountain fare. In their respective seasons, you can dine on mushrooms, mountain greens, and river fish. You may also be served small orange river crabs (*kani*), from which the hot spring originally got its name. (Today the name no longer means "Crab Spring," although the pronunciation is the same.) More exotic touches to the menu are bear sashimi, deer sashimi, and bear brain.

98 Meotobuchi

Although the walk from Meotobuchi Hot Spring to Kaniyu is worthwhile, especially if you spend the night and sample the waters at Hatchō-no-yu, don't dismiss Meotobuchi itself. This outdoor-bathing heaven at the end of the bus route from Kinugawa Onsen Station has one ryokan—Meotobuchi Onsen Hotel—and lots of weak sulphur water. Not only will you heal any skin diseases or neuralgic problems afflicting you, but the riverside rock pools and masses of tangled foliage on the banks will keep you happy indefinitely. This area of several remote springs is the answer to a hot-spring-buff-cum-hiker's wildest dreams.

99 Araki

LOCATION: Araki is in southern Saitama Prefecture, near Chichibu City. Take the Seibu Ikebukuro Line from Ikebukuro Station in Tōkyō to Seibu Chichibu Station. From there it's 25 minutes by bus to the hot spring.

THE WATERS: Araki, a spring in the Takashino group, was discovered by one of the current proprietor's female forebears two hundred years ago in a dream. The water is sodium hydrogen-carbonate with sulphur, good for almost anything, especially skin problems. It has a sulphur smell, a greenish yellow tinge, and a somewhat slimy feel to it. But don't judge a bath by its color and texture: the best are usually not the most appealing to the eye or the nose.

AROUND AND ABOUT: The best way to see Chichibu is to follow part of the Chichibu Pilgrimage route, which goes to thirty-four temples in all. It starts at Shimabuji Temple, not far from Araki (the bus there from Seibu Chichibu Station takes 30 minutes), and ends at Suisenji Temple. Since 750 years ago, many Buddhist believers, dressed in white and carrying canes, have walked the route from temple to temple. Some do it annually. At Shimabuji Temple you can purchase the proper accoutrements for the pilgrimage—things like a hat, sandals, a cane, and white clothing. Araki is between the third and fourth temples, which are not far apart. The pilgrimage is a pleasant walk through cypress and pine trees punctuated by damp, woody smells and the haunting booms of temple bells. At Shimabuji Temple notice the faded vermilion interior and the black dragon painted on the ceiling of the Inner sanctuary. At Kinshōji, the temple nearest Araki, you can see 1,319 stone Buddhas (*sekibutsu*) erected in the seventeenth century to honor Buddha and beseech him to console the souls of those killed in natural disasters. They are mossy and all have different faces. One has been likened in appearance to the Virgin Mary. ■ NAGATORO: To shoot some quite rapid rapids and have a good time dodging water flying everywhere, try the boat trip at Nagatoro. (Just hold on tight; they'll do the navigating.) The scenery is exciting, too. To get there take the Chichibu Tetsudō Line from Chichibu Station to Nagatoro Station, 20 minutes away. The boat ride takes 20 minutes and runs from April through December:

ACCOMMODATIONS: Araki Kōsen is a comfortable, renovated ryokan, which serves mountain vegetables and wild boar stew.

100 Fukuroda

LOCATION: Fukuroda is in the town of Daigomachi in northern Ibaraki Prefecture. Take the Suigun Line from Mito City to Fukuroda Station. The hot spring is within walking distance of the station.

THE WATERS: Fukuroda lies on the Taki River, a tributary of the Kuji River, which traverses Ibaraki. The water, simple thermal with sodium chloride, is well known for its soothing effects on the skin. It is said to eliminate bags and sags and give the complexion the well-known, much-sought-after look of peaches and cream. The spring came up with the rice in a field and was used by local ʼfolk as far back as the Heian period. The Mito daimyo used it in Edo times; it didn't become public again until this century.

AROUND AND ABOUT: Daigomachi is known for three things: its hot spring (a rare thing in Ibaraki), its waterfall (one of the biggest in Japan), and its konnyaku (devil's-tongue plant). The waterfall falls in four stages and is termed masculine, meaning the water is fast and voluminous. One more attraction is the moon peeping bewitchingly over the shoulder of Tsukiore Hill, named for this moon view.

ACCOMMODATIONS: Fukuroda Onsen Hotel is a Japanese-style ryokan with a marble tub. For dinner it often serves wild boar. It overlooks the river and has a large garden. Another possibility is Takimisō, which features views of small waterfalls from the tubs.

101 Rokuryū

LOCATION: Rokuryū is in Ueno, an eastern subcenter of Tōkyō. Ueno is one of the major railway and subway junctions in Tōkyō so there are many ways to get there in addition to the standard route via the Yamanote Line that circles Tōkyō. From the station the bathhouse is about 15 to 20 minutes on foot, depending on how quickly you find the right exit and get to the back gate of Ueno Zoo. While in the station, ask for the park exit (kōen guchi) and surface there. Once above ground, walk through the park to the back and locate the back gate to Ueno Zoo. The bathhouse is opposite this gate down a narrow lane near a noodle shop. The bathhouse is not particularly eye-catching except for its tiled roof over the entranceway. Leave your shoes outside the bathhouse proper in the lockers provided, and then head right if you're female, and left if you're male. At the entrance to the dressing room pay the attendant ¥250—a reasonable fee considering that public bathhouses charge the same for bathing in ordinary tap water. Rokuryū is closed on Mondays and open other days from 3:30 P.M. to 11:00 P.M..

THE WATERS: The current proprietor's father learned of this spring sixty years ago while at prayer one day. Until this happened he had operated an ordinary bathhouse and the cost of the water was driving him deeper into debt. If only he could procure his own water source he had thought, and a mineral one at that, he would be set for life. After being told by Buddha about a spring he started digging. He dug to a depth of 500 meters and was ready to give up when black water gurgled forth. This was no comfort, however, since he couldn't imagine such water being good for anything. How wrong he was! Today this thermal spring is known for curing more than thirty ailments, from heat rash to rheumatism to too much poison in the system. These ailments are listed above the bathhouse mirrors so you can choose a few to work on while you soak and gossip with the regulars who come here daily. The water is classified as sodium hydrogen-carbonate water, although it actually contains more than thirteen different minerals. It is 23° C (73° F) at the source and is heated to 40° C (104° F) or more for bathing. Don't be put off by the color, which resembles black cola, for Rokuryū is the perfect way to end a day dashing about Ueno's parks and art galleries, or struggling through the throngs to get the best deal in the markets that are nearby.

AROUND AND ABOUT: Many northern Japanese got their first look at the none-too-gentle, gritty side of commercial Tōkyō at Ueno, where they disembarked from long-distance trains. Some of this mercantile excitement will no doubt mesmerize you, too, at least on first encounter. Suffice it to say you'll never be short of shops, shows, and eateries in Ueno while you wait for the bathhouse to open. Ueno Park offers some more traditional types of tourist attractions, the zoo, with its nationally revered giant pandas, several art museums, a concert hall, and magnificent cherry blossoms in spring. These blossoms should be approached with caution, however. If you harbor a serene, pastoral image of pink blossoms and quiet, strollable lanes, you might want to avoid Ueno altogether. The more tolerant are advised to go before 4:00 P.M., while the crowds are still navigable.

ACCOMMODATIONS: Tōkyō's accommodation facilities run the gamut from elegant Western-style hotels to park benches and number in the thousands. To select one that suits your budget and your itinerary, contact the Tourist Information [(03)3821-3826].

102 Ōshima

LOCATION: This hot spring is on Ōshima Island, the biggest of the seven Izu Islands, south of Tōkyō. From Tōkyō's Takeshiba docks (near Hamamatsuchō

Station) it takes about 8 hours by ferry. From Haneda Airport in Tōkyō it takes 30 minutes by air. You can also ferry or fly to Ōshima from several other ports on the mainland, including Yokohama and Ōsaka. Other ferries to the islands leave smaller cities like Atami and Itō on Izu Peninsula. All of these transportation lines leave you at Ōshima's port town of Okada, from which the hot spring is 30 minutes by bus.

THE WATERS: The spring is on Mount Mihara in a cave overhung with twisted roots, vines, and creepers. The simple thermal water is good for aching joints, upset stomachs, and carefree holiday-makers in general.

AROUND AND ABOUT: Ōshima is known for its women—usually young, pretty, dressed in blue-and-white kimono, and carrying baskets on their heads. In former times the baskets held camellia nuts, the source of the hair oil that glossed the hair of Japanese beauties, but now the baskets are for the sake of tourists. Fortunately, the camellia bushes themselves remain, enhancing the already-beautiful tropical island environment. Apparently the island's developers have been influenced by images of Hawaii—if deluxe hotel bars, souvenir shops, and crowded beaches aren't your cup of tea you may prefer spending your time in more rural Ōshima. You can also rent bicycles, fish, surf, swim, or fish.

ACCOMMODATIONS: Ōshima Onsen Hotel is Japanese style and serves fish, meat, and vegetables cooked in camellia oil.

103 Jinata and 104 Ashitsuki

LOCATION: Jinata and Ashitsuki lie on the southern coast of Shikinejima Island, which is near (but not one of) the Izu Islands, south of Tōkyō. In summer you can take a ferry from Tōkyō's Takeshiba docks directly to this island, but at other times you must go via Ōshima Island. The ferry from Tōkyō to Nobushi takes about 10 hours. From the port of Nobushi, Jinata and Ashitsuki are 30 minutes on foot or 10 minutes by taxi. The two springs are 10 minutes by bus from each other.

THE WATERS: Jinata means "land" (*ji*) and "big axe" (*nata*), and the combination is meant to suggest the serrated rocky coastline, so well known here. Ashitsuki is geographically similar. At both places the sea washes into the shoreline springs between cracks in the rocks, and the retreating tide leaves many natural, hot pools for bathers who like to combine minerals with the surf and the sandy beaches not far away. The result is a mixture of spring water, classified as iron, diluted with brine, which adds sodium chloride. The combination plus the sun and the beauty of the setting would seem to cure practically anything, but anemia, rheumatism, neuralgia, and insect bites are the ailments best treated here. The water at Jinata has a reddish tinge and Ashitsuki pools contain wisps of floating black seaweed. In both it is a good idea to wear swimsuits for protection when sitting on the rocks, since they are sharp and can scratch (and since neither spring includes cuts and scratches in its list of cures).

AROUND AND ABOUT: Shikinejima, about 12 kilometers in circumference, was formed by a tidal wave that cut it off from the larger island Niijima, one of the Izu Islands. Besides eating, bathing, swimming, and sleeping there's not much to tax you on this island.

ACCOMMODATIONS: Not all the inns here have spring water in their baths, but if you intend to use the beach pools it doesn't matter. Two places that do use spring water are Mimatsuya at Jinata and Ashitsukiya, a ryokan, at Ashitsuki. They are close to the beach and comfortable.

FOOD: You'll see racks and racks of drying fish (*himono*) on Shikinejima. Salty and strong-smelling, they may not be to your liking. The alternatives include shellfish and grilled white fish, both of which often go into making tasty soups.

105 Shioma

LOCATION: Shioma is on Hachijō Island, the most southern of the Izu Islands. Hachijō Island is 300 kilometers south of Tōkyō—11 hours by ferry and about 1 hour by air. You can also get there by island hopping among the Izu Islands, or by using other ports on the mainland. The hot spring is 15 minutes from the airport by taxi and 35 minutes from the port town, Kamiminato, by bus.

THE WATERS: The water is weak sodium chloride, recommended for skin and stomach problems, nervous disorders, anemia, and constipation. Like Shikinejima, there are natural outdoor pools on the craggy beach that can be located and used at low tide. Many of the inns and the hotel have indoor hot-spring baths, too.

AROUND AND ABOUT: Again the key word is Hawaiian. The island is publicized as yet another of Japan's little Hawaiis, but it's really not necessary. There's enough local color to make this island inviting without relying on Hawaii. From early Edo times political exiles and samurai fallen from grace lived here. These swordless warriors used to sing and beat drums to compensate for their boredom and military impotence. Their songs and dances remain as part of this island's cultural heritage. Another bit of the bygone is the mansion where the governor Katori lived and officiated for the Edo government. Apart from historical pursuits, you can go snorkeling and even see bull sumo, staged during the year to give the bulls exercise and the tourists excitement. Hot-spring buffs may want to go dipping at another, nearby coastal spring—Hachijōjima Hot Spring, 5 to 10 minutes by bus to the south

ACCOMMODATIONS: There is only one modern hotel, Nangoku Onsen Hotel, and that is near Hachijōjima Hot Spring. Inside you'll find a man-made jungle bath of dangling ferns and tropical trees, where you can soak in style with your cocktail and mango slices—just like in Hawaii. There are no accommodations at Shioma Hot Spring itself.

106 Hakone Yumoto

LOCATION: Hakone Yumoto is the gateway to the Hakone group of sixteen hot springs, all located near Lake Ashi, southwest of Tōkyō in Kanagawa Prefecture. This hot-spring area is contained in the Fuji-Hakone-Izu National Park. From Tōkyō take the Tōkaidō Main Line or Shinkansen (bullet train) to Odawara and then a bus for 15 minutes. You can also take the Odakyū Line from Shinjuku Station in Tōkyō to Hakone Yumoto (1½ hours).

THE WATERS: Hakone Yumoto was mentioned in *Man'yōshū*, a historically important anthology of poems compiled in the eighth century. Hakone Yumoto is the oldest in the Hakone group and the biggest. In the Edo period, bathers from Edo (Tōkyō) set off for Hakone carrying their food and walked the 82 kilometers in two to three days. Those too sick to walk, or rich enough to afford it, hired *kago*—the small boxlike palanquin the good guy always springs out of in samurai movies, usually carried by two unfortunates with huge calf muscles. The hot spring became popular with foreigners in the late nineteenth century. One Frenchman and his friends, walking along the Tōkaidō Road, were amazed to see naked men and women scrubbing up and soaking in the open air all together. What was even more astounding was the length of time they spent doing it. Some of the foreigners wanted to try it, others thought the water might be full of floating diseases, but because it wasn't ordinary water, they finally agreed it was probably safe enough and so they doffed their robes and started splashing. They liked it so much they continued on to Miyanoshita Hot Spring, but because the empress was in residence, they had to forgo this bath. Thus began foreigners' excursions to Hakone Yumoto. The water is simple thermal with sodium chloride—good for everything. Several ryokan here let the public use their tubs for a small fee before 5:00 P.M. One such ryokan is Hatsuhanasō in Oku Yumoto, 5 minutes by bus from Hakone Yumoto. It has an open-air bath complete with waterfall and is a scenic, tranquil bathing spot away from the commercial activity of this area. For an entrance fee you can also bathe at one of the famous *senninburo* (baths capable of holding a thousand people) in the center of Hakone Yumoto.

AROUND AND ABOUT: Nowadays Hakone Yumoto is known as a resort spring, catering mainly to Tōkyōites escaping for the weekend. There's a lot for them, and you, to see in this part of the Fuji-Hakone-Izu National Park. Lake Ashi (40 minutes east of Hakone Yumoto by bus), the shimmering centerpiece, is worth a cruise on an ordinary ferry or on a Spanish-style galleon that shuttles sightseers about. The red shrine gate standing in the water at the edge of the lake could form a backdrop for an unusual photograph of you and your friends sailing Ashi the Spanish way. For those who like reliving the past, there's a walk along some of the old Tōkaidō —the highway to Edo (Tōkyō) constructed to channel daimyo and their money and respect to the shogun. To keep their enemies out and to keep hostage members of the daimyo families in, the government set up a checkpoint near Lake Ashi. No one could get through without a passport and it was difficult to sneak around it. Many of the hostages were wives and daughters, who occasionally tried to get through illicitly and return to their hometowns. In fact a lake nearby—Otomegaike—gets its name from one such woman, who was caught and threw herself into the lake rather than go back to Edo. Today cedars still loom over the route and patches of the walk are rough enough to create something of the old atmosphere. The walk starts between Moto Hakone and Hakone-machi on the southern side of Lake Ashi, and continues toward Hakone Yumoto. The area is also famous for its wood carvings and inlay work, good examples of which can be seen and purchased at Taichi, a shop in Hakone Yumoto.

ACCOMMODATIONS: Tenseien is a grand ryokan that has a stroll garden with miniature waterfalls for after-bath relaxation. The open-air bath is surrounded by bamboo fencing. Another traditional ryokan, high in the mountains along the old Tōkaidō Road, is Hōeisō. The Sukumo River runs past it, providing a pleasant setting for a riverside open-air pool. For dinner you can choose between duck and pheasant.

FESTIVALS: During the Suwa Shrine festival on March 27 at nearby Sengoku-bara the spirits of the hot spring are presented with hot water. This festival also features a lion dance, Yudachi no Shishimai, by people dressed in lion costumes. On November 3, the Hakone Daimyo Parade is held to reenact the journey along the Tōkaidō to Edo. The participants wear full dress and carry all they need for such an expedition.

107 Tōnosawa

LOCATION: Tōnosawa is 600 meters up the Haya River from Hakone Yumoto (106), to the west. From the Tōkyō area you can take the Tōkaidō Main Line, Shinkansen (bullet train), or Odakyū Line to Odawara Station. The bus to the hot spring takes 15 minutes. If you transfer at Odawara Station to the Hakone Tozan Tetsudō Line and get off at Tōnosawa Station, it's a 10-minute walk to the spring.

THE WATERS: The water is simple thermal, good for stress, aches and pains, and skin problems. If it's imbibed, it will aid digestion and stomach problems. In the seventeenth century, it is said, a monk living in a riverbank cave to practice self-discipline found this spring.

AROUND AND ABOUT: The atmosphere of Tōnosawa is quite different from that of Hakone Yumoto, even though they're so close geographically. The ryokan clustered along each side of the river hang out over the bank, competing for waterside viewing positions. The views can be seen out the large glass windows of the small sitting rooms attached.to the guests' rooms. There's tradition in the air—you can almost feel it as you walk about. The mountain temple Amidaji, a 20-minute walk from the hot spring, stands quiet in the dark, cool shade of the surrounding cedar trees. The roof of the main shrine is thatched, and in June, when the hydrangeas bloom, the misty rain, the deep blue blossoms, and the shrine make a very Japanese picture. This is the kind of hot spring you need when the razzmatazz of Hakone Yumoto gets to you.

ACCOMMODATIONS: Kansuirō is a three-story, deluxe Japanese inn that was named by the former Meiji prime minister Itō Hirobumi. They serve excellent food. The ryokan Fukuzumirō has wooden cottages built in different architectural styles. The main building houses both marble and wooden tubs.

108 Miyanoshita

LOCATION: Miyanoshita is in the center of the Hakone group of hot springs east of Hakone Yumoto (106). From Tōkyō take the Tōkaidō Main Line, Shinkansen (bullet train), or Odakyū Line to Odawara. The hot spring is 30 minutes by bus from Odawara Station. At Odawara you can transfer to the Hakone Tozan Tetsudō Line and get off at Miyanoshita Station; the spring is a 5-minute walk from there.

THE WATERS: Miyanoshita witnessed the Westernization of Japan during the Meiji era. After its discovery by wandering Frenchmen and Englishmen who spread the word, the two most deluxe establishments at the time, the Fujiya Hotel and the ryokan Naraya, commenced a commercial war dedicated to attracting foreigners to Miyanoshita. However, in true Japanese style they reached a compromise, which gave the foreigners to Fujiya and the Japanese to Naraya; the catch was that Fujiya had to pay Naraya a certain percentage to cover their loss each year. Thus Fujiya Hotel became the hot-spring hotel patronized by more non-Japanese than any other in the country. Still now it's considered one of the grand establishments that those who can afford it should visit when they come to Japan. The water at Miyanoshita is simple thermal, which treats rheumatism, neuralgia, and skin diseases, but this particular spring is also said to be beneficial to those with catarrh, nose, throat, or respiratory problems. There is a roped-off rock pool which was once used by Toyotomi Hideyoshi's. It is not used now.

AROUND AND ABOUT: The atmosphere of Miyanoshita is that of an expensive, elegant hot-spring town reminiscent of Japan a century ago, when Western culture was all the rage. In fact, the Hakone area is known for its Western-style accommodations, architecture, and menus. It is also known for its many hiking courses. Some walks, like that up to Fuji Lookout, are gentle; others encompass longer distances and steeper slopes. The hotels, ryokan, and tourist offices will gladly give you maps and pats on the back, and point you in the right direction. Autumnal colors can divert your attention somewhat from the blisters. Summer is cool and refreshing at Miyanoshita; it's high in elevation (417 meters), well shaded, and slow-paced.

■ CHŌKOKU NO MORI MUSEUM: Chōkoku no Mori literally means "Sculpture Forest." Fittingly, this outdoor sculpture garden and art gallery is in a superb natural setting on the side of a mountain. The works are by Japanese and foreign artists, and are positioned to contrast and blend alternately with the trees, bushes, water, and rocks in the garden. By catching good light conditions and moving around the objects, you can maximize your enjoyment of this man-nature combination of artistic beauty. To get there, take the Hakone Tozan Tetsudō Line for Gōra and get off at Chōkoku no Mori Station—a 10-minute ride. There is a bus from Miyanoshita as well, which takes a little longer.

ACCOMMODATIONS: There are many hotels with a Western touch in this area. Fujiya Hotel serves French cuisine, has a golf course, and has a superb garden. The Naraya Ryokan has all-weather tennis courts.

109 Dōgashima

LOCATION: Dōgashima, on the Jakotsu River, which connects many of the Hakone springs, is reached via Miyanoshita Hot Spring (108). Follow the directions to Miyanoshita and proceed down the hill to Dōgashima by cable car or overhead gondola.

THE WATERS: The great general Toyotomi Hideyoshi used the natural rock pools of Dōgashima for healing his men before they resumed fighting in nearby Odawara against the other great general, Tokugawa Ieyasu. White steam from the spring can be seen rising up from the dense green surrounding the only two ryokan here. The water is weak sodium chloride—recommended for stomach ailments, women's disorders, and nervous tension. Both ryokan have their own rock pools in the river that are fenced off by heavy stones shaded with leafy green foliage that struggles out of the cliff faces.

AROUND AND ABOUT: Unless you take up paddling in the river or scaling the cliffs up to the ryokan, there's not a lot to distract you here. This is a fine state of affairs considering the pleasure of sinking down into the numerous secluded, open-air pools here. Dōgashima offers another of the once-in-a-hot-spring-lover's-lifetime chances to have a bathing experience you'll never forget.

ACCOMMODATIONS: The two ryokan sit on top of cliffs like fortresses on impenetrable stone foundations. Their posture, however, belies their structure—large windows, white walls, and brown wooden shutters, hardly the material to fend off the enemy. The white walls contrast beautifully with the luminous green around, particularly in summer. The ryokan Taiseikan has a rock-encircled outdoor pool, a women-only outdoor pool, and twenty-eight more tubs both indoors and outdoors. Staying at Yamatoya Hotel is also a treat.

110 Ubako

LOCATION: Ubako is west of Hakone Yumoto (106) on the overhead cable car from Gōra down to Lake Ashi. Take the Hakone Tozan Tetsudō Line to Gōra Station, then the cable car to Sōunzan, and finally the overhead cable car to Ubako Onsen. You can also reach the spring by bus from Sōunzan—a 25-minute ride.

THE WATERS: This hot spring gets its water from Ōwakudani, the so-called hell that is visible (and smellable) from the overhead cable car. It's the usual billowing yellowy-white clouds, parched gray earth, and little old men and women selling thermally boiled eggs. Fortunately, Ubako is nothing like this; its surroundings are green and its water devoid of sulphur smells. A medicinal spring, Ubako was originally known as a place for curing eye disorders. The water, simple thermal, probably still heals eyes, but is also good for insomnia, rheumatism, and nervous breakdowns. If you don't like heights you might arrive at Ubako in a somewhat stressed state, so take advantage of the water.

AROUND AND ABOUT: The trip over hellish Ōwakudani, along the scenic cable-car route, and across Lake Ashi by ferry will give you a good picture of the Hakone area. Hakone is made for tourists with some extra yen and a desire to do things like go cruising in a white, swan-shaped paddle boat. However, up beyond the souvenir shops, away from the stand-up eateries selling roasted corn, basted squid, and soft ice cream, the mountains are calm and beautiful, ample compensation for commercialism which may temporarily offend.

ACCOMMODATIONS: The moderately priced Shūmeikan offers mountain views from its windows. It is small with thirteen Japanese-style rooms.

8 HOKURIKU REGION

An Island within an Island

Hokuriku, consisting of Fukui, Ishikawa, and Toyama prefectures, has been called a cultural island within Honshū Island. This is because during the Edo period the Maeda family, ruling for the Tokugawa shoguns, made Kanazawa, capital of Ishikawa Prefecture, into an artistic and cultural oasis—a little Kyōto, whose reputation lives on. Geographically, too, the Hokuriku Region is isolated. It is cut off by the rugged mountains straddling its boundaries as well as by severe winter storms that unload masses of snow onto its mountains and plains. This means that even now, in the age of air travel and snow plows, easterners, from warmer climes, do not venture into Hokuriku until they are quite sure winter has gone to rest. Not that this should deter the hot-spring visitor; provided the hot spring is not too far from a station on a main rail route, there is no better way to spend winter than snug and rosy in a hot thermal tub.

Although Ishikawa, by virtue of its capital, possesses the lion's share of cultural attractions, lingering traditions can be found in all three prefectures of the Hokuriku Region. The following is a brief introduction to some of the cultural assets treasured by the people of Hokuriku and admired by those who visit it.

Ishikawa Prefecture: Kanazawa was spared from the bombs of World War II and so today something of a castle town remains there. Very little of the castle itself still stands, but the twisting roads that don't lead to it and the house belonging to the samurai who guarded it do remain. The Maeda family

8 HOKURIKU REGION

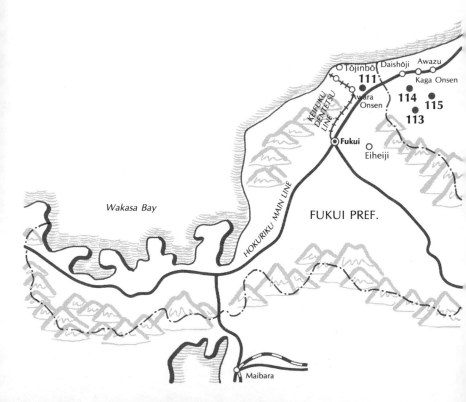

SEA OF JAPAN

Wajima

Noto Pen.

ISHIKAWA PREF.

117

Noto Island

Wakura

Nanao Bay

Toyama Bay

NANAO LINE

Tomari

Takaoka

Kurobe

112

JŌHANA LINE

Uozu

118

Kanazawa

Toyama

TOYAMA CHIHŌ
TETSUDŌ LINE

119

Jōhana

Unazuki Onsen

120

TAKAYAMA LINE

122

121

Kanetsuri

116

Kurobe Gorge

Hakusan-shita

TOYAMA PREF.

*KUROBE KYŌKOKU
TETSUDŌ LINE*

▲ MT. HAKU

were given the richest rice-producing area in Japan, and in order that the shogun wouldn't think they were spending their yen on arms and insurrection, the Maedas decided to devote their energies to making Kanazawa a city of the arts. They encouraged the performance of Noh theater, traditional music, and storytelling—all of which thrive in Kanazawa today. They also supported the potters who made soft yellow, dark green, and lavender Ko-Kutani pottery, which can still be found in antique shops; modern pottery is brighter, cheaper, and called Kutani ware. They landscaped Kenrokuen, one of the most beautiful stroll gardens you will see in Japan, and they built stately, traditional houses—like Seisonkaku in Kenrokuen. As well, they cast a benevolent eye upon the manufacture of Kaga Yūzen silk, exquisite, softly patterned, and still priceless, and they drank lots of *matcha*—the thick, green tea used in the tea ceremony. All of these delights can be seen, touched, or tasted by visitors to Kanazawa. The traveler can incline his head, scramble through a low door, and have tea in a garden that once belonged to a samurai. Or he can stop off in a restaurant and try Ishikawa's *jibuni*—a stew of duck, lily bulbs, small, soft dumplings, and vegetables—followed by grilled small fish (*gori*) from Asano River bounding Kanazawa, or *kaburazushi*—sushi rice topped with fermented turnips and yellowtail fish.

Another remnant of the past in Ishikawa is the *gojinjōdaiko* style of beating drums still performed on July 31 and August 1 near Wajima on Noto Peninsula. The drums recall the battle between local villagers and the daimyo Uesugi of the neighboring Echigo Province (now Niigata) in 1576. The locals beat their drums furiously and dressed themselves in masks of tree bark with tresses of kelp from the sea. As might be expected, they secured a formidable victory.

Toyama Prefecture: During an obligatory visit to the shogun in Edo (Tōkyō), the daimyo of Toyama, Maeda Masatoshi, took along a sample of the local apothecary's brew, called *hankontan*, meant to instill strength of will in the recipient. As chance would have it, an important advisor to the shogun fell ill, but upon swallowing some *hankontan*, he miraculously recovered, thus ensuring a great future for the humble, hometown concoction. This medicine, gleaned from bear kidney and herbs, among other things, is still made by pharmaceutical companies in Toyama, although they add more modern chemicals to their brew today. It is sold throughout Japan by salesmen who leave a chest of medicine at a shop and return a year later to replenish it, and to collect their money. The system of "consume now and pay later," along with the Toyama medicine man, is well known in Japan.

In southern Toyama near Gokayama, the terrain is rough and inaccessible. In this area the Taira clan hid after fleeing from their Minamoto clan opponents during the battles of the twelfth century. Their life style and defeat is retold today in dances and songs, performed during some of the many festivals held throughout Hokuriku during the year. (See Ōmaki Hot Spring, 121, for more details.)

Fukui Prefecture: Most Japanese used to know Fukui for its *habutae* silk, a very fine, sheer cloth said to be the best in Japan and used for making formal kimono. Today Fukui tourist shops sell *habutae mochi*—smooth, silky rice cakes meant to duplicate the texture of the desirable silk.

Besides silk, Fukui is known for Eiheiji Temple, symbol of the Buddhist fervor still very much alive in Hokuriku. Twenty minutes from Fukui on the Keifuku Dentetsu Line, this temple was constructed in the thirteenth century by the ruler of Echizen (now Fukui). Around that time the monk Dō-gen, founder of the Zen Buddhist Sōtō sect, trained two thousand acolytes here. Despite the renovations, the traditional layout of the buildings and the seven-hundred-year-old cypress trees remain. Travelers are welcome to stay if they can rise at 3:00 A.M.; they are permitted to join in Zen medita-tion sessions after a stay of three days. The very secluded, vast, and silent surroundings of the old temple are perfect for meditation.

Hokuriku, an island within an island, can be a cultural oasis for the traveler who is willing to spend the time to seek out and immerse himself in the treasures remaining from the region's past.

111 Awara

LOCATION: Awara is near the northern border of Fukui Prefecture, not far from the coast. From Kanazawa take the Hokuriku Main Line to Awara Onsen Station. The bus from there to the hot spring takes 10 minutes.

THE WATERS: This hot spring took its name from the surrounding terrain: *awara* means marshy grasslands. The spring was found by accident when an unfortunate farmer looking for water for his rice fields unearthed spew-ing hot thermal water. Later, in 1883, a ryokan was opened near the spring, and since then the community has flourished. In 1956 a devastating fire prac-tically destroyed the entire town, but it was rebuilt in an elegant, modern style with neat traditional gardens and subdued, deluxe hot-spring facilities. Many Japanese like this kind of hot spring—just enough tradition without the signs of age, deterioration, and dirt that usually go along with it. Many of the local baths have modern shiny taps, smooth marble, and patterned tiles and look out over traditional gardens. The water is sodium chloride—good for rheumatism, women's ailments, and neuralgia.

AROUND AND ABOUT: Awara, the biggest hot spring in Fukui Prefecture, stands guard at the start of Tōjinbō, a spectacular strip of jagged coast, steep cliffs, and menacing waters. Tourists are invited to clamber over the pitted rocks and dabble in the rock pools where slimy, boneless creatures lurk in the shadows. The rocks come in giant, vertical slabs whose crevices and cracks tempt the brave rock-hopper but send the more timid straight back to the restaurant sitting above. Fifteen minutes by bus from Awara is Mikuni, a port town that dates back to the eighth century, when ships from all parts of Japan, Hokkaidō in particular, called here. Later Mikuni became an important trading port for Chinese and Korean vessels. The women who fought over the sailors' attention gave Mikuni a certain reputation since they were courageous and bold, qualities uncommon in prostitutes at the time. These women are immortalized in local stories and ballads. Something of the old port-town atmosphere can be felt during the grand Mikuni Festival on May 20. In the highlight of the festival, a parade, men dressed in samurai garb swagger along to the beats of huge drums and the shouts of enthusiastic onlookers. Some of them also carry large warrior dolls in full military regalia.

ACCOMMODATIONS: The traditional ryokan Kaikatei has a Japanese-style garden and has been patronized by imperial family members. The ryokan Beniya, a modern structure, has also had illustrious guests. Kameya is a less expensive ryokan. All of these inns have outdoor baths.

THE TRUTH ABOUT TŌJINBŌ: In Heisenji Temple, near Awara, there lived an extremely wayward monk named Tōjinbō, who drank great quantities of saké, womanized, and fought at the drop of a hat. His fellow monks despised him and plotted his demise. One day they took him on a drinking picnic at the top of a cliff overlooking the sea, and when he was sufficiently inebriated, they pushed him over. That very night, around midnight, a man walking along this cliff was grabbed around the ankle by a giant hand that emerged from the sea and pulled him down into the murky depths, where he drowned. A week later his body was found washed up on the rocks. This was only the beginning of a spate of similar "hand" incidents that caused great turmoil in the temple. The monks decided to come clean and confessed, hoping to stop the weird happenings that clearly had been instigated by the murdered monk. They also named the cliff Tōjinbō after the monk, bringing an end to the killings. Still, they say, strange things happen here, so don't go rock-climbing when you are drunk or when it's dark.

112 Yuwaku

LOCATION: Yuwaku is just south of Kanazawa City, the capital of Ishikawa Prefecture. From Kanazawa Station on the Hokuriku Main Line, it takes 40 minutes to reach the hot spring by bus. Buses to the spring leave from many other parts of the city, too.

THE WATERS: Yuwaku was apparently known and used as far back as the eighth century. In the Edo period, it was a health resort for the ailing members and friends of the Maeda clan, the shogun's representatives who ruled from Kanazawa City. The water, containing sodium sulphate and sodium chloride, has always had a good reputation with those suffering chronic skin, muscular, and respiratory diseases. It does wonders for skin disorders, rheumatism, arthritis, and burns. The several public baths, like many in this region and elsewhere, have been neglected. Local people seem to prefer their own tubs or the exotic, deluxe facilities at the ryokan and hotels, who open their baths to the public for a small fee.

AROUND AND ABOUT: Yuwaku sits on high ground, at the foot of Mount Iō overlooking the Asano River. For a city suburb, the area is lush and peaceful. If you don't stay at Haku-unrō, at least take a walk by this Spanish-style ryokan with banquet rooms filled with Japanese screens, paintings, scrolls, and pottery. Its square tower, stained glass windows, and carved ballustrades date to the Meiji era. Not far from the Yuwaku inns—a short walk, about 500 meters across the road—is Edo Mura, a village of rebuilt and renovated houses from the Edo period, many of which have been disassembled, moved here, and reassembled. This cross-section of samurai, merchant, and farm houses is complete with old tools, cooking utensils, articles of clothing, and personal ornaments. The grounds are authentically landscaped and the souvenir offerings are minimal. ■ KANAZAWA: The Maeda clan were great patrons of the arts, making Kanazawa something of a mecca for artists. Traditional arts and crafts still thrive there today, although at first glance around the station, at the tangle of shops, advertisements, and coffee shops, you may be dubious. To see some of Kanazawa's cultural offerings, take a walk through the castle remains, Kanazawa University, Ishikawa Prefectural Museum, the Noh theater, or the old samurai quarters. The white plaster walls, tiled roofs, cobblestone streets, and fortress gray are all remnants of the past. For a change of pace, visit Ninja-dera ("Ninja Temple"), an amazing house of tricks where you had better stick close to the guide to avoid brushing against hidden knobs that could send you hurtling several floors down into a well. Worse still, you might get lost forever in a maze of real and false doors. Officially named Myōryūji, this temple was actually a refuge for the Maeda clan and had nothing to do with ninja. To think about how you can redecorate and burglar-proof your own home in a similar fashion, take time off in a teahouse. Kanazawa's exquisite teahouses, complete with tables and chairs for those who get pins and needles in their legs from sitting on tatami mats, serve bitter green tea complemented by tasty sweets decorated with the teahouse crest or a seasonal motif. Before you leave Kanazawa, stroll through Kenrokuen Park, considered one of the three most beautiful landscape gardens in Japan. The well-contrived design includes Edo-style lanterns lining pathways, stone bridges arching over sparkling streams, and artfully arranged and pruned trees and shrubs.

ACCOMMODATIONS: Haku-unrō, the Spanish-style ryokan mentioned above, is a fine choice. Kanaya is another deluxe ryokan.

FOOD: Kanazawa is the place to go for culinary adventure—whole areas of the city are devoted to the enjoyment of food. Near the rivers or in the center of town, you can dine at restaurants with miniature gardens on view, private tatami rooms, hanging cooking pots and kettles over open hearths, or pottery on display. A never-ending series of plates will be placed before you— seafood, vegetables, and other local delicacies all arranged to visual perfection. The dishes vary with the seasons, of course, and seasonal propriety receives much attention here. For a somewhat pricy excursion into gourmet nirvana, try the restaurant Goriya on the Asano River. Reservations are advised.

113 Yamanaka

LOCATION: Yamanaka, one of the Kaga group of hot springs, is in Ishikawa Prefecture, somewhat inland from the Sea of Japan. Take the Hokuriku Main Line from Maibara and get off at Kaga Onsen Station. The bus from the station to the hot spring takes 40 minutes. By taxi, it is 20 minutes.

THE WATERS: They say Yamanaka was discovered either a millennium ago by the monk Gyōki or five hundred years ago by another monk, Rennyo. Whatever its origin, this hot-spring town boomed in the eighteenth century, was destroyed by fire in 1931, and is now enjoying a modern revival. Like many of the hot springs in the Kaga group, Yamanaka has been the object of efforts to put new life into the bath, so don't be surprised at some of the deluxe trappings you'll see in this out-of-the-way community. The water, containing weak calcium and sodium sulphate, is particularly effective in treating stomach ulcers, surface wounds, rheumatism, and sciatica. If you suffer none of these complaints, lie back and enjoy your luck and the sweet but faint smell of the water here. Bashō, the haiku poet, wrote that he wouldn't pick chrysanthemums at Yamanaka because he couldn't bare to contaminate the lingering fragrance of the thermal water on his hands. You can try out this water anywhere here, including at the segregated baths at the public bathhouse: Kiku-no-yu for men and Ashi-no-yu for women.

AROUND AND ABOUT: Yamanaka is an odd combination of oblong concrete hotels and old ryokan with benches covered in red cloths set up in the gardens where guests are served tea. No matter how self-consciously Yamanaka may try to appeal to tourists, its location on a very scenic part of Kakusen Gorge should guarantee its survival. Ryokan picturesquely line both sides of the Daishōji River below. To see the best features of the gorge, follow the 1-kilometer walking course that begins at Kōrogi Bridge in the center of town and ends at Kurotani Bridge. The cliffs are steep and rocky, and in spring, pink cherry blossoms peek over the clifftops—you can see them if you look up. While you're out walking, you might stop at Iōji Temple and Hakusan Shrine. In Iōji Temple there is a statue of Yakushi Nyorai, the Buddhist deity of medicine, carved by Gyōki. Hakusan Shrine is near the statue of Jizō—the Buddhist patron god of travelers, children, and pregnant women—where the *yuna*, female bath attendants, used to bid farewell to their favorite clients. They hid their sadness at parting behind a shawl wrapped around their face, somewhat like the covering over the lion's head in Asian lion dances. Because of this similarity, these women were, and still are, called *shishi* (lion). Some of the ballads about this hot spring tell of the painful love affairs that the *shishi* had with men who visited them frequently over the years but who never stayed on. According to the ballads, the women tried to hide their sorrow, but the Jizō saw their tears. Although the geisha here are still called *shishi*, they no longer attend male clients in the baths. But as attendants at dinner, they are famous—geisha at the Kaga group of hot springs have their own portable shrine in the Yamanaka Koikoi Festival held September 22 to 24. Those in need of elegant gifts might want to purchase some of the local lacquerware, called *Yamanaka-nuri*.

ACCOMMODATIONS: The ryokan Yoshinoya is famous for its Noh stage and garden where tea is served. It's expensive but worth the money. Two popular ryokan with lots of natural wood and bamboo incorporated into their structures are Kayōtei and Kajikasō. All of these inns serve "boats," plates, and baskets of the superb fish and sashimi that are so well known in this part of Japan.

FESTIVALS: During the Bon Festival in mid-July you can participate in the procession of dancers, which starts in front of the public bathhouse. Just don your yukata, and when you hear the music, it's time to step out.

114 Yamashiro

LOCATION: Yamashiro, one of the Kaga group of hot springs, lies slightly north of Yamanaka Hot Spring (113), in Ishikawa Prefecture. From Kanazawa take the Hokuriku Main Line to Kaga Onsen Station. The hot spring is a 10-minute bus ride from the station.

THE WATERS: This area is mentioned in the first history of Japan (*Nihon Shoki*), written in the eighth century, and seems to have been known in prehistoric times as well. Chances are that the spring itself, though not mentioned specifically in ancient documents, has been soothing people for quite a few centuries now. The water, containing sodium chloride and calcium sulphate, is good for women's disorders, neuralgia, and hemorrhoids as well as for stress and fatigue, which may very well describe your physical state if you've made the journey here from the eastern coast of Japan.

AROUND AND ABOUT: You can still see evidence of the past in Yamashiro, though not from prehistoric times. The primary evidence is the so-called *bengaragōshi* style of windows on some of the ryokan. The vertical slats of wood placed at close intervals across the window openings allow air and light to pass through while providing some privacy. Dating to the Edo period, these windows can be seen on several ryokan around Yokuden, the public bath. Inside these same ryokan is other evidence of Edo—wooden columns blackened by smoke and contrasting walls painted with reddish lacquer. The relatively short *noren*, or entryway curtains, are a style admired by the Maeda, who once ruled the Daishōji clan in Edo days. This town is very keen on promoting hot springs and has been improving the baths, accommodation facilities, facilities for drinking thermal water (small wells with ladles), and hot-spring festivals and customs. The result is a bathing buff's hot spring.

ACCOMMODATIONS: If you can, stay at Araya, a first-class ryokan established 250 years ago that comprises elements of both old and new Japan. The food is good and the bath is large. It is expensive, though, and advance reservations are necessary. Yamashiro Grand Hotel, however, takes the prize where novelty in the bath room is concerned. One side of the room is modeled after the Ishikawa Gate of Kanazawa Castle. As you soak, you can imagine yourself as a lean, catlike ninja scaling the wall to attack unsuspecting guards. . . . The less aggressive bather might prefer the outdoor bath set in a bright, flowery garden.

FOOD: Food preparation here is the object of much competition. In season, crab meat, fresh bamboo shoots, and *matsutake* mushrooms are among the delectable morsels you'll find arranged beautifully on your plate.

DRUMS OF SORROW: Yamashiro seemed to be the perfect hot spring, with not a blot on its character, until the caretaker at Senshōji Temple fell in love with a local bath attendant some six hundred years ago. Such liaisons were taboo in those days, so the lovers had to meet surreptitiously. Every day Ikuzō, the caretaker, would strike the bell at the temple, the signal to the woman, Omitsu, to meet at their usual place. Inevitably, one day Omitsu didn't show up. Ikuzō struck the bell frantically time and time again, but to no avail. Omitsu was dead and would never come again. Followed by curious villagers, the distraught Ikuzō ran off to the temple pond and threw himself in. Today the story of their doomed love affair is retold by a narrator to the accompaniment of the local style of drum beating called *yunohanadaiko*, which you can hear being performed at most of the inns for private groups in banquet rooms at dinner time. However, it may be possible for foreign travelers to obtain special permission to sit in and listen to the performance.

115 Awazu

LOCATION: Awazu, one of the Kaga group of hot springs, is southwest of Kanazawa City in Ishikawa Prefecture. From Kanazawa take the Hokuriku Main Line to Awazu Station. The hot spring is 10 minutes by bus from the station.

THE WATERS: The oldest established spring in the Hokuriku Region, Awazu dates back to the early eighth century, when it was discovered by the Buddhist monk Taichō Daishi. The water, containing sodium sulphate, treats arteriosclerosis, rheumatism, and women's ailments. Imbibing the water is good for diabetes and obesity. There is a public bathhouse in the center of town called Sōyu. Awazu's waters are plentiful; many establishments have their own private springs on the premises. The ryokan Kametani has an open-air bath.

AROUND AND ABOUT: The famous haiku poet Bashō is among the many who have waxed lyrical about this hot spring. Yosano Akiko is another; this Meiji poet wrote a poem in an effort to capture the old, authentic atmosphere she found here. To find it yourself, try walking to Nata Temple, established more than a thousand years ago. Adding to the air of antiquity is the weather-beaten wood, moss, and cracks. Awazu is a medium-size town that abounds in leafy greenery.

ACCOMMODATIONS: The ryokan Hōshi, with *bengaragōshi* window grates and sliding glass doors, is the oldest ryokan in Japan. The same family line has managed it for forty-six generations now. Its several baths include a rocky open-air pool in a garden. The ryokan Tsujinoya is more deluxe but more expensive.

FESTIVALS: Long ago, farmers in the area sat in their rice fields at night with torches and drums, warding off insects with flames and drumbeats. Boredom led to drum-beating contests and the Kaga style of beating, called *ideyudaiko*, which is performed today at the hot-spring festival on August 26 to 28.

116 Chūgū

LOCATION: Chūgū is northwest of Mount Haku in the southeastern corner of Ishikawa Prefecture. From Kanazawa take the bus for 1 hour to Hakusanshita Station. From there the bus to Chūgū takes about 40 minutes. The hot spring is open from mid-May to October.

THE WATERS: Chūgū was discovered by the Buddhist monk Taichō in A.D. 717, when he was led there by a dove. The spring was originally named Hato-no-yu after the dove (*hato*), but following a facelift, it was renamed Chūgū after a building in the precincts of nearby Shirayamahime Shrine. In former times, this was a medicinal spring patronized mainly by those suffering from stomach troubles. The water is very hot and contains sodium chloride and calcium hydrogen-carbonate. The pleasant taste and presumed effectiveness mean many take home the water in plastic containers for treating their next stomachache. A 4-kilometer walk away is an open-air public bath, but this one is out in the wilds with a waterfall and lots of noisy birds to keep you company.

AROUND AND ABOUT: Nowadays Chūgū is less of a medicinal spring and more of a vacation spot, despite its inaccessibility in winter. On one of your walks, drop by the five-hundred-year-old Shirayamahime Shrine. Under the stately cypress trees beyond the stone steps, two carved wooden dogs, designated as cultural treasures, guard the simple shrine buildings. The complementary pair—one with its mouth open, the other with it closed—ward off evil spirits. Known as *Koma inu*, the dogs are variations of the lion guards used in Korea. In old Japan miniature versions of the pair were employed as weights to anchor screens in the imperial palace.

ACCOMMODATIONS: Miyamura Ryokan and Yamada Ryokan are both comfortable, inexpensive, and closed in winter. Their menus include a wide variety of river fish, mountain vegetables, and, in an exotic touch, bear sashimi. The raw bear meat is not for the squeamish and not always available—order in advance.

117 Wakura

LOCATION: Wakura, one of the biggest hot springs in the Hokuriku Region, lies on the eastern coast of Noto Peninsula on Nanao Bay, Ishikawa Prefecture. From Kanazawa take the Nanao Line to Wakura Onsen Station. The bus from the station to the hot spring takes 5 minutes.

THE WATERS: Although discovered on land in the ninth century, the source of Wakura's thermal waters was moved several meters out to sea by an earthquake in the eleventh century. As a result, the water had to be trapped in a man-made rock pool maintained at great expense just offshore. The financial support came from members of the ruling class, who sought out the water for its effects on sexually transmitted diseases that were sweeping this class at the time. Water was even transported in barrels to daimyo in neighboring provinces. In 1868 the land around the spring's source was reclaimed, but some inns were still built so that their porches extended over the water. Not only is this aesthetically pleasing but it also means that guests today can do a spot of fishing from the windows of some of the ryokan if they feel so inclined. The sodium chloride water is good for chronic digestive disorders if imbibed, and for anemia and rheumatism, as well as problems in more sensitive regions, if bathed in.

AROUND AND ABOUT: In an attempt to encourage young tourists to stay here before continuing on around the peninsula, the town of Wakura has built sports facilities, a boat harbor, and after-dark dining and dancing venues.

As a result, Wakura looks like a modern pleasure resort but on a small scale—a stark contrast to the wild, rocky coastlines that characterize most of Noto Peninsula. But the views from the ryokan rooms, especially the baths, are picturesque, aided by Wakura's position on the tip of Cape Benten in Nanao Bay. The baths often face the calm, sheltered bay and the yacht marina, which sunrises and sunsets paint in glowing pink and red. If Wakura is too fast-paced for you, escape to the rest of the peninsula—small fishing villages, farmhouses surrounded by glassy rice paddies, stormy seas, and long, spacious beaches on the western side. Or walk across the bridge to Noto Island (15–20 minutes), and swim, walk in the park and aquarium complex, or fish.

ACCOMMODATIONS: The ryokan in Wakura have put a lot of effort into promoting "hot-spring living." The facilities are therefore quite good and not as expensive as resorts on the eastern coast of Japan. A good example is the large, very modern ryokan Kagaya, which has both Japanese- and Western-style accommodations. Its open-air pools are really something: meandering streams, waterfalls, and a lot of space surrounds you as you bathe. The management will arrange a display of drum beating if you and some friends can arrange the money; it's not expensive for a group. If you are looking in the middle price range there is the small, homey ryokan Ryoso Hamanasu.

CRAFTS: Noto Peninsula has a number of artists' enclaves, including Wajima, famous for its exquisite lacquerware—chopsticks, stationery boxes, trays, screens, small chests of drawers, bowls, and so on. The prices are dear, but accurately reflect the time and skill involved in the complex lacquering process. Wajima is on the northwestern coast of Noto Peninsula, 1 hour 40 minutes from Wakura Station on the Nanao Line. Another craft product you will see throughout the Hokuriku Region is Kutani ware (*Kutani-yaki*), porcelain decorated in bright, handpainted glazes—typically, red, gold, and black.

118 Ogawa Motoyu

LOCATION: Ogawa Motoyu lies on the Ogawa River, at the foot of Mount Yakushi in northeastern Toyama Prefecture. From Toyama take the Hokuriku Main Line to Tomari Station on the coast. From there, a bus to the hot spring takes 35 minutes; a taxi takes 20 minutes.

THE WATERS: Ogawa Motoyu was discovered in 1626 by the monk Shūkei, who was led to it in a dream by Yakushi Nyorai, the deity of medicine (and hot springs). The sodium chloride water soothes stomachs, especially if you drink it over a period of time. It's also good for infertility, and is visited by many would-be grandparents who want grandchildren! The single hotel/ryokan complex here offers both indoor baths with large glass windows looking out on nature and an outdoor cave bath. The spacious limestone cave, down the hill from the hotel, looks out on the river. Three thermal waterfalls have been created with pipes coming through the cave walls. Half of the pool is outside the cave, in broad sunlight. Although it's all good clean jungle fun, if you are shy you might want to go with a group. The bathing is mixed, and the cave recesses aren't sufficiently dark for hiding.

AROUND AND ABOUT: Throughout the years the cave bath at Ogawa Motoyu has been very popular with local people—formerly fishermen, nowadays summer mountaineers and employees of YKK, the world's biggest zipper manufacturer, which has factories nearby. Tourists, too, like this spring because they can stay in the ryokan part of the hotel and do their own cooking, saving considerable expense. The hotel complex is sufficiently surrounded with greenery to give it the air of a hideaway. Appropriate souvenir gifts from Ogawa Motoyu include *wakame* (seaweed), *himono* (dried fish), *sansai* (pickled mountain greens), and *wakame yōkan*, sweet-bean gelatin garnished with seaweed.

ACCOMMODATIONS: Your only choice here is the first-class Hotel Ogawa or the adjoining ryokan Kashimabu, where you must do your own cooking. You can buy groceries for your gourmet meals at the shopping mall that is part of the hotel complex. You can also get a haircut or a massage at the mall. The ryokan management provides after-dinner entertainment—singers, storytellers, musicians playing the shamisen—to help make up for culinary genius that went awry in the kitchen and to encourage good rapport among guests who may have had to compete for cutting boards and elbow room before dinner.

119 Unazuki

LOCATION: Unazuki is inland from Kurobe City in northeastern Toyama Prefecture. From Toyama take the Hokuriku Main Line to Uozu Station. Transfer to the Toyama Chihō Tetsudō Line and get off at Unazuki Onsen Station. The hot spring is a 5-minute walk from the station. Or, you can get off the Hokuriku Main Line at Kurobe Station and catch a bus from there—a 50-minute ride.

THE WATERS: Unazuki's very hot, plentiful water is pumped in from Kuronagi Hot Spring, 8 kilometers away. The water is classified as simple thermal, considered good for anything, especially convalescence.

AROUND AND ABOUT: Unazuki is another of the new, modern hot springs to rise out of the ashes of fires. Thirty years ago, the spa town was burned to the ground. Now, in its place, a group of high-rise luxury hotels stands on the riverbank between the towering mountains. While its location at the entrance to Kurobe Gorge, counted among the Three Most Spectacular

Gorges in the country, is superb, Unazuki owes its popularity to a dam-construction company that laid in the main attraction—a small-gauge railway, the Kurobe Kyōkoku Tetsudō Line, that originally carried workers and supplies in and out of the gorge. Now this train is rushed by tourists who want to see the gorge in a novel way. The open carriage comes precariously close to the edges of steep cliffs, affording thrilling views of deep ravines below. The trip (1 hour 40 minutes) ends at Keyakidaira, in the heart of the gorge, where you can picnic, hike around, and regain your composure before braving the ride back. The train is mobbed in summer, spectacular in autumn, and closed in winter (November through May). Whatever the season, it's slightly unnerving. A less hair-raising option is to follow the foot trail along the tracks. It takes 4 hours to reach Keyakidaira on foot. Other attractions include skiing at nearby slopes in winter, a snow carnival on the first weekend in February, and, for when the train is booked for several days, Kōchi Museum, which houses all types of antiquities, including swords, paintings, scrolls, statues, and ceramics. The museum is in the center of the town. Then, of course, there are always the three B's—bed, breakfast, and bathing—to keep you occupied while you wait your turn for a train ride. In the evenings, at Unazuki Grand Hotel, you can hear a performance of the fiery, energetic drum beating that is so popular in this part of Japan. The music is performed nightly, at 8:30 P.M.

ACCOMMODATIONS: The modern ryokan Entaijisō has a small Japanese garden and a tea room. Women will particularly like this ryokan as they have placed the women's bath on the seventh floor, where it looks out on a magnificent view. The men's tub is on the first floor. Hotel Kurobe has deluxe rooms and features a view of the train from its lobby. The ryokan Enraku also offers views of the gorge.

FOOD: If you're homesick, try the local watermelons. They're oval in shape and red inside, a change from most Japanese watermelons, which are as round as a basketball. Mountain vegetable dishes combined with fish from the Sea of Japan make a tasty main course. Only the adventurous should try the *wasabizuke*—finely cut vegetables pickled in Japanese horseradish (*wasabi*). This slippery, gray-green paste will either put hairs on your chest or take your tongue out.

120 Kanetsuri

LOCATION: Kanetsuri is in the Kurobe Gorge, very near Unazuki Hot Spring (119), in northeastern Toyama Prefecture. Take the Hokuriku Main Line to Uozu or Toyama Station. Transfer to the Toyama Chihō Tetsudō Line and get off at Unazuki Onsen Station. Transfer again, to the Kurobe Kyōkoku Tetsudō Line, for a scenic 70-minute train ride through Kurobe Gorge to Kanetsuri Station. One of the two ryokan is by the station. Note that the

Kurobe Kyōkoku Tetsudō Line is closed from December through May.

THE WATERS: This hot-spring hideaway opened in the early nineteenth century when a spring was discovered in the cliff face overlooking the Kurobe River. A rock pool was built with white rocks taken from the cliffs and the river to trap the thermal waters. Today this same technique is used to form haphazard barriers between clear pools of hot, simple thermal water and clear pools of cold river water. Because the river is narrow and the banks are covered with thick, overflowing growth, the waterside pools are shaded and sheltered. The banks change color with the seasons—autumn is the best—and the rocks form secret passageways and pools, like the small private area reserved for women nervous about sharing the largest, communal pool with a crowd of men. You don't have to stay at the ryokan (or pay a fee) to use the riverside pools, so you can make this a day trip—a scenic, sometimes thrilling, ride combined with a relaxing bath.

AROUND AND ABOUT: Besides the pools, the gorge, and the river, there's not much in the way of diversion here. The energetic traveler can skip stones on the river, redesign the rock walls around the pools, or walk up and down stream. For the hedonist, there's sky gazing, sunbathing, and birdwatching—all from the comfort of the hot pools, of course.

ACCOMMODATIONS: Miyamasō, a solitary, sturdy mountain ryokan, is comfortable and has an indoor thermal bath for when you want a change of venue. By choosing a less elaborate menu and staying in a less desirable room (for example, one without a view), you can regulate your budget.

FOOD: If you like sampling local brews, try Iwana Kotsushu, or grilled fish saké. Don't let the name put you off, for it tastes very much like saké usually does.

121 Ōmaki

LOCATION: Ōmaki is in western Toyama Prefecture. From Toyama take the Hokuriku Main Line to Takaoka Station. From the station take a bus to the Komaki Entei stop—a 1-hour trip. From there it's a 30-minute ferry ride across a man-made lake to Ōmaki Hot Spring. Note that the ferry makes the round trip only four or five times a day.

THE WATERS: In 1183 a fierce battle was fought between the Taira and Minamoto clans at Kurikara Pass, not far from Ōmaki. The Taira followers were defeated, and one badly injured warrior, Fujiwara Yorihide, barely managed to escape into the surrounding mountains. He prepared himself to die, since he was alone and there was no hope of anyone finding him in the inaccessible mountain forests. As he lay near a pool, he saw one pigeon after another fly down and bathe in the water. They didn't drink it, however, so he wondered if it could be a thermal pond. With this in mind, he summoned his strength and dragged himself to the edge of the pond to drink.

Indeed it was thermal water, and it's said he stayed here and recovered in a very short time. What better praise could spring water receive! Local people used the pond for years afterward and it wasn't until this century, when the river was dammed to form an artificial lake, that a ryokan was built for outsiders. The hot-spring pool has been refashioned into quite a sophisticated jumble of mammoth rocks holding in clear, sodium chloride water containing calcium sulphate. If the idyllic location doesn't cure your ills, the water will work wonders on your stomach, skin, muscles, and any cuts or wounds. It is also good for weak, battle-scarred bodies that may happen to drag in.

AROUND AND ABOUT: The lone ryokan occupies a very choice position overhanging the water, so you can drop a line from your window and catch your dinner (other food is provided for those without a talent for fishing). When you tire of the Robinson Crusoe life you can go to Inami, a town down the Shō River that's 10 minutes away by bus. There you can spend unwanted yen in the souvenir shops and go sightseeing. Among the sights is Saishōji Temple, with its double-tiered, thatched gate. Part of the temple was built by Hida workmen. It has heavy wooden beams and a double, thatched roof on the main gate. As you stroll about town, you'll see a lot of chiseling by local artists carving wooden toys, ornaments, and household utensils.

ACCOMMODATIONS: Ōmaki Onsen Ryokan is a comfortable, traditional-style building. Their menu includes river fish, mountain vegetables, dishes flavored with *miso* (fermented bean paste), and grilled fish saké to wash it all down with.

FESTIVALS: Very near Ōmaki, there is a town, Gokayama, which is famous for a samurai dance performed by five men in formal kimono. They tie their sleeves under their arms and wear headbands and sashes. Wielding swords, they sing to the accompaniment of traditional instruments—drum, shamisen, *shakuhachi* (a wooden flute), *yotsudake* (percussion), and *kokyū* (a Chinese shamisen). The song "Mugiyabushi" tells the story of Taira samurai fallen from grace and forced to do menial tasks. See it at the Mugiya Festival on September 15 and 16. On September 26 and 27, during the Kokiriko Festival, you can see young women in white kimono and white *hakama* (flared pants) perform this dance at Hakusan Shrine in Gokayama, 30 minutes by bus from Ōsaki (note that there are only two buses a day).

122 Rindō

LOCATION: Rindō is on the southern end of the Tonami Plain, in southwestern Toyama Prefecture. From Toyama take the Hokuriku Main Line to Takaoka Station. Transfer to the Jōhana Line and get off at Jōhana Station. The bus from the station to the hot spring takes 15 minutes.

THE WATERS: What's remarkable about this hot spring is its water. It bubbles like a carbonated drink—in fact, it's known as soda-pop water—and if you drink it you can easily taste and feel the similarities. Technically, it is carbon-dioxated water and was at first feared since the gas emitted, carbon dioxide, killed birds and animals that inhaled too much and since unwary humans got incredibly drunk from its fumes. It was known as *saké ike*, or saké pond, around A.D. 700, when the whole area was volcanically active. Only in 1475, when the Buddhist monk Rennyo came here and blessed it, was the hot spring officially opened up. Whether it was Rennyo's blessing or time, the waters stopped getting people drunk. In the late nineteenth century, the local folk decided to build inns and share the water with visitors, as it had proved extremely effective in rejuvenating complexions and healing wounds and burns. Today, the water is said to be good for stomach, nervous, and heart problems, including stress. The baths using thermal water (not all of them do) are in rooms where the windows are always open to allow air to circulate freely. This is to protect bathers from any negative side-effects of the carbon dioxide, although today this is not a problem and there's no need to worry about carbon-dioxide poisoning—even members of the imperial family have patronized Rindō. While the bubbly water is good for human skin, it eats away at tubs, even marble ones, over the years.

AROUND AND ABOUT: Rindō is a small hot spring with very few ryokan. Besides the water, not much moves around here. Only Mount Takashimizu, visible in the distance, produces an occasional rumble. Pleasant walking paths go by ponds overgrown with water lilies, but the more scenic spots can only be reached on foot by avid hikers. The rest of you will need a car to fully explore the plain and mountains.

ACCOMMODATIONS: The single ryokan is Kagaya, which though small has a big tub.

9 TŌHOKU REGION

The Real Japan

Tōhoku means "Northeast," and is an apt name for this region of Japan that comprises the six prefectures on the top third of Honshū. The area was once called Michinoku, or "Back Roads," meaning the back country and in a way the back of beyond. To Japanese people, Tōhoku conjures up visions of "real country." The way of life here, the scenery, and, of course, the people are of the same hue: close to the land and the customs of old. Modernity moves fast, though, like the bullet train, which has recently been extended into Tōhoku. So how long these nether regions will remain a treasure trove of winding mountain tracks, thatched roofs, water wheels, crazy festivals, and strange tales is something you should think about—and soon.

Tōhoku's terrain has it all, from ashy white wastelands (the product of temperamental volcanoes) to lush green valleys, glassy paddy fields, and all-enveloping winter snow blankets. Winter deals harshly with Tōhoku, so travel plans are best left for warmer months. But you'll hear all about winter, and see what people do during the snowed-in months as you browse in Tōhoku's many crafts shops where homemade wooden toys, ornaments, domestic utensils, garments, paintings, kites, and masks are on display. You'll also come across the Tōhoku legends and folklore that fill many a winter's fireside evening, teaching and amusing as they strive to make some sense of nature and man and the spirits in between. Some stories are light and colorful like the winter festivals and make the mood a jolly one, but others are somber and moving and make you look behind the door, and in the

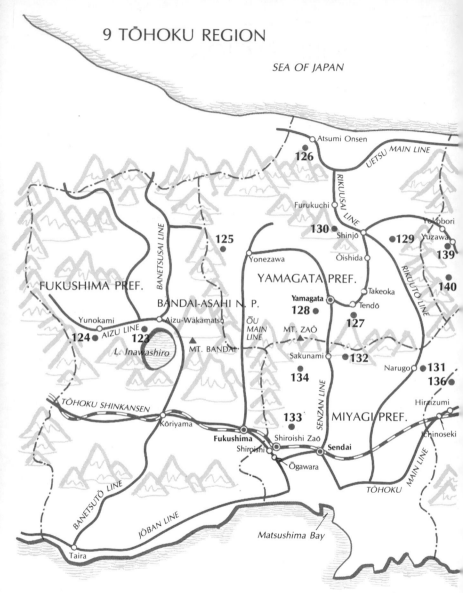

9 TŌHOKU REGION

SEA OF JAPAN

Atsumi Onsen

126

UETSU MAIN LINE

RIKUUSAI LINE

Furukuchi

130
Shinjō

Yokobori

129 Yuzawa

139

BANETSUSAI LINE

125

Yonezawa

Ōishida

140

YAMAGATA PREF.

Yamagata
128

Takeoka

RIKUUTŌ LINE

FUKUSHIMA PREF.

BANDAI-ASAHI N. P.

Tendō

127

ŌU
MAIN
LINE

Yunokami

Aizu-Wakamatsu

MT. ZAŌ

Sakunami

132

Narugo **131**

136

124 AIZU LINE **123**

L. Inawashiro

MT. BANDAI

134

SENZAN LINE

Hiraizumi

TŌHOKU SHINKANSEN

133

MIYAGI PREF.

Kōriyama

Fukushima
Shiroishi

Shiroishi Zaō

Sendai

Ichinoseki

TŌHOKU MAIN LINE

Ōgawara

TŌHOKU

BANETSUTŌ LINE

JŌBAN LINE

Matsushima Bay

Taira

PACIFIC OCEAN

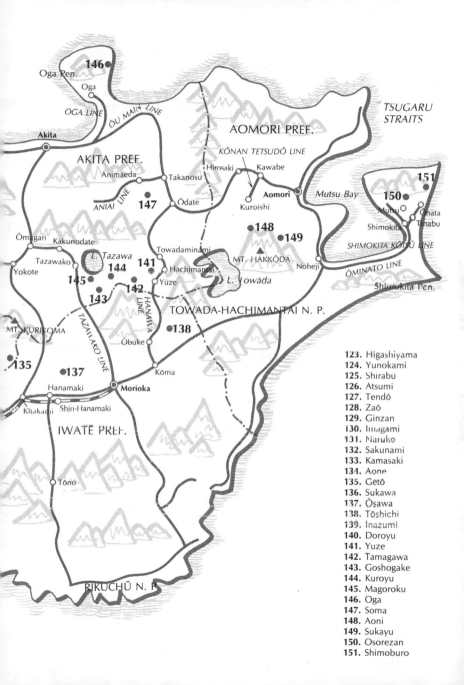

cupboards of your ryokan room, before you get into your futon.

It's easy to see why thermal pools have proved so popular in the north. Not only do they cleanse and heal bodies tired of bending over seedlings in muddy fields, but they have often been the only place to gather and chat with friends. In many small mountain towns, soaking in the bath is the highlight of the working day. Here bathers relax together, men and women often in the same tubs, getting themselves fit and happy for the next few days or weeks of toil.

While Tōhoku may be the place to go to for authentic hot-spring experiences, remember that many of the baths mentioned on the following pages are remote, basic, and largely the haunts of local people. Sometimes they're just natural pools with nothing between you, the water, and the clear blue sky. So if mixed bathing, cooking for yourself by lamplight, or walking several kilometers to the inn is not what you want, read and choose carefully. There are, of course, many hot-spring towns in Tōhoku with all the home-style comforts laid on. But it would be giving up a lot to forgo visiting the smaller ones, for these are the places you'll remember. In the same way that the hot springs of Tōhoku will strike you as being very memorable, so will the natural splendors of its landscape. The following examples of visual beauty are well-known ones and can only serve as a brief introduction to Tōhoku's impressive offerings. Many of them lie hidden in remote locations.

Matsushima: This bay of rocky islets with pine trees growing out of them at pleasing angles is near Sendai in Miyagi Prefecture, and is a fitting place to begin. Together with Amanohashidate on the Sea of Japan and Miyajima near Hiroshima, Matsushima is considered one of Japan's three great beauty spots and has been celebrated over the centuries in song and verse as well as reproduced in miniature in Japanese gardens. From various vantage points around its edge you are invited to view the scroll-like scenery and to compose your own poetry. You can also visit several temples, shrines, and bridges that span the still water.

Morioka: This city, capital of Iwate Prefecture, is a mixture of old and new. An old castle town, it retains the narrow streets and many of the crafts its feudal residents practiced. Here, for example, you'll see a variety of intricate ironwork, such as the traditional tea kettle (*nanbu tetsubin*) and the wind bells now made for tourists. Exquisite reminders of what went into making kimono for the samurai are the mats, clothing, *noren*, and other textile objects made by Ono Saburō using dyeing and patterning processes from three hundred years ago. You can actually see this work being carried out, or if you're just window-shopping there are several museums and display rooms with exhibits. While you're at the Iwate Prefectural Museum visit its *magariya*, or L-shaped house, a typical Iwate dwelling still seen in these parts. The farmer and his family occupy the longer section and the animals the shorter section when it is too cold for either to go outside in winter. The houses are usually rambling structures with huge, thatched roofs, and many of the tales of this area exploit their floor plans by telling exactly where the spirits of the dead appear or into which room the wicked fox comes. There is even one small room where blind musicians wait before performing, called the blind room.

Before leaving Morioka, you might like to try *wanko soba*. Morioka eaters go for downing as many bowls of these thin noodles as they can in the shortest time possible. No biting the noodle—there's no time for it—just swallow! The average is 30 portions, the record around 200!

Tōno Basin: Southeast of Morioka in Iwate Prefecture, the Tōno Basin is where you'll see the above-mentioned *magariya* set in quiet fields next to creaking wooden water wheels. It's an area where you can lose yourself and satisfy all your romantic cravings for what you always imagined the Japanese countryside to be. Don't wander around after dark, though, since all manner of strange creatures live here. You might come across a *kappa*, for example. These red or green monsters with webbed feet and hands live in the pools of Tōhoku, especially those around Tōno. They like to drag people in, and to impregnate women with their none-too-pretty offspring. About ten years ago, in fact, a woman from this region killed her baby because "it was a *kappa*." If one approaches you, bow low, and its bow in reply will send the water pouring out of its dented head, and since it's a water creature it'll have to leave you and jump back into its pool! To find out more and truly frighten yourself, read *The Legends of Tōno* by Yanagida Kunio. Also in the Tōno Basin, at Atago Shrine, you can see some of the 380 Buddhist images carved by a priest in the 1780s to appease the souls of those who died in a terrible famine that swept through the region. If you listen carefully, they say, you can hear the distressed souls talking to each other.

The Rikuchū Coast: This is a 200-kilometer stretch of excellent seascapes along the eastern edge of Iwate Prefecture. Most people make for its midway point, Jōdogahama ("Paradise Beach"), with its white sand, well-carved cliffs, rock islets, and seaweed hung out to dry in the sun, all of which can be taken in from a boat or a stroll on the beach. Goishigahama, 100 kilometers south of Jōdogahama, is so called because of its smooth, black pebbles (*ishi*) resembling those used for playing go (*go*), a board game of strategy like checkers that was favored by a daimyo of the Daté family who lived near here. Besides a wealth of delicacies for the eye, the Rikuchū coast offers food—lots of shellfish cooked at stalls on the beach or served more decorously in the restaurants that overlook the beach.

A description of the attractions of Tōhoku would not be complete without a word on its alluring women, especially the Akita *bijin* (beauty). She is said to be one of the most beautiful women in Japan. Her skin is smoother, whiter, and finer, her nose tilts more bewitchingly, and her eyes are bigger. Why she is made so, no one knows, although she has strong competition from her sisters in Niigata, Kanazawa, Kyōto, Tottori, and Yamaguchi—all on the same side of Japan and all renowned for their beauties. Is it the wind from the sea? If you go to one of these areas will the beauty rub off? Observe the Akita women carefully as you travel about Tōhoku, and your sojourn in the back country could mean not only a body revitalized by thermal water, and a mind filled with folklore, but also an insight into the beauty secrets of Japanese women.

123 Higashiyama

LOCATION: This hot spring is in the suburbs of the city Aizu-Wakamatsu in northwestern Fukushima Prefecture. It is accessible from Aizu-Wakamatsu Station on the Banetsusai Line, and from other directions by private lines. From Aizu-Wakamatsu Station the bus to the spring takes 20 minutes.

THE WATERS: The origins of Higashiyama are controversial; some say the monk Gyōki discovered it while he was chasing a three-legged bird, others say he followed a five-hued cloud to its source. Today Higashiyama is a resort spring with its fair share of deluxe high-rises as well as traditional accommodations. At one time there were as many as ten springs in Higashiyama with ryokan bearing their names clustered around them. Some have disappeared, but the hot-spring town atmosphere still remains. This is partly due to the reputation of its geisha (*geiko*), who came here in the latter half of the Meiji era when Higashiyama was patronized by the rich and well-heeled—the only ones who could afford to have geisha attend their dinner tables. Still today the geisha here are highly skilled musicians, dancers, and singers, much in demand by those who yearn for past graces. As you walk along the river you will hear the shamisen in the distance—that may be as close as you can afford. The water contains sodium chloride and calcium sulphate, good for skin irritations, rheumatism, neuralgia, women's problems, and winter colds.

AROUND AND ABOUT: Aizu-Wakamatsu has a lot going for it. An old castle town, it has a reconstructed castle, Tsuru, originally built in 1384 as the headquarters of the Aizu clan; a rebuilt samurai manor, the Buke Yashiki; an old but still thriving saké industry; and many other traditional arts and crafts centers where paper, pottery, and cloth are made. At the Aizu clan headquarters you can see armor, scrolls, and prints and enjoy a view of the city. Buke Yashiki is a rambling complex of samurai living quarters complete with mannequins dressed in the garb of the day. For saké lovers, a museum in Aizu-Wakamatsu explains the brewing process. Before you leave Aizu, you should down a drop along with a charcoal-grilled carp (*koi*). To fill you up you'll need some *wappa*—rice topped with mountain greens, mushrooms, or *yamadori* (a mountain pheasant). ■ OYAKUEN HERB GARDEN: The bus from Aizu-Wakamatsu Station to Higashiyama passes this garden (the stop is Oyakuen Iriguchi). Planted by the Matsudaira family, it has over three hundred varieties of herbs growing in it, which are still used to make herbal remedies. It is quite unlike a traditional Japanese garden, and its walkways provide quiet, strolling venues where you can mull over Aizu-Wakamatsu's past.

ACCOMMODATIONS: Mukaidaki is a first-rate traditional ryokan, but it has a porcelain bath with graceful nude carvings of women on one side. For a less exotic tub try the ryokan Arimaya with its rock bath.

FESTIVALS: A huge Bon Festival with folk dancing begins on August 13 and lasts a week. On September 23 you can see the Byakkotai Parade, which is a procession of young men dressed in battle garb—headband, sleeves tied up with a sash, baggy pants, and swords.

124 Yunokami

LOCATION: This hot spring is west of Lake Inawashiro, Fukushima Prefecture. Take the Aizu Line from Aizu-Wakamatsu Station to Yunokami Station and walk 10 minutes. From Aizu-Wakamatsu Station there is a bus that takes about an hour.

THE WATERS: Yunokami is a medium-size Tōhoku hot spring. There are about seventeen ryokan in all and one open-air bathing pool in the river that is free, open to the public, and communal. During the Edo period this was a major stop on the Aizu Nishi Kaidō, the main route to Edo. At that time there were many inns and private houses; some of them have been preserved, and their steep thatched roofs and squeaky sliding doors and shutters re-create that era well. It is unusual to see so many old-style buildings in one place nowadays. The ryokan sit among the foliage along the riverbank, some all but covered by tall, floppy trees or obscured by rocky outcrops in the Ōkawa River. Autumn is particularly scenic around here, and from the river's bathing pool you can gaze up at slopes of red and gold or enjoy their wavering reflections in the water around you. The water, alkaline simple thermal, is good for stress; so is the fishing you can engage in from the tub. Other maladies treated are rheumatism and neuralgia.

AROUND AND ABOUT: When the fish aren't biting, you can go off to the post town, now a folk village called Ōuchijuku, which houses hundreds of bits and pieces from daily life in the Japan of olden days and displays the development of this Oku Aizu area. Cutting, digging, cooking, and farming tools and utensils are all arranged to acquaint you with life in the back country. The folk village is 20 minutes by taxi from Yunokami Station. You can also visit Tōnohetsuri, a natural rock formation 10 minutes by taxi from Yunokami. Tōnohetsuri looks like a continuous indentation carved out of the rocky riverbank above and parallel to the water.

ACCOMMODATIONS: The ryokan Kasuikan is an old wooden structure near the river. Another ryokan, Tōsenkaku, overlooks the gorge and a suspension bridge across the water. Its food is good, its views superb.

FOOD: Fish—fresh from the river—is what it's all about here. You'll be served salted, grilled carp, trout, and other catches depending on the season. If you like fishing you are encouraged to catch your own and barbeque them on the riverbank. Don't be surprised by the crowds drawn to the site by your success and the aroma wafting over the water.

125 Shirabu

LOCATION: Shirabu is a little south of Yonezawa City in southeastern Yamagata Prefecture. Take the Ōu Main Line to Yonezawa Station and then the bus to Shirabu Yumoto. Get off one stop before the terminal at Shirabu Onsen. The bus ride takes 50 minutes.

THE WATERS: Seven hundred years ago this hot spring was just an open-air pool in the wilds. About four hundred years ago three inns were put up. The remains of these three inns still stand, along with about ten more built to cope with the area's new prosperity. The water contains hydrogen sulphide and calcium sulphate, and you'll smell it from the bus as you approach. It will fix just about any ailment, although stomach complaints are recommended targets for those imbibing.

AROUND AND ABOUT: Surrounded by green, red, or white as the seasons pass, and with brown thatching and clear blue skies for contrast, Shirabu is a relaxing, rustic mountain hideaway. Its location on the Ōtaru River in a valley, near Mount Azuma and north of Mount Bandai, is one of the most scenic parts of Yamagata Prefecture. A ropeway nearby will take you up the western side of the Azuma Range. Those queasy about swaying cable cars ascending volcanic slopes may prefer the tropical-plant garden at Shirabu that uses the thermal waters to grow bananas, pineapples, and other exotic fruits and flowers. ■ YONEZAWA: Besides beef, textiles, and carved wooden hawks, Yonezawa City is famous for the Uesugi family, who took up their rule here from the seventeenth century. The first lord was Kenshin, a great warrior renowned for his battles against the equally illustrious Takeda Shingen in the sixteenth century. The Uesugi castle is now part of Matsugasaki Park, where there is a museum, the Uesugi Keishōden, that displays materials of the Uesugi era, especially anything remotely connected with Kenshin. Or take a stroll through the attractive garden in the grounds of Risen Temple.

Afterward, enjoy some Yonezawa beef done any way you fancy, from sashimi (raw) to grilled with special sauces. Such a treat will lighten your day, and your wallet—but it's worth it.

ACCOMMODATIONS: Nakaya, one of the three original ryokan, has a waterfall bath and the mood of olden times, with long, wooden corridors opening onto a courtyard garden. The other two old ryokan, Higashiya and Nishiya, share this mood, helped in part by their thatched roofs and rattling, wooden sliding doors (be sure to ask for the old building, *honkan*, if the past is what you want—the modern annexes make life too easy).

FOOD: Try the local fruit in season: cherries, apples, and the above-mentioned more exotic varieties. Before or after the meal choose one of the specially designed sweet cakes. Carp is also good, especially in autumn.

126 Atsumi

LOCATION: This hot spring is on the Sea of Japan coast in southwestern Yamagata Prefecture. Take the Uetsu Main Line to Atsumi Onsen Station and then a bus for 7 minutes to the ryokan area.

THE WATERS: Atsumi is the most popular seaside hot spring in Yamagata Prefecture. Situated on the banks of the Atsumi River with Mount Atsumi to one side, it is in a very scenic location, and of course the sea is within walking distance. Two main theories explain its discovery. One credits a dream of the great Buddhist priest Kōbō Daishi in the ninth century in which he was led to the source by a child. The other claims that a woodcutter saw a crane dipping in a pond and discovered it was really hot water the bird was washing its feet in. It is known, however, that Atsumi was operated as a hot-spring town by Niigata's Shōnai clan in the Edo period. The water here is famous for the way its color changes with the weather. It contains hydrogen sulphide, calcium sulphate, and sodium chloride and is particularly good for skin problems, from minor blemishes to hives, burns, and cuts. If you drink it, it will get your bowels moving. There are two public baths, conveniently named Number One and Number Two.

AROUND AND ABOUT: Besides the sea and fish, there are other natural delights here: avenues of cherry blossoms in April, rose gardens abloom in June, and gentle slopes for skiing in winter. Of special interest are the morning fairs, held from April through November, where local people sell fresh and dried fish, seaweed, vegetables, pickles, *mochi* (pounded rice), and other foodstuffs locally caught, grown, or made at home. Many visitors choose their dinner ingredients at these fairs and have them cooked at their ryokan. Kumano Shrine, just near the fair, has broad steps leading up to its buildings, which are somber and simple, stone and wood, and overgrown in places with weeds. From the top you can look out over the town. The shrine houses a monument to Yosano Akiko, a well-known Meiji poet and essayist.

ACCOMMODATIONS: Tachibanaya is three hundred years old and has a Japanese garden and good bathing facilities. It also has a separate, cottage-like building, where you may stay if you reserve it. It is more expensive than similar rooms in the main building, but it is private and in an attractive setting. Atsumi Grand Hotel cooks fish at your table and serves them with special sauces. It has a Panorama Bath and a Roman Bath.

127 Tendō

LOCATION: Tendō is a little north of Yamagata City, Yamagata Prefecture, along the Ōu Main Line. The ryokan are short walks from Tendō Station.
THE WATERS: Tendō was a castle town ruled by the lord of the Tendō clan in the Edo period. It did not become the thriving resort it is today until local businessmen stumbled upon the idea of combining its cottage industry, making *shōgi* pieces, with making bathtubs. *Shōgi* is a game like chess and Tendō developed into a *shōgi* resort, a place where men, but not women, could play the game in the tub on floating boards. There was even an inn built with windows, tubs, and rice crackers in *shōgi* designs. These days a game is held in spring using young men and young women as the "pieces," who are moved about the oversized board by local government officials and other VIPs. This is all part of the Shōgi Festival—and what began as a means to tide impoverished samurai over until payday is now Tendō's *raison d'être*. The water contains calcium sulphate and sodium sulphate, and treats rheumatism, cuts, and constipation—the latter no doubt the result of long periods spent sitting at the gaming table.
AROUND AND ABOUT: Near Tendō Hot Spring there is a kurhaus, Goten, which would be an enjoyable extension to your bathing experiences here. It is 15 minutes by bus from Tateoka Station on the Ōu Main Line, which is a 20-minute train ride from Tendō Station. This sports and bathing complex was the first of its kind to be built in Japan, and has excellent facilities. For a few hundred yen you can exercise and treat your body to a variety of hot thermal baths—cascade, bubble, steam, and the like—all in the same place. Tendō is also 20 minutes by bus from Yamadera, a series of temple buildings spread over the slopes of Mount Hōju. This beautiful mountain has attracted pilgrims for more than a thousand years. A winding path of chipped stone steps climbs to the summit, passing small temple storehouses, shrines, and monuments. Bashō, the itinerant seventeenth-century haiku poet, came here, and in one of his most famous poems he wrote about how the song of the cicadas on this mountain seemed to penetrate the very rock faces, in stark contrast with the peacefulness all about them.
ACCOMMODATIONS: Tōshōkan has male and female *shōgi*-shaped tubs and tubside boards for playing the game. Futamikan is less exotic; a traditional inn, it has regular-shaped tubs.

128 Zaō

LOCATION: Zaō is east of Yamagata City, the capital of Yamagata Prefecture, near the border with Miyagi Prefecture. Get off at Yamagata Station on the Ōu Main Line. It's a 50-minute bus ride from there to the spring.

THE WATERS: Zaō, a National Health Resort, comes close to being the perfect winter vacation spot. Not only does it have some of the best skiing in Japan but it has abundant, mineral-rich water to soak away the exhaustion of a day on the slopes. Just be sure to avoid getting the thermal water in your eyes since it's very acidic and likely to cause smarting. The water is, however, good for your skin, your stomach, après-ski bruises and cuts, high blood pressure, and nervous tension. There are three public baths: Kami-no-yu, Shimo-no-yu, and Kawara-no-yu.

AROUND AND ABOUT: Although Zaō is a popular ski resort, it is mercifully free of ski-bunny boutiques. Instead its steep, winding streets, smelling of sulphur and lined with rickety ryokan, make you very aware that this is a place where tradition lives on. Skiers, of course, have the best of both worlds. Sightseers in winter can admire the *juhyo*, strange snow sculptures that are in fact trees so completely covered in hoarfrost and dripping ice that they resemble weird monster men. They are formed by swirling monsoons from the Japan Sea that became fierce snowstorms as they rise against the Asahi Mountains. Don't view them at night when moon shadows seem to bring them to life. In summer, Zaō is cool and beautiful. Unfortunately many other people have discovered the delights of ski spots in the off-season, so you and the fields of dahlias won't be alone, but at least you can walk about without dodging stray skiers. At Lake Sakazuki, also close by, you can rent a rowboat and let your arms do the walking.

ACCOMMODATIONS: The deluxe Ōhira Hotel has an open-air bath. Matsu-kaneya is built in the older Momoyama style and has fine wooden screens with depictions of Kabuki actors. A tub of Japanese cypress takes pride of place here.

129 Ginzan

LOCATION: Ginzan is in northeastern Yamagata Prefecture. Take the Ōu Main Line to Ōishida Station and then a bus for 10 minutes to Obanazawa. From there, the bus to Ginzan takes 40 minutes.

THE WATERS: Ginzan was a thriving silver mining center in the fifteenth century, and then the veins ran out. The search for more silver uncovered something else, not as profitable but some consolation nevertheless. It was thermal water, and Ginzan became a medicinal spring (*tōjiba*). Its location in a valley on the Ginzan River, its hot water, and its cold winter have in succeeding years made it very popular, despite the loss of its ore. The water contains sodium chloride and sulphur and is good for sluggish blood, diabetes, and skin irritations. Of the three public baths, two are reserved for the use of local patrons. The third, Ginzan Onsenkan, is open to the public.

AROUND AND ABOUT: In winter you can ski and in summer you can walk. The ski slopes are open from December through March. Walking courses starting from the hot-spring area take you to Shirogane Waterfall or to Senshinkyō Gorge. Ginzan is in a part of Yamagata that is very picturesque, especially in summer. Three- or four-story ryokan line the river and simple bridges connect the banks, making for a quaint relaxing atmosphere. You'll feel as if you've just traveled back in time to the Meiji era, particularly when you walk near the old ryokan at night and look up at the windows where dim light barely illuminates the paper screens behind the glass. Another aspect of the past is the craftsmen carving *kokeshi* dolls, a trade handed down from father to son. The wooden lady wears a painted "dress" of yellow and green lotus flowers, and her smile is demure. You can browse among the many dolls on display and perhaps choose one to take home. There are also several temples nearby—the goddess Kannon at Ginzan is the twenty-fourth along the route of a pilgrimage of thirty-three made in this region—which only the very faithful and the very fit should attempt.

ACCOMMODATIONS: The traditional Notoya Ryokan has oval tubs and a viewing lounge on the top (fourth) floor for taking in the sights. The ryokan Fujiya is old and, like the Notoya, traditional in decor.

130 Imagami

LOCATION: Imagami is southwest of Shinjō City in northern Yamagata Prefecture. Take the Rikuusai Line to Furukuchi Station. (The Rikuusai Line meets the Ōu Main Line at Shinjō.) At Furukuchi take the bus to Tsunogawa, the terminal—a 25-minute ride—and then walk for about 3 hours (10 kilometers) to get to the spring. Imagami is accessible only from June to October.

THE WATERS: Situated at the foot of Mount Imakuma, Imagami is a unique hot spring. Besides the walk to get to it, you are required to do other things that only serious bathers would consider acceptable. You must wear a white kimono-like garment in the bath, you mustn't eat meat or drink wine, and you are expected to talk quietly and about serious topics while in the tub. This is because Imagami is a religious spring where people come to chant sutras in the bath and to place offerings at the small altar just outside the tub. Imagami has its own power plant and water supply. Everything is quite simple and is centered on the kind of religious bathing experience that many ailing people have claimed works miracles. The water, hydrogen carbonate with sodium chloride, is especially good for rheumatism and gout. People who arrived with canes have been able to walk away unaided after bathing here. The water is only 36° C (97° F)—not as hot as it usually is at Japanese hot springs—and some people sit in the bath for many hours praying and then chanting with the other bathers. Note that cameras are not allowed in the bathroom.

AROUND AND ABOUT: The proprietor of the single lodge here at first wanted to make this a resort spring, for the location is very scenic (he planned a bus service, too). But after meeting the people patronizing Imagami, he changed his mind and left the area as the rustic, out-of-the-way, spiritual place it is. The candlelight shadows and the murmuring bathers may puzzle you, but if you are interested in seeing a religious aspect of hot springs, Imagami offers a very authentic experience. Imagami is not for those wanting any luxury, wild night life, or even mild night life. It's a plain and serious hot spring that offers great benefits to those who believe in its powers.

ACCOMMODATIONS: The solitary inn, Imagami Onsen, is always able to accommodate visitors, although in summer more young people are coming now to try the water. It's not likely to be booked up, but a telephone call beforehand might save you a long, unnecessary hike.

YAMABUSHI: The religious atmosphere of Imagami is further enhanced by the knowledge that *yamabushi* lived near here in the past. These mountain dwellers were members of a religious sect dedicated to purification through rigorous living. They lived frugally, sleeping outdoors in the bitter cold and meditating. When they came down from their abode in the Yamagata Mountains near Dewa Sanzan Shrine, they were immediately recognizable by their baggy pants, monk's coat, "one tooth" mountain-climbing geta, cane, and conch shell, and by their aura, a product of their spiritualism as much as of the legends that grew up around their rugged way of life. No one is sure how many mountain men remain—it would take an extraordinary young man to live such a life today.

131 Naruko

LOCATION: Naruko is in northwestern Miyagi Prefecture. Take the Rikuutō Line to Narugo Station. The hot-spring area is a few minutes' walk away.

THE WATERS: When a volcano erupted here in the ninth century, whole forests slid down the mountainsides and hot springs burst forth out of the rubble. This was the start of Naruko—*naru* can mean to create a mighty din (and it also can mean the squeaking noise of a Naruko *kokeshi* doll). Knowing they were dealing with powerful forces, the people who developed the waters also built a shrine to the gods of the springs. Today Narugo is a popular medicinal hot spring with research facilities, although this aspect of the town has been somewhat overshadowed by the limbless, squeaking, wooden dolls (*kokeshi*) that are made here. The *kokeshi* trade has brought to Naruko deluxe accommodations, countless souvenir shops, and many hardworking craftsmen. These all make Naruko an interesting place, but the excellent thermal waters shouldn't be overlooked; they're there under the wood shavings somewhere. There is a public bath, Taki-no-yu, and countless fun and serious baths line the wide, stony Arao River. Naruko is easily the best-known hot spring in Tōhoku. The water is simple thermal, sulphur, or sodium chloride depending on the tub. All the waters have a unique skin-softening effect. When you're in it the water seems slimy, but once out your skin feels smooth and tight and clean. Nervous tension, indigestion, and stiff joints are just some of the maladies treated at Naruko.

AROUND AND ABOUT: Naruko is a popular tourist stop, particularly in autumn when it's at its best with radiant foliage and shrine and *kokeshi* festivals. Nevertheless, crowded or not, it is a Tōhoku hot spring you shouldn't miss. The hot-spring area is in the Naruko Gorge—a woody, picturesque valley, perfect for between-bath strolling. The rocks are odd shapes and sizes, and make good conversation starters. At one time the nearby town Iwadeyama was the headquarters of the Daté clan, powerful rulers of this northern region during the Edo period. A relic of that era is an old checkpoint gate, the Shitomae no Seki-ato, through which travelers in the area or en route to Edo had to pass. Next to the gate is an engraved stone, one of many in Tōhoku inscribed with a haiku by Bashō, the poet of the back country. When you return to Naruko you'll be curious to see, and maybe buy, a *kokeshi* doll. A good place to get an idea of the many varieties of *kokeshi* is in the Nihon Kokeshikan, where thousands are arranged in a fascinating display. There you will see why Naruko is the *kokeshi* capital of Japan.

ACCOMMODATIONS: Narugo View Hotel, with both Western- and Japanese-style accommodations, overlooks the river, and one of its baths features a slippery dip (slide) entrance. A more traditional stopping place is Yusaya Ryokan, where food and banquet facilities are the main drawing card.

FESTIVALS: September is bonanza month—the shrine festival and the All-Japan Kokeshi Festival coincide; the shrine festival is on September 7, the Kokeshi Festival runs from September 7 to 9. During the shrine festival special rituals mourn the passing of *kokeshi* abandoned, broken, and discarded during the preceding year. Newly carved *kokeshi* are also presented to the shrine gods. It's a crowded but exciting few days.

KOKESHI: These cylindrical dolls made from a solid piece of wood originated in Tōhoku, although imitations are now found everywhere in Japan. To be considered authentic, a *kokeshi* must be modeled after one of the recognized *kokeshi* styles registered with one of the Tōhoku *kokeshi* guilds. There are ten such guilds, and Naruko is one of them. The origin of *kokeshi* is a mystery. Since guilds are always in hot-spring towns, perhaps *kokeshi* were the original souvenirs taken home by visitors to the baths. Another theory is that *kokeshi* were fashioned by fathers for their children during the long Tōhoku winters.

Yet another says they were originally fertility symbols, and still another says they were made to replace daughters sold into prostitution when times were very hard, as they often were up here. No one knows for sure. The Naruko *kokeshi* is joined at the neck, and if you twist the head, she squeaks. Her dress consists of painted red and green chrysanthemums, and her face wears a pert expression.

132 Sakunami

LOCATION: Sakunami is on the Hirose River, west of Sendai, the capital of Miyagi Prefecture. Sendai is on the Tōhoku Main Line (and a Tōhoku Shinkansen stop), and Sakunami Onsen is a 35-minute bus ride from there. You can take the Senzan Line from Sendai Station to Sakunami Station and then a bus (20 minutes) to the spring.

THE WATERS: The celebrated monk Gyōki came this way in the eighth century and found and blessed a spring coming out of the riverbank. Even in those early times people were bathing in the rock pool Iwatsubo-no-yu, which is today part of the Iwamatsu Ryokan complex and one of Sakunami's main attractions. The bath is made of wood and separated from the river by rocks and cement set to keep it in place. It is partially covered, but there's still a fine view of the stream. Bathing is communal, but the old wooden stairs to the pool will squeak whenever others approach the pool, and you can then discreetly move to a shaded nook if you want to remain hidden. The water is simple thermal, good for rheumatism, skin irritations, women's problems, and neuralgia. The sheer beauty of the location, with its great old trees settled into an ancient rock wall, also guarantees a spiritual lift and a renewed confidence in your fellow man. Several other outdoor bathing pools in Sakunami offer a change of bathroom decor.

AROUND AND ABOUT: Sakunami is too close to Sendai to have remained exactly as Gyōki found it, and now it's full of concrete, charter buses, and souvenirs, the most famous souvenir being a *kokeshi*—a wooden doll with a big head, slender body, no arms or legs, and a dress patterned in twirling chrysanthemums. You will have noticed a giant *kokeshi* standing by the roadside welcoming you into town, and you can see the workshops where they are made as you stroll about the streets after your bath. Another place in Sakunami offering succor to the troubled—albeit of a different kind from the baths—is Saihōji Temple, home of the god of matchmaking and safe childbirth. ■ SENDAI: This city of modern, cosmopolitan people and places also boasts a very authentic historical section. From the beginning of the seventeenth century until the Meiji Restoration 250 years later, the Daté clan presided over the Sendai area from their castle, Aobajō. Museums, monuments, and gardens have now taken the place of the castle, which was all but destroyed in the Meiji era and later bombed in World War II.

Other historical sites in Sendai include the Daté Mausoleum, or Zuihō-den, and a monument to Hasekura Tsunenaga, one of the first Japanese to sail to Europe. Sent in 1613 by Daté Masamune to Rome to see the Pope, Hasekura returned seven years later only to find that in his absence Catholicism had been strictly outlawed by the shogun. Another memorial is to Lu Hsün, a Chinese who studied medicine in Sendai at the turn of this century. Such is the flavor of Sendai: cultural, outward-looking, and scholastic, all in an easygoing, pleasant environment. Much of the city was destroyed in World War II, and afterward rows and rows of trees were planted to bring life back to its streets. Today, Sendai is justifiably called the "city in a forest" and offers the modern tourist numerous attractions, not the least of which are its several museums, art galleries, and crafts shops. Be on the lookout especially for Sendai's famous heavy chests (*keyaki tansu*) made of zelkova wood and with black iron fittings. After your exhilarating days in the physical splendor of Tōhoku's back country, Sendai offers just the right mix of rural tradition and modern culture to ease your transition back into city environments.

ACCOMMODATIONS: Iwamatsu Ryokan, whose famous tub is mentioned above, is 180 years old and has a modern annex for those who want noise-proof rooms at night. The plush Hotel Ichinobō has chandeliers in the foyer and good bathing facilities. The ryokan Senzansō has a thermal pool big enough to stretch out and exercise in before breakfast . . . or after. Food in all these places consists of beautiful arrangements of mountain vegetables, river fish, and small cakes.

FESTIVALS: One of the most dazzling and energetic festivals in all Japan takes place in Sendai on August 6 to 8. Day and night there is dancing, processions, and street revelry. Shops and street vendors sell anything and everything. All around are bright streamers of red, green, yellow, and purple, made up of thousands of handmade cranes, stars, and other shapes that shimmer in the breeze as they flutter down from towering arrangements of paper flowers. These rainbow streamers represent the threads woven by the star Vega who meets her lover, the star Altair, once a year at festival time, called Tanabata. Sendai's Tanabata Festival is spectacular, but the tale of Vega and Altair is similarly celebrated throughout Japan in summertime. The original story is Chinese and tells how the god of heaven banished the weaver and her man, the herdsman, to opposite sides of the River of Heaven (that is, the Milky Way) because they were spending too much time on love and not enough on the loom or the lamb. The two are permitted but one meeting a year when these two stars cross in the sky—the original star-crossed lovers! Another Sendai festival, at Ōsaki Hachiman Shrine on January 14, features New Year decorations being burned in a huge bonfire. A building constructed 380 years ago by the Daté family still stands in this shrine complex.

133 Kamasaki

LOCATION: Kamasaki is west of the city Shiroishi, on the edge of the Zaō Mountain Range in Miyagi Prefecture. The bus to the spring takes 30 minutes from Shiroishi Zaō Station on the Tohoku Shinkansen (bullet train), or 20 minutes from Shiroishi Station on the Tōhoku Main Line.

THE WATERS: Kamasaki is for serious bathing and consists of a group of four ryokan huddled together in a basin plateau surrounded by mountains. It has a long history as a medicinal hot spring, and although it attracts its share of summer wanderers and winter skiers, the place is primarily a center of healing. You will find local people in its waters, as well as out-of-towners seeking cures for such things as whiplash and broken bones. The efficacy of Kamasaki is legend, and the premises of the ryokan Ichijō are awash with neck and leg braces that have been discarded there in the hope of quick recuperation. The water is sodium chloride with sulphur, and it also helps heal wounds, cuts, bruises, indigestion, and anemia.

AROUND AND ABOUT: There's not a lot to tempt you from the bath, but that's as it should be in such a hot spring. Much thought has been put into the tubs to add aesthetic enjoyment to your physical well-being as you soak. For example, the renovated hotel Kimuraya has a moon-viewing pool on its top floor, so there's no need to go staggering about in the nighttime snow looking for good gazing ground, and the communal bath inside is fitted out to resemble a *tengu*'s house! A *tengu* is a small, red-faced, fiercely frowning demon who strikes fear into your heart until you see his ludicrous long and phallic nose. His house—the bath room—has a tub with a pebbled bottom and walls made up variously of trees, stones, and a display of *tengu* masks. The cavelike atmosphere might well appeal to a *tengu*. The ryokan Ichijō's bath—the oldest at Kamasaki and once used by all the other ryokan when the hot spring was getting on its feet—boasts garden views and an illustrious history that saw the local feudal lords relaxing in its tubs. If you tire of the tub and your skin starts to pucker, visit the park with a parasol-shaped pine tree and a path that in 20 minutes will lead you to the Yajirō *kokeshi* area, where you can browse around watching the craftsmen at work. Nearby Shiroishi is known for its *sōmen* (wheat noodles), made without oil and easy to digest, that were developed by a kind child who wanted to help his father, who had a delicate stomach, be able to enjoy his favorite food. Obara Hot Spring is also close by and is situated in a beautiful gorge on the Shiroishi River. To get there take a bus from Shiroishi Station—a 20-minute ride.

ACCOMMODATIONS: Ichijō Ryokan has a 24-hour communal bath and serves shellfish delicacies. Mogamiya Ryokan is a traditional two-story wooden inn where saké is served in bamboo cups to make you feel like a feudal lord of old.

134 Aone

LOCATION: Aone lies east of Mount Zaō and southwest of Sendai City, Miyagi Prefecture. Get off at Shiroishi Zaō Station on the Tōhoku Shinkansen (bullet train) or at Ōgawara Station on the Tōhoku Main Line. Then take a bus for about an hour to reach the spring.

THE WATERS: Situated on a plateau in the mountains, Aone was discovered in 1528 by a landowner in the area, who was then granted rights to its operation as a hot spring by the region's powerful ruler, Daté Masamune. Masamune himself was very fond of Aone and built a wee weekend cottage here to use when he came to bathe and plot strategies. Aone's simple thermal waters are good for your skin, aching limbs, and jangled nerves. There is a public bath in addition to the different kinds offered by the ten or so ryokan. An especially fine one is the tub at Yumoto Fubōkaku, which took thirty workmen over two years to build and features intricately inlaid stones. Such painstaking rock work may be responsible for the bath's alleged ability to increase the intelligence of those who dabble in its waters. Don't be nervous, though—no one but you will know whether it works or not.

AROUND AND ABOUT: There's not a lot to do other than bathe, browse, and eat. Between baths you can visit Daté Masamune's wee cottage that has been faithfully reconstructed on the grounds of the ryokan Yumoto Fubō-kaku. Two stories high and built of wood in the traditional Momoyama style, it contains a most impressive display of armor, artwork, and domestic utensils actually used by the Daté when they stayed at Aone. If you want to get farther out and about, tell the ryokan master how much time and stamina you have and he will direct you to one of the recommended hiking courses and give you colorful maps of the area with recognizable landmarks duly noted. Be honest about your stamina—this is not Sunday strolling country. In winter many hot-spring guests spend the day on Zaō ski slopes.

ACCOMMODATIONS: Yumoto Fubōkaku is a first-rate ryokan. Seireikaku is also a traditional wooden inn with a rural atmosphere.

135 Getō

LOCATION: Getō is in southwestern Iwate Prefecture near Miyagi and Akita prefectures. Take the Tōhoku Main Line to Kitakami Station and then one of the three daily buses for the hour trip to Getō. The hot spring is closed from mid-November to mid-May.

THE WATERS: Originally known as Take-no-yu, this National Health Resort is a giant among medicinal springs, owing to its water's fabled ability to settle uneasy stomachs. The efficacy of the water, which is calcium sulphate, was first tested by some large white monkeys who were seen drinking it in 1335 by the monk Jikaku Daishi. Descendants of the Heike clan also claim the honor of its discovery, as do others. There are several open-air baths on the river's edge and a cave bath at Getō, and as at many Tōhoku hot springs they are communal—except for one open-air bath that is for women only. Elsewhere, if you want a bit of privacy, any ryokan will lend you a big towel to screen out the curious eyes of peeping Toms and the occasional white monkey. Getō lies in a deep gorge and is still patronized more for its cures than its water games. Doctors come here in summer to organize special bathing routines that typically include the waterfall bath, the bubbling bath, and the "pressure" bath where water is piped onto the patient in a broad, strong stream. A novel touch is the walking bath, a spacious, shallow pool made for thermal strolling. Long-legged bathers may find its effects stop at the ankle. Getō Onsenkan follows the German model of a kurhaus and offers exercise routines and various thermal baths for ¥300 a day. On Thursdays a doctor is in attendance. Accommodations are not available at the kurhaus. For further information, call (0197)64-6989.

AROUND AND ABOUT: Getō Gorge is attractive, cool even in summer, and full of trees alive with the tunes of nightingales, cuckoos, and other melodious birds. But besides a walk here, it might be better to spend time taking full advantage of the bathing facilities.

ACCOMMODATIONS: Kokuminshukusha Getō Sansō and Kankōsō are both inexpensive. In summer you can camp and use their tubs for a charge.

136 Sukawa

LOCATION: This hot spring is just inside Iwate Prefecture, near the point where Iwate, Akita, and Miyagi prefectures meet, north of Mount Kurikoma and west of Hiraizumi. The scenic bus ride to Sukawa from Ichinoseki Station on the Tōhoku Main Line takes 1½ hours. The bus doesn't run from November to sometime in April depending on weather conditions.

THE WATERS: Sukawa is very high up, unlike the many valley hot springs found in Tōhoku. The air is clear and dry, making Sukawa ideal both for those with respiratory illnesses and others who must live and breathe in Japan's less-than-savory industrial environments. The spring smells of sulphur but not strongly, and the water is so abundant that as much as a third of it is allowed to flow around the town, down the street, past the station, and into the Yujiri River. This makes for an extravagantly large bath that holds as many as a thousand people at the Sukawa Kōgen Onsen Hotel—you won't know what's swimming toward you from the other end until it's right up next to you . . . so beware of sharks and mermaids! The dressing rooms are segregated, but the doors out of them lead into the same pool. The name Sukawa, literally "Vinegar River," comes from the acidity of the water, which also contains acid-aluminum sulphate and hydrogen sulphide. The combination will heal just about anything: heart, circulatory, respiratory, gastroenteric, rheumatic, and nervous problems. There's also a special bath with a "rack" built over steaming holes in the ground where you can lie down and bask in the natural vapors—5 minutes of this strong treatment is plenty. These facilities are all part of the Sukawa Kōgen Onsen Hotel. You can also bathe at a public pool or a kokuminshukusha with hot-spring facilities.

AROUND AND ABOUT: On a clear day you can see the Pacific Ocean, way above and beyond the red rooftops and green pines. On an autumn day this region is at its best: a blaze of red, orange, and gold, with a nip in the air that drives you back to the tub. A car will take you the short distance to Hiraizumi City and to Genbikei and Geibikei Gorges (where you can rent a flat-bottomed boat in the tourist season). ■ CHŪSONJI: One of the most interesting temples in Japan, the Chūsonji complex includes a nine-hundred-year-old Golden Pavilion and a priceless trove of treasures from the Heian period. In the twelfth century, Fujiwara Kiyohira, who had prospered off local gold fields, determined to create an earthly paradise here where men could lead a peaceful and culturally rich life in accordance with Buddhist teachings. He began the construction of the temples Chūsonji and Mōtsūji, and launched Hiraizumi as the cultural city of northern Japan. Try to combine gazing at the temple's gold leaf and inlaid mother-of-pearl with one of its many events: on January 20, Heian dances performed in the Mōtsūji Temple precincts; on May 1 to 5, the Fujiwara Spring Festival; June 25 to July 15, the Iris Festival; and November 1 to 3, the Fujiwara Autumn Festival with Noh performances. The temple complex is in Hiraizumi, on the Tohoku Main Line.

ACCOMMODATIONS: Sukawa Kōgen Onsen Hotel, with its gigantic bath, one of the biggest in Tōhoku, allows you to order meal courses depending on your budget. The hotel also offers inexpensive lodgings that resemble a kokuminshukusha. However, it is only open from May to mid-October.

137 Ōsawa

LOCATION: Ōsawa, near Hanamaki City in the center of Iwate Prefecture, is part of the Hanamaki group of hot springs. Take the Tōhoku Main Line to Hanamaki Station; the bus from there takes 30 minutes. Or, take the Tohoku Shinkansen (bullet train) to Shin-Hanamaki Station; the bus from there takes 40 minutes.

THE WATERS: The main attraction here is a magnificent open-air bathing pool separated from the river by a higgledy-piggledy line of rocks. Whether under the stars or in blazing daylight this large pool with mossy green banks will tend your body with its simple thermal goodness. For hedonists it's perfect: natural, hazy, steamy, and hot. For the infirm it's good for rheumatism, neuralgia, and skin irritations.

AROUND AND ABOUT: There's nothing much here in the way of distraction, just river, ryokan, and mountains. The single ryokan has two sections, one being for those who want to cook for themselves. Its buildings are old, rickety, and simple, befitting the Ōsawa atmosphere—nothing too modern or automatic. The kitchen is where people gather to chat, cook, and swap vegetables while dreaming up healthy and exciting delicacies from the produce the local farmers' wives brought in to the market that morning. Both sections of the ryokan have huge indoor baths. If you can·bring yourself to stir from the ryokan, visit the poet-sculptor Takamura Kōtarō's cottage—25 minutes by bus from Hanamaki Station—where are stored some of his manuscripts, letters, and also some of his wife Chieko's paper collages.

ACCOMMODATIONS: There is only one ryokan, Sansuikaku, described above. Costs will depend on your kitchen skills as well as your pocketbook. If you are making your own food, note that apples and rice crackers are especially good around here.

138 Tōshichi

LOCATION: Tōshichi, south of Hachimantai Plateau in northwestern Iwate Prefecture, is a little over an hour by bus from Ōbuke Station along the Hanawa Line. Get off at Tōshichi Onsen (the bus comes from Morioka Station). The hot spring is closed from November through May.

THE WATERS: Tōshichi is said to have been discovered in 797 by the general Sakanoue Tamuramaro while he was out chasing robbers on his mission to subdue the "northern territories." Another story has it being discovered as late as the middle of this century by the owner of the nearby hot spring Yuze (141). Tōshichi, whatever its origin, is today a highly regarded health spring up in the mountains, serving both those on the mend as well as people looking for a quiet, scenic place to relax in, away from the cares of the workaday world. The water is described as "thick," meaning that it feels as if it could support you if you wanted to float—don't try, unless you want to swallow several mouthfuls of hydrogen sulphide water. This water—for soaking, not drinking—is good for skin problems, rheumatism, female disorders, and anemia. There is a steam bath and an open air bath at Matsukawa, two not-so-high mountains away. The idea is to combine 4 to 5 hours (one-way) hiking with serious bathing—recommended only for the hardy.

AROUND AND ABOUT: There's nothing extravagant about this hot spring or its surroundings. In winter it's covered with snow and skiers and in summer with masses of pine, Japanese hemlock, and other greenery, and, of course, the occasional climber. Most summer visitors come only to bathe, but the natural wonders of the Hachimantai Plateau are a good excuse to stay over and get some exploring in. Mount Iwate, Mount Mokko, and Hōrai Gorge—rocky with low bushes and steep ravines—are all close by.

ACCOMMODATIONS: The ryokan Saiunsō is a long building with high windows to keep out the snow and a steep roof to prevent snow from accumulating. It is typical of this area where winter comes with a vengeance. Here you can enjoy *horohoro nabe*, a stew containing the meat of the *horohorochō*, a bird that looks like a peacock and tastes like a chicken.

139 Inazumi

LOCATION: Inazumi is in the southeastern corner of Akita Prefecture, near the city of Yuzawa. It is a 40-minute bus ride from Yokobori Station, which is on the Ōu Main Line.

THE WATERS: Inazumi is a remote spring known for the abundance of its water, which is piped to other hot-spring towns in the area, and for its own bathing facilities, ranked among the best in Tōhoku. The lone ryokan here has several large baths, modern but of wooden construction and with superb views from the windows. The waters are good for aches, pains, stress, skin problems, and neuralgia, and offer a variety of bathing styles with superb views from the windows. One bath contains acid-aluminum sulphate and hydrogen sulphide. One bath is for women only, one is a cascade bath, and one is an all-season open-air bath (especially nice in the snow).

AROUND AND ABOUT: Inazumi is an ideal place to indulge in baths, food, and a bit of culture. If it's winter or anywhere thereabouts, you won't stir from the tub, but if it's spring or summer and you tire of the bath it might be fun to take a saké tour of Yuzawa, known for its excellent water and rice and its many brewers of Japan's national drink. Not all people like saké—or its fierce hangover that punishes the overindulgent. But it's a drink worth getting to know, and if you're going to suffer, why not do so in the fine castle town of Yuzawa with one of its authentic local brands: Ryōzeki, Ranman, Hakusan, or Senryō? Back in Inazumi you're once more in a small hamlet of red roofs, white walls, and green pines. In winter everything is shining white and dripping with icicles.

ACCOMMODATIONS: Inazumi Onsen, the only ryokan here, stocks your room refrigerator with free chilled thermal water in summer. The proprietor has a good collection of *kokeshi* dolls and of the squares of stiff cardboard called *shikishi*, written or painted on by well-known artists and calligraphers. These are all on display in the foyer, where you can while away cold evenings between your warm and soothing baths. There are also five cottages with tea ceremony facilities. The meals—trays of vegetable and fish stew, served with slightly sweetened boiled mountain greens, preserved vegetables, rice, and *miso* soup—and long luxuriant baths and some Yuzawa saké may make a stint here one of your most memorable escapades in Tōhoku, or even in Japan.

FESTIVALS: Yuzawa accentuates its old-time feeling during its festivals.

Painted lanterns are carried aloft on poles during the Tanabata Edōrō Festival on August 6 and 7. On August 24 a procession in Yazawa vividly re-creates the entourage of a feudal lord setting out on a journey to Edo. All daimyo were required to maintain a residence near the shogun's castle and spend time there every other year—it kept them out of mischief.

140 Doroyu

LOCATION: This hot spring is in southern Akita Prefecture, southeast of Yuzawa. Get off at Yuzawa Station on the Ōu Main Line and take a bus to the spring—a ride of 1 hours 20 minutes. Doroyu is closed in winter from November to sometime in April depending on the weather.

THE WATERS: There used to be three public baths here: the Waterfall Bath (Taki-no-yu), the Mountain Bath (Yama-no-yu), and the River Bath (Kawa-no-yu). They were known to few, and even now this area is remote and undisturbed. The baths have been handed over to three ryokan proprietors to look after, but visitors can still bathe in all three no matter which inn they are staying at. The sulphur water is a bit slimy and opaque but like all medicine, the worse it looks, the better it is for you. People treated here include those with respiratory ailments, stiff limbs, nervous disorders, and common colds. The waters are more effective if you can stay a few weeks; many people do, and use the cook-for-yourself facilities all the ryokan have. Long stays are typical at many Tōhoku hot springs, which attract the serious bathers. Local vendors bring in fresh vegetables and meat each day, set them out, and sell them to the guests. The busy kitchen provides a change of pace and conversation after a quiet day of restful bathing.

AROUND AND ABOUT: Hidden in a valley, too deep in snow to be reached for much of the year, Doroyu and its environs don't provide casual strolling venues. For those who prefer rugged treks anyway, there's the Mount Kiji region, which is most famous for its *kokeshi* with a pronounced nose, red and black plum-blossom petals down the front, and the appearance of a cape over small, gently sloping shoulders. The dolls are made today by only one man, and he is getting on in years; so don't delay if you want a *kokeshi* inscribed by Ogura-san.

ACCOMMODATIONS: Ogura Ryokan is a homely, small inn with cook-for-yourself facilities. If you don't fancy slaving over a hot stove, try ordering the inn's mushroom dishes; the variety of fungus served is amazing, healthy, and delicious to boot. For long-staying guests bent on cures, Hōmeikan is a good choice.

FESTIVALS: The Kamakura festival, held in Yokote City in Akita Prefecture in mid-February, is famous for its small igloos where children sit and eat cakes and sip sweet saké. Originally places where offerings were made to invoke the gods' blessings on the rice harvest, the igloos are now playgrounds for children, who in the harsh winter sit snugly inside near a brazier in front of a small altar, playing cards and eating and drinking and talking with the adults and tourists who come to look at their snow houses. Yokote is 25 minutes from Yuzawa Station on the Ōu Main Line, which makes it a convenient place to stop on your way to or from Doroyu.

141 Yuze

LOCATION: Yuze is south of Lake Towada, in northeastern Akita Prefecture. Take the Hanawa Line to Yuze Station, from where you can walk to the ryokan.

THE WATERS: Situated along the Yoneshiro River, Yuze is known for its deluxe facilities, and despite being on a much smaller scale than southern and central Honshū resorts its fine hotels and spacious baths do make it similar to a resort hot spring. There are two kinds of water here, simple thermal and sulphur. Both are good for skin problems, paralysis, and female disorders. Simple thermal is often recommended for neuralgia and rheumatism, while sulphur is good for stomach disorders, asthma, and anemia when imbibed. Most places offer both waters, so you can wander from tub to tub as your ailments dictate.

AROUND AND ABOUT: Near Yuze is the old castle town of Kemanai, with its narrow streets, gates with peaked roofs, and a huge Bon Festival from August 21 to 25. But probably the most interesting place in the vicinity is the site of the old Osarizawa mines. There you can walk 7 kilometers underground. In eery, reddish green light you will see lifelike moving wax models: Edo women in baggy pants and happi coats strike at the rock with picks, while others cart or sort ore in dark hovels fit only for moles. These gruesome depictions of the miner's life are not pleasant, but they are nevertheless impressive renditions of the era of gold and silver in days gone by.

ACCOMMODATIONS: Various accommodations and bathing facilities line the banks of the river. One, the Yuze Hotel, has wings on both banks connected by a covered walkway. This deluxe hotel also has a rooftop swimming pool, a restaurant-theater, and good tubs. Hime-no-yu Hotel is a modern building with a traditional Japanese garden and a huge, round tub. A quieter family place is Hotel Taki-no-yu, which has large tatami rooms.

FOOD: *Nabe* (stew), called *shottsuru*, made with *hatahata* fish and vegetables, is served at the ryokan and hotels. The apples (*kazuno ringo*) in the region are also well known. What do they taste like? Not unlike apples in most apple regions in Japan: sweet, hard, and juicy.

SOAP: The lusciously fragrant apple-and-honey soap produced in this region makes a useful gift to take home to your loved ones. It contains sinter, the mineral deposit frequently found near the mouths of hot springs—not a very appealing thought, but it makes for a wonderful creamy complexion.

142 Tamagawa

LOCATION: This hot spring is on the Tama River in Akita Prefecture on the northern part of Hachimantai Plateau, a national park. It is an hour ride by bus from Hachimantai Station on the Hanawa Line, which branches off from the Tōhoku Main Line at Morioka Station. You can also approach the spring by bus—a 1½-hour ride—from Lake Tazawa.

THE WATERS: Tamagawa, one of the three best hot springs in the Hachiman tai group—the others being Goshogake (Akita Prefecture) and Tōshichi (Iwate Prefecture)—is off the beaten track and has a long history of healing. Its very hot water—98° C (208° F)—is extremely abundant, and so is the acid it contains. Fortunately, ordinary water is added to cool it down, which dilutes its chemical nature as well. Even so, don't be shocked if rubbing your skin in the bath makes some of it peel off and float away. (People with sensitive skin should be sure to rinse off after bathing.) Not only acidic, the water also contains sulphur and is radioactive—a dynamic combination used by hot-spring physicians from several universities in the Tōhoku region to treat illnesses like poliomyelitis. The cure here is aptly referred to as a form of shock treatment, much like the one at the hot baths of Kusatsu (86), used to shock the nonfunctioning part of the body into action. The water is also good for less-serious ailments like rheumatism, whiplash, asthma, and gastroenteric disorders. The last is aided by imbibing, but once again it's best to take it diluted and in small doses; too much could cause vomiting or tooth-enamel erosion. If you're wondering about the safety of bathing at Tamagawa, don't—there are more real doctors running around and layman doctors sitting in the tubs than you'll see at any other hot spring in the land. Besides, the steam bath and mud bath are excellent—you'll feel great afterward . . . all aglow. The water in the open-air bath is white, another unusual feature; with the somber faces arranged around it, gazing into the distance, you can be sure that Tamagawa is a serious health spring.

AROUND AND ABOUT: Around Tamagawa and Goshogake (143) is some of the wildest terrain found on Hachimantai Plateau. If the bath fills you with unbridled energy and a desire to get into open spaces, you might like to walk to Goshogake. This will give you 5 hours of looking up at steep, rocky mountain slopes whose peaks are always hidden by mist and whose crevices shelter the last dregs of winter snow even in summer. The growth is scrubby, even dead in places where it didn't make it through the cold weather. All Hachimantai is like this—a place for those wanting something untamed on a vast scale, with the added touch of danger and the unexpected that volcanic areas possess. The walk will make you aware of a different aspect of Japanese mountain country where all is not lush green.

ACCOMMODATIONS: Tamagawa Onsen, with a mixed outdoor bath, is divided into three sections—ryokan, kokuminshukusha, and cook-for-yourself inn—all of which are closed from November through April. The building, although big enough to hold a thousand people, is wooden and simple, harmonizing nicely with its surroundings.

143 Goshogake

LOCATION: This hot spring is almost in the center of Hachimantai Plateau in eastern Akita Prefecture. From Hachimantai Station on the Hanawa Line, the bus to the spring takes 45 minutes.

THE WATERS: Like Tamagawa, Goshogake is a hot-spring buff's hot spring, offering serious bathing and authentic thermal experiences. One such experience is its "heated floor" bath, a long room with a naturally heated earthen floor (*ondoru*)—the area is quite active volcanically—kind of like a giant electric griddle covered with tatami mats. Just lie on the tatami and let your body relax, revive, and heal. Another novelty is a little wooden house, windowless but with holes in its roof through which poke heads lined up like those of felons confined to a place of primitive torture. But these heads are smiling . . . this is, in fact, a marvelous old-fashioned sauna tub that really heats and cleanses your skin and relieves any ache, anywhere. Both of these baths belong to the Goshogake Onsen Hotel. In the ordinary bath the water contains sulphur, and besides rheumatism and neuralgia is particularly good for respiratory ailments like asthma.

AROUND AND ABOUT: The wonders of Goshogake don't stop with the baths. Outside the ryokan there is a "volcanic study trail" that takes you on a fascinating half-hour walk through Kōya Jigoku, a "hell place" with a striking navy blue pond, as it winds its way past bubbling, boiling gray mud and water, all overhung with steam and the pungent smell of sulphur. The immediate surroundings, rocky and grayish, soon give way to spring or summer green—and there sits the hot spring, in fields of bobbing white and yellow flowers. The small town is typical of snow-country hamlets. Its handful of buildings are plain oblong boxes with high, small windows and steep roofs. There's nothing extravagant about life here; nature is in control for most of the year.

ACCOMMODATIONS: Neither of the two places to stay at Goshogake is very expensive. Goshogake Onsen has cook-for-yourself facilities, while the Hotel Sansui is more modern.

FOOD: Akita Prefecture is known for its stews (*nabemono*) cooked over an open fire. One special variety is called *maitake nabe—mai* means to dance and *take* means mushroom, suggesting that these mushrooms are so good you'll dance for joy when you find them in the wild (and never tell anyone else where they're hidden). Another delightful stew, called *kiritanpo nabe*, has a long stick of *mochi* (glutenous rice pounded into a soft mass) cooked in the stewpot. To wash these delicacies down you might try Akita saké.

Ranman is for those who like a touch of sweetness, and Aramasa for those who like it dry. Both are made from water that was once pure, mountain-top snow.

144 Kuroyu

LOCATION: Kuroyu is northeast of Lake Tazawa in central-eastern Akita Prefecture. Get off at Tazawako Station on the Tazawako Line, which extends from Ōmagari on the Ōu Main Line to Morioka on the Tōhoku Main Line. From the station take a bus for 55 minutes to Kuroyu Onsen and then walk 20 minutes to reach the hot spring.

THE WATERS: Like so many Akita hot springs, Kuroyu is a quiet, lonely place accessible only in spring and summer (the area is closed from December through May). All around spirals of steamy vapor curl upward. Through this trudge the farmers who live nearby, lugging their bedding and cooking pots and anything else needed for a summer vacation at the healing waters. During the day they work the fields, and in the evenings they bathe, chat, sing, drink, and moon gaze. Some stay at the single inn, a simple thatched affair, for up to a month. This all makes for a very enlightening experience for the foreign guest or even the Japanese person from the city. It's basic rustic bathing in the company of long-time hot-spring aficionados. In fact being in Kuroyu is one of the rare times you'll feel you're really getting to the heart of back-country Tōhoku, where the bullet train leaves precious few villages untouched nowadays. Kuroyu belongs to the Nyūtō group of hot springs and features both sulphur and simple thermal baths, both recommended for high blood pressure, rheumatism, and surface cuts and scrapes. Probably the most visited tub is the cascade bath (*takiyu*): The bather stands on wooden planks in a rocky alcove and exposes the ailing part of his anatomy to powerful cascades of hot water that issue forth from open pipes. This bath is communal and small, so you have to wait your turn; but it's well worth it!

AROUND AND ABOUT: Kuroyu is a small village of wooden houses built to cope with plenty of snow. Near the town is a sinter field, or *yubatake*, where open wooden pipes crisscross the boiling mineral water and catch the sinter, which is scraped off and used to make souvenirs or sold to those wanting to make a hot spring in their apartment tub. Along the edge of the hot pool there is a line of Jizō statues, small stone figurines representing the guardian god of travelers, among others. It's a slightly eery, but intriguing, sight.

■ KAKUNODATE: Thirty-five minutes south on the Tazawako Line from Tazawako Station is Kakunodate, a town known for its lovely cherry trees that were originally brought from Kyōto and now extend for several kilometers along the river. This is an old castle town, and in the Uchimachi section it's possible to see houses and gardens from former days of glory remaining more or less intact. Another remnant of the Edo period is *kabazaiku*, the art of scraping, smoothing, and molding cherry bark into decorative objects like tea caddies, scoops, small boxes, trays, and ornaments. Out-of-work samurai, especially after the Meiji Restoration of 1868, developed the art as a means of paying their rent. The Kyōto-like aspects of this place are in part the result of its having been the seat of the powerful Satake family, one of whose "sons" was adopted from the imperial family.

ACCOMMODATIONS: Kuroyu Onsen is Kuroyu's sole ryokan. Built of natural materials, it is simple and comfortable; the cascade bath mentioned above belongs to this inn.

LAKE TAZAWA: Lake Tazawa is the deepest lake in Japan and poses something of a mystery because it never freezes over. Another oddity is that it is always full but is fed by very few rivers. No doubt these things have a lot to do with Princess Tatsuko, a delectable dragon, once an Akita beauty, who resides somewhere in its murky depths. This lady dragon is married to Hachirō Tarō, a handsome male dragon, once a man, who lives in Hachirō-gata Lagoon. The two spend their summers apart and meet at princess Tatsuko's place from the autumnal to the vernal equinox. The local people say their passion is so fierce that Lake Tazawa is too hot to freeze over! Geologists will have you believe otherwise, though. On July 20 and 21 each year there is a dragon festival, when two long, billowy, green-blue dragons with huge golden horns are carried into the lake by men in blue and white happi coats. This riotous, fun spectacle lends support to the lovemaking theory, as does the bronze statue nearby of a curvaceous lady, a reminder of how beautiful Tatsuko was before she became a dragon.

145 Magoroku

On the bus to Kuroyu you'll pass the hot spring Magoroku. Its mineral water, simple thermal, is particularly good for eye problems. The inn here has cook-for-yourself facilities and is a place for those willing to forgo modern conveniences to get a taste of raw Akita mountain life. If you've studied your basic traveler's phrasebook, don't be surprised if the dialect used by the locals is incomprehensible; even southern Japanese patrons can't understand it!

146 Oga

LOCATION: The Oga Peninsula is a noticeable bump on Akita Prefecture's western coast, and this hot spring is on its northern side, just where the land begins jutting out into the sea. Take the Oga Line from Akita Station to Oga Station, and then a bus for about an hour to reach the spring.

THE WATERS: Oga is a medium-size hot spring near Akita City and a good place to stop off during a tour of the peninsula. A mixture of old and new, of deluxe ryokan and humbler ryokan, minshuku, and kokuminshukusha, it copes with the needs of most people passing through. The water contains sodium chloride and hydrogen carbonate. It's good for hardening of the arteries and neuralgia, and for stomach disorders if imbibed.

AROUND AND ABOUT: Being on the sea, Oga provides a change of scenery from the mountain hot springs so numerous in Akita. Oga Peninsula, too, is another face of this prefecture, a perfect balance of mountains, sea, food, and culture. In appearance it resembles a clenched hand, thumb pointing upward. Halfway down the western coast are rough, pitted, jagged brown rocks half-buried in the sea, dense well-watered forests climbing up mountain slopes to restaurants and lookout towers, and views of a clean blue sea and lakes in their natural state. The boats that leave Toga Bay, below the hot spring, offer a prime vantage point for sightseeing.

ACCOMMODATIONS: The Japanese-style Hotel Yūzankaku is good for families and serves a "demon" stew called *namahage nabe*. The ryokan Hakuryūkaku also serves unusual food; its *ishiyaki* is made by dropping stones heated to 1,000° C (1,832° F) into a wooden bowl containing fish and a *miso* broth. It tastes great.

FOOD: The *hatahata* fish swims in about November and is caught, pickled, and added to seasoned cooked rice and vegetables to make a kind of sushi — not for those who dislike salty-sour tastes. The pickling brine is saved and used like soy sauce as a seasoning for winter stews. The cold-weather hot pots—called *shottsuru nabe* or *shottsuru kaiyaki*—of fish, vegetables, and tofu are famous in Akita.

FESTIVALS: If you are here on December 31, you may see the *namahage*, wild beastlike creatures who race about villages terrorizing children and drinking up their fathers' saké. The name *namahage* derives from the word for a blotch on the skin caused by sitting near the fire for a long time. The *namahage* are out to get lazy people who do just that: sit near the fire when they should be out working. They really are an awful sight, covered in black-green hair a foot long, with demon faces and horns. Fiercely frowning, they have several teeth missing and wield knives. Heaven help those who've misbehaved, or children who cry, or people who haven't prepared enough saké, fish, and *mochi* to appease these maniacal beasts. Once fed, they calm down remarkably quickly, bless the house and harvest, and then leave, striking up their usual din just before reaching the next house. They don't visit ryokan at the hot spring, so if you can't get an invitation to someone's house, go to Shinzan Shrine (in the center of Oga City) on February 13–15 and see them frolicking at the Seto Festival: a sight not to be missed (if you're well behaved!). If you are in this area in the summer, however, you might like to catch the Kantō Festival in Akita City—on your way to or from Oga Hot Spring. This festival of strength held before the rice harvest to invoke the gods' blessings upon the yield, takes place in Akita City on August 5 to 7. To a tall vertical pole are attached numerous horizontal crossbars, from which are strung up to 46 lanterns representing kernels on a giant ear of rice. The whole affair, standing 10 meters tall and weighing almost 60 kilograms, sways precariously back and forth as a village strongman attempts to keep it upright by balancing the pole on various parts of his anatomy. As you watch, you will find yourself gasping in fear as the tower tips and almost falls but it never—well, hardly ever—does.

147 Soma

LOCATION: Soma is south of Ōdate in northern Akita Prefecture. Get off at Animaeda Station on the Aniai Line, which you can transfer to at Takanosu Station on the Ōu Main Line. An hour-long bus ride will take you the rest of the way. The baths are closed in winter, from November to sometime in April, depending on the weather.

THE WATERS: If there are any "secret" hot springs remaining in Akita, this is surely one. Located in the Moriyoshi Mountain Range, where water tumbles down in strange, tortuous, twisting routes along smooth stone beds, it was known as a sacred place, inhabited by higher beings and avoided by all others. In fact, the area was opened up just thirty-five years ago, and the spectacular mountains and the hot spring are only now being visited by travelers. The simple thermal, weak alkaline water is good for diabetes, skin problems, female disorders, and heart disease.

AROUND AND ABOUT: While the hot-spring area, hidden in a gorge, is quiet and relaxing enough on its own, you simply must get out and about in this area, it's so beautiful. Moriyoshi Prefectural Park boasts masses of green slopes, sometimes with white snowy tops even in summer. It's utterly open here, with just a few cows and the odd group of school children or others on sketching excursions, squatting in the grass and trying to put the flowers of spring on paper. For flowers are all about, dancing spots of white, yellow, pink, and mauve, delicate and dainty, but remarkably sprightly after the harshness of winter. The rocks and waterfalls provoke a quite different mood, with their heavy, stark, thundering compositions of white water and shining granite. Light filters through the new leaves, and all you need is a boat on the mirror-smooth lake to think you're in paradise. In winter the land is buried under snow and the skiing is good.

ACCOMMODATIONS: Soma Onsen is a very comfortable ryokan built in the traditional way.

148 Aoni

LOCATION: Aoni lies east of Kuroishi City, almost in the center of Aomori Prefecture. From Kawabe on the Ōu Main Line take the Kōnan Tetsudō Line to Kuroishi Station. Then take a bus for 30 minutes, get off at Aoni Iriguchi, and walk 2 more hours to reach the hot spring. If you let the proprietor know you're coming he'll pick you up at the bus stop.

THE WATERS: Like most Aomori hot springs Aoni is way away from things, but it's even a bit more remote than most, a perfect place if you want to relax in a quiet (lights out at 10 o'clock), beautiful setting without any modern trappings. The single ryokan here was built fifty years ago by Niwa-san, a poet, and although he has since died, his inn is still what he meant it to be—a simple place close to nature to come and bathe and stay. The clear, odorless, and tasteless water is simple thermal with a dash of radium and is good for neuralgia, rheumatism, and skin problems. There are two rocky outdoor bathing pools set in the side of the river and partially covered with makeshift roofs. In the Ryūjin-no-yu tub inside, there are floating wooden *konsei-sama*, giant penis-shaped fertility symbols that you can dodge while singing and throwing water over your head—some fun!

AROUND AND ABOUT: Aoni is very beautiful with its fast-flowing river and wooden bridges stretching from bank to bank. The one ryokan complex, about the only sign of life, blends in nicely with its traditional thatched roof and large, shuttered windows. You can walk along the river (and try to catch your own dinner) or just sit and chat with the natives. The local brew is called *yamameshu*—a powerful liquor into which a grilled fish has been dunked to give it its unforgettable flavor, and perhaps its remarkable ability to get you talking even if you don't speak a word of Japanese. As you sit with your friends around a sunken fireplace, beneath a thatched roof, you pour the *yamameshu* into a wooden dipper and pass it from person to person until the stories run out—or until the narrators can take no more. Outside the sky is filled with stars bigger than any you've ever seen in Japan, but their size has got nothing to do with how much you've tippled. ■ LAKE TOWADA: Lake Towada, a caldera lake half in Akita and half in Aomori, is one of the best-known places to visit when in Tōhoku. It is 1 hour by bus from Aoni and presents one of the most beautiful vistas in the north, unmatched except by the off-the-beaten-track panoramas that belong to only the most intrepid travelers. The lake's water is clear, and the colorful reflections of autumn hillsides are superb. Its banks, however, have suffered their share of less beautiful invasions. Dozens of gaudy food stalls, ferry-boat docks, hotels, restaurants, and, of course, souvenir shops disfigure the landscape. But it's unrealistic to expect that a lake as beautiful as Towada could remain untouched in today's world, or that you could be its sole surveyor. Yet above the summer campers, the grilled *mochi* coated in *miso*, and the saccharine voices of taped information, the pine-clad mountains stand in quiet, benevolent relief. On the shore, past the shops, you'll see the famous statue of two identical nude women carved in bronze by Takamura Kōtarō. This twentieth-century poet-sculptor was sometimes criticized for his treatment of his wife, Chieko, a native of Tōhoku who gave up her desire to be an artist and the beauty and freedom of her home territory, to be with him in Tōkyō. She died a depressed schizophrenic in a mental hospital, yearning for the skies of the north. Some say her husband's grief and remorse was in part responsible for his placing the "Maidens," as the statue is called, out in the open on the banks of Lake Towada. Takamura's lyrical love poetry, telling of his feelings, have made him a tragic figure in Japan, one who most Japanese feel suffered as much as his wife did.

ACCOMMODATIONS: Aoni Onsen ryokan, your only choice, is popular with local folks who stay here for weeks at a time. If you're lucky, you can enjoy their folk songs and folk dances in the dining room. Reservations can be made with the travel agent listed in Appendix 2.

TSUGARU JONGARABUSHI: This is a well-known folk song from western Aomori, also called the Tsugaru region, and is played on the shamisen, a long, thin-necked instrument whose strings are hauntingly resonant when plucked. The music is rhythmical and rousing, but the lyrics are strange, stirring, and of unknown origin. One theory says the words were sung to protest the cruel warfare carried out by a local castle lord, Tsugaru Tamenobu, in the eighteenth century. This might explain the frenzied tones that make this music so popular throughout Aomori.

149 Sukayu

LOCATION: This hot spring, by Mount Hakkōda, is between Aomori City (the capital of Aomori Prefecture) and Lake Towada. The bus to the spring from Aomori Station, on the Tōhoku Main Line, takes 1½ hours. In winter the bus still runs, albeit irregularly.

THE WATERS: The waters of Sukayu are superb; this was the first National Health Resort in Japan, and a research team from Hirosaki University works here most of the time. The waters, acidic with hydrogen sulphide and calcium sulphate, treat poliomyelitis, heart diseases, dermatitis, asthma, wounds, cuts, rheumatism, neuralgia, and, if imbibed, constipation and metal poisoning. There is only one ryokan, and researchers encourage bathers to enter its four baths in a set order determined by their malady, immersing themselves in each for a specified time. For best results, treatment should be undertaken for about a week, but even casual bathers can follow a routine, alternating between cascade, hot, and warm baths as instructed. It is also possible to have a massage in the ryokan. The bathroom is huge and copes with hundreds of serious and not-so-serious summer guests. You might also like to try the Manju Fukashi bath a few minutes' walk from the ryokan. The name means "Bun Steamer," and if you change the last letter in "bun" to "m" you'll get the picture—namely, a spot to sit over soothing vapors. It's great for hemorrhoids.

AROUND AND ABOUT: Sukayu dates back to the seventeenth century and has always been a health spring, although many of the people passing through in the warmer months are perfectly healthy and just like bathing. Winter is very nice, though, with snow all around and hot tubs to keep the cold at bay.

ACCOMMODATIONS: The only inn is Sukayu Onsen Ryokan, a simple place, with costs depending on how keen you are to do your own cooking and on how many extras you eat and drink. Even if you don't stay here you are welcome to enjoy the baths for a small fee.

FESTIVALS: The spectacular Nebuta festival is held in Aomori City in early August. The Nebuta is one of Japan's largest and most colorful spectacles. The gorgeous, grotesque, papier-mâché dummies carried through the streets at this time are thought to have been used to scare the Ezo people by Sakanoue Tamuramaro, a general sent from the south to subdue these local tribes in the eighth century. Today several thousand dancing people cavort through the streets following the dummies, which are lit from inside by candles or, increasingly, electric bulbs. The dancers wear patterned, blue-and-white yukata and flowers on their pointed bonnets, and everyone has a great time—no one seems at all frightened of the monsters, just of the noisy crowds of tourists. Nearby Hirosaki City stages a similar, smaller-scale version—the Neputa Festival—in early August.

150 Osorezan

LOCATION: This hot spring is near Mount Osore in the center of the "blade" of axe-shaped Shimokita Peninsula in Aomori Prefecture. Take the Ōminato Line from Noheji (where it meets the Tōhoku Main Line) to Shimokita; then transfer to the Shimokita Kōtsū Line and get off at Tanabu Station. A bus from there to the spring takes 40 minutes.

THE WATERS: Situated in the shade of ominous Mount Osore, a crater mountain in a scarred, bubbling hell land, this hot spring is actually within the precincts of Entsūji Temple, which was established in the ninth century, and comprises several buildings including four bath huts. This is definitely not your picturesque, relaxing bathing venue. It is possibly one of the least appealing bathing spots in all Japan. But that's as it should be, for Osorezan's main purpose is to provide baths for pilgrims who have come to comfort the spirits of the dead that wander in this place. From July 20 to 24 and September 1 to 5 are the Itako Festivals, named after the blind women mediums who gather there and contact deceased family and friends for living relatives. This has become a great tourist attraction, with many outsiders coming only to have their spines chilled, thus devaluing what the priests and many local folk still consider a serious and deeply religious hot spring. As you will soon recognize by the smell, the water contains sulphur.

Treatments are for stomach ulcers, skin complaints, and, strangely enough for a temple precinct, venereal disease.

AROUND AND ABOUT: It's exactly as hell should be: white, ashy, and barren, with just the quiet emerald green of Lake Usori for visual relief. The pitted earth bubbles with pools of various shades, and the entire area swelters under a shroud of sulphur fumes. People construct small mounds of stones on the ground to help the departed souls who must build similar mounds on their way to the next world. Unfortunately, their piles are continually knocked down by devils bent on torturing these suffering spirits. It is easy to see why this place has from ancient times been associated with the land of the dead and hell. But for the foreign visitor it is one, admittedly unpleasant, way to understand the back country and a little-seen aspect of Japanese religious practices.

ACCOMMODATIONS: Since this is not a regular tourist hot spring, there is no accommodation of the usual sort. However, it is possible to stay at Entsuji Temple. Lodgings are simple, comfortable, and inexpensive.

151 Shimoburo

LOCATION: Shimoburo (sometimes called Shimofuro) lies north of Osorezan (150) on the coast of Shimokita Peninsula, in Aomori Prefecture, on what is almost the northernmost point in Honshū. At Noheji Station on the Tōhoku Main Line transfer to the Ōminato Line and go to Shimokita Station; transfer there to the Shimokita Kōtsū Line, which will take you to Ōhata. The bus to Shimoburo from Ōhata Station takes 30 minutes.

THE WATERS: Shimoburo used to have several public baths for the local fisherfolk. It's still a fishing village, but the public baths have dwindled to two, the rest being housed in ryokan built to accommodate visitors, many of whom come from southern Hokkaidō. The two original baths are Ōyu and Shinyu, but they are patronized today mainly by the elderly of the village. The water contains sulphur and is pungent, but works well for skin problems, cuts, bruises, rheumatism, and stress. Although Shimoburo is a health spring it looks more like an ordinary, wintry coastal town—only the smell and the spirals of steam give it away.

AROUND AND ABOUT: In Aomori Prefecture the sea is constantly changing, and the waters around Shimoburo are an excellent place to catch all of its varied moods. In summer and autumn the fishermen set out to catch squid. This is done at night since these creatures are attracted to light. The small boats bobbing about with their lights on look like a fairy tale at sea, and the air is crisp, clear, and cool. In winter it's freezing cold, and all but the thermal hot spots are blanketed in thick white snow. From several ryokan baths you can watch the winter in comfort and warmth. If it's not winter and you feel like getting out and about, you can take a 2-hour round-trip ferry ride to Hokkaidō or a 40-minute bus ride to Ōmasaki, the lighthouse at the tip of Honshū. Another boat trip takes you west to view the white cliffs pounded and shaped by the sea, along the Tsugaru Straits between Hokkaidō and Honshū. This stretch is called Hotokegaura, and the curves of the giant rock sculptures are impressive when viewed from below.

ACCOMMODATIONS: Kakuchō Ryokan was mentioned in a popular novel about this area written by Inoue Yasushi and therefore conjures up a romantic atmosphere among many Japanese. A modern ryokan is Shimoburo Kankō Hotel, which has sea views from its tub where mineral water from the mountains and sea water are mixed together. On a good day you can see Hokkaidō from the window.

FOOD: *Ika, ika,* and more *ika.* (That is, squid.) You can have it fresh from the sea when it's slightly sweet, almost transparent, and a little chewy—and most delicious—or you can have it basted and grilled, or dried, or as tempura, or mixed with any number of other foods such as vegetables or fermented soybeans (*nattō*). If you're not a squid lover, there's also a delightful array of fish, sea urchin, and shellfish like abalone and scallops served in a large "boat" at a very reasonable cost. This is a treat you can't forgo.

10 HOKKAIDŌ ISLAND

Wilderness and Ainu Traditions

The "godly" couple given the task of creating Hokkaidō split up to do the work. The husband went east while the wife went west. He worked methodically, carving smooth, curved bays and promontories; but she dallied, talking to friends and wasting time. When she finally realized how late it was, she became frantic, hurriedly hacking out jagged inlets and jutting cliff faces. Her coastline, the western side of Hokkaidō, was a careless work, while his, the eastern side, was a joy to behold.

This is a tale told by Hokkaidō's first settlers, the Ainu people, to explain the shape of their island. The Ainu are racially and culturally distinct from the Japanese, and in centuries past were driven to Hokkaidō from the main island as Japan's political and military forces pushed up from the south. As the tale suggests, Hokkaidō is a land of striking contrasts. It is a place where nature has had the luxury of space—on a scale found nowhere else in Japan—and has fashioned vast wild landscapes. Not content to rest with unrivaled natural splendor, nature continues to make its presence felt; the earth rumbles and quakes, water in rivers and pools boils, volcanoes explode or fissures appear in the middle of some unfortunate farmer's potato field, and winter takes up more than its share of the year in a none-too-gentle way. But nature here is magnificent. Green slopes and blue lakes, sandy beaches and fishermen's bays, virgin forests and wild flowers, snow and ice and storm—all are untamed delights. Even the inevitable soda machines, everywhere else so obtrusive, sit here in relative oblivion, unable to challenge their surroundings.

"The bear is not a god itself, but it is the form the spirit of the god assumes. To release the spirit, so that it may return to the heavens, the bear must be killed. The *kamui* (spirit) is then freed." This is what the Ainu believe about the bear and its death. Dressed in long brown and black coats and skirts edged in square border chains, the Ainu hunters killed and worshiped in accordance with strict religious laws. The bear was a central object of their worship and, like the fox, the wolf, or the snake, a demon until "saved" by the hunter's arrow or otherwise made into a force of good rather than evil. The Ainu world was the world of men, animals, and gods, where man did his utmost to please the gods and survive the catastrophes of nature. The Ainu offered food and unrefined spirits to the gods, to the fire god first and then to others like the water god; through the observance of such rituals they tried to ensure the gods' benevolence here in this temporary world.

Ritual and tradition permeated Ainu community life as well. Before her wedding day, a young Ainu bride-to-be's grandmother would give her a chastity belt made from grass. This the bride would wear until her death, and it would be burned with her body at her funeral. Around her mouth she would be tattooed in blue, another sign of her modesty and status as one "possessed" by her husband. An Ainu woman always married within her tribe, but never within her family. On her wedding day, she and her husband ate from a special bowl of rice. After this her life of child-bearing and parenting began. Cultivating, gathering, and preparing food and spending time in worship, dance, and song were the substance of her life. After she died her spirit would penetrate the dreams of those she left behind, and they would hold memorial services for her, praying to the fire god at an altar adorned with a carved piece of wood much like a totem pole. Her ancestry, like that of all Ainu, was preserved intricately and faithfully in song, passed down through the generations.

Today attempts are made to preserve these beliefs and customs, but with very few pure Ainu remaining and all their legends and folklore being passed on orally, it is proving to be a difficult task. Not many Japanese scholars are fluent in the Ainu language, and until recently the Ainu people were unwilling to break traditions of silence where outsiders were concerned.

While the Ainu world has all but disappeared, much of the raw nature in which the Ainu lived and worshiped still remains, and it is up to you to find it and imagine for yourself how it must have been for people in centuries past. You won't find it difficult. You can visit famous lakes like Mashū, Akan, Kussharo, Tōya, and Ōnuma, or great mountains like Shōwa Shinzan and Usu, or picturesque peninsulas like Shiretoko, Nemuro, Erimo, and Shakotan. Wilder spots include Noboribetsu's Hell Valley, the Rebun and Rishiri islands off Wakkanai. In winter you should go see the *ryūhyō*, massive

10 HOKKAIDŌ ISLAND

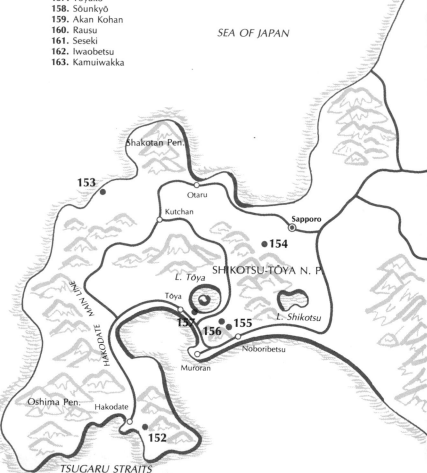

OKHOTSK SEA

Wakkanai

Shiretoko Pen.

SHIRETOKO N. P.

Asahikawa   Kamikawa   Abashiri

163

162   **161**

SEKIHOKU MAIN LINE

Shari

MT. RAUSU

160

158

MT. DAISETSU

DAISETSUZAN N. P.

L. Kussharo

AKAN N. P.

L. Mashū

Nemuro Shibecha

L. Akan   Teshikaga

SHIBETSU LINE

159

Naka Shibetsu

SENMO MAIN LINE

NEMURO MAIN LINE

Shibecha

Nemuro

MURORAN MAIN LINE

Nemuro Pen.

Kushiro

PACIFIC OCEAN

ice floes that make their way down Hokkaidō's eastern seaboard from the Okhotsk Sea. They touch land anywhere from Abashiri to Wakkanai, and as they pack up against the shore and crunch together, they sound uncannily like people weeping. This is in January. By February the ice is still, and you can actually go out and walk on it. The Ainu used to come here to catch seals trapped on the floes and brought down from the north.

While it's unlikely you will ever have to take on a bear in the Hokkaidō wilds, you'll be aware of animals here as you can be nowhere else in Japan. Deer, racoons, sheep, cows, horses, birds, and fish will all find their way into your camera lens and, in some cases, onto your plate. Hokkaidō's lingering frontier, its remnants of Ainu culture, its patches of wilderness filled with an abundance of plant and animal life, are what make this northern island distinct from the rest of Japan and an invigorating place to visit for travelers weary of the cramped and tourist-filled beauty spots to the south.

152 Yunokawa

LOCATION: This hot spring is in the southern suburbs of Hakodate port, in the southernmost part of Hokkaidō. From Hakodate Station (on the Hakodate Main Line) take a taxi, bus, or streetcar—it's only about 15 minutes to the spring.

THE WATERS: Being in the suburbs of what used to be a thriving port and the main connection point for travelers going north and south between Hokkaidō and Honshū, Yunokawa has developed into a resort spring. Located on the Matsukura River overlooking the Tsugaru Straits, it is the oldest hot spring on record in Hokkaidō, and was used by the clan that settled in this region from Honshū and ruled it for the Tokugawa shogun in the seventeenth century. The Japanese liked the healing qualities of the water, which contains sodium chloride and calcium sulphate. No doubt in those days fighting men had plenty of opportunities to put it to the test. In addition to battle scars, it's also good for rheumatism, neuralgia, and muscle aches and pains. And if you drink from one of its seventeen sources, you can clear up your allergies at the same time that you help your digestive system.

AROUND AND ABOUT: In the daylight hours take a walk on the beach or up Mount Hakodate—really just a hill—or snoop around the wharves. At night you can take the same path up the hill and see the lights of Hokkaidō and Honshū. At night you can also catch glimpses of geisha shuffling through the streets on their way to entertain guests. Something you shouldn't miss is Goryōkaku Fort, built in the mid-nineteenth century. This is where Enomoto Takeaki waged the last battle against the restoration of Emperor Meiji, and his defeat here marks the end of the Tokugawa period. The huge star-shaped fort, made from earth and stones, was modeled after pictures in an old book on Dutch architecture. It withstood a month-long seige before falling. Today its cherry and lilac trees are admired as much as its imposing fortifications. For those passing through and in need of a bath, the Hōrai Hot Spring, 20 minutes by bus from Hakodate Station, has a public bath. The water is hot, salty, and just right for grubby, travel-weary wanderers.

ACCOMMODATIONS: Wakamatsu is a small "samurai"-style ryokan situated on the coast. It has twinkling nighttime views. Chikuba is another traditional inn, which has its own moss garden.

FOOD: Salmon is good in Hokkaidō, and in Hakodate it is used in *sanpei-jiru* soup. Made with saké lees, this delicious soup is unlike any other Japanese soup you've had. Butter and cookies made by members of the Trappist religious community are also good here. A French priest started the community in the nineteenth century. Today Trappist nuns live near Hakodate, farming and leading an austere life of prayer and solitude.

FESTIVALS: A hot-spring festival is held on the second Saturday of August. The Hakodate Port Festival is also held at the beginning of August.

153 Raiden

LOCATION: Raiden is a little way down the southern side of Shakotan Peninsula in western Hokkaidō. Take the Hakodate Main Line to Otaru Station and then catch the bus to the spring—a 50-minute ride.

THE WATERS: Raiden sits between massive green slopes and the sea on a very beautiful stretch of the peninsula. The mountains jut out into the sea forming endless bays and inlets that make excellent silhouettes in sunset photographs. The water, calcium sulphate, is good for skin irritations, lifeless complexions, obesity, neuralgia, menstrual pain, and respiratory problems like asthma. Drinking it clears up constipation. The spring dates back to the days of Minamoto Yoshitsune, a samurai, and Benkei, his retainer, in the twelfth century. Yoshitsune, one of Japan's great tragic heros, supposedly fled to Hokkaidō to escape death at the hands of his brother, Yoritomo, the ruler of Japan in Kamakura.

AROUND AND ABOUT: Watching the sea and the sky change moods and colors throughout the day would probably be pleasant enough, but if that smacks too much of debauchery, then you might check out Benkei's sword holder, a rock called Katanagake, or, further away toward Hakodate, the pine tree where Yoshitsune sat—Koshikake no Matsu—only worth the trip if you're a real history buff. After your serious wanderings you might want to let your mind rest a bit and just visit Narukami Waterfall or clamber over the rocks on the beach. If you yearn for the traditional Japan—and there's not much of it in young Hokkaidō—there is a *daibutsu* (Great Buddha) statue nearby called Kikōin.

ACCOMMODATIONS: Kankō Katō is a modern ryokan with a hot-spring swimming pool. It overlooks the sea. Hotel Raiden, also modern, has good bathing facilities. If you just want to bathe, you can stop off at Iwanaicho Raiden Onsen Center; no accommodations are available there.

FOOD: In Raiden they make a *nabe* (stew) of cod, *miso* (fermented bean paste), and vegetables. It's just what you need on cold evenings after the bath. Tuna, octopus, squid, herring (*nishin*), and fish eggs are good here, too. For those not partial to fish there is asparagus.

154 Jōzankei

LOCATION: Jōzankei is about 30 kilometers southeast of the capital, Sapporo, in western Hokkaidō. The bus to the hot spring from Sapporo, which is on the Hakodate Main Line, takes a bit more than an hour.

THE WATERS: The spring takes its name from its discovery in 1869 by a monk from Okayama Prefecture called Jōzan, who, it is said, was led to the water by Ainu people. Because it is so near Sapporo, Jōzankei is a very popular resort spring and has inevitably obscured a lot of its vistas with concrete. What is lacking in scenery, however, is made up for in the bath room. Jōzankei Grand Hotel claims it has the "biggest bath in the cosmos," the Uchū Saidai. Some of the water here contains sodium chloride, while other tubs contain hydrogen sulphide water. Chronic skin problems, rheumatism, and women's problems are treated in the glamorous bath rooms of Jōzankei. If you drink mineral water instead of Sapporo beer, your digestive system will be pleased and your stomach will be at peace.

AROUND AND ABOUT: The Jōzankei area is not all ugliness, despite its resort status. The spring is in a valley on the Toyohira River surrounded by steep mountains. A little way from the concrete, the environs are quite pleasant indeed, and the snow does a good job of prettifying the area in winter. In summer you can walk around or take a trip to Sapporo, and in winter you can ski—or take a trip to Sapporo. Skiing facilities nearby are the top attraction along with the baths, but Sapporo is definitely worth a visit, especially for sampling the unique way it blends modern urban hustle with the uncomplicatedness of the lingering frontier. ■ SAPPORO: In Sapporo, stroll down the pedestrian mall toward the tower or past the famous clock. Visit the Botanical Gardens and the University Museum, or go to Hitsujigaoka, an agricultural center where sheep will entertain you as you look out over the city. Sapporo is casual, and if you really want to relax, try the Sapporo Beer Garden and wash down a "Genghis Khan" mutton barbeque with mugs of Sapporo's best-known export.

ACCOMMODATIONS: The deluxe Jōzankei Grand Hotel has an assortment of huge, sculptured baths: Uchū Saidai ("Biggest Bath in the Cosmos") or the Versailles Bath, the ultimate in grand tub decor. Hotel Shika-no-yu has a women's tub that is as big as the men's. Another superb place to stay with big tubs and good cuisine is Shōgetsu Grand Hotel.

FESTIVALS: The Sapporo Snow Festival features an impressive display of exquisitely carved ice sculptures of life-size proportions. Held the first week in February, this popular festival attracts great crowds of people from all over Japan.

155 Noboribetsu

LOCATION: This hot spring is south of Sapporo on the southern coast of Hokkaidō. Take the Muroran Main Line from Muroran to Noboribetsu Station. The spring is a 15-minute bus ride from the station.

THE WATERS: No matter what ails you, Noboribetsu can help—you can take a dip in almost every mineral water known in Japan, from radioactive to acidic, sodium chloride, sulphur, sodium hydrogen-carbonate, sodium sulphate, and acid-aluminum sulphate. It also has simple thermal and mineral-free hot water. There are several hospitals where research into medicinal-water therapies is carried out. For example, Hokkaidō University's balneological facilities here offer treatments for such things as motor disturbances, diabetes, rheumatism, and chronic digestive problems. But Noboribetsu is not just for serious bathing. The inns and hotels provide some of the most extravagant and "fun" bathing facilities in Japan, and in the back streets of the town you can find all manner of food, drink, and night life. The springs were probably discovered by the Buddhist priest and woodcarver Enkū in the sixteenth century—one of his carved images of the Kannon goddess is enshrined in nearby Jigokudani. More closely associated with Noboribetsu, however, is Takimoto Kinzō, who in 1857 found thermal waters here when he was searching for just such a place to cure his rheumatic wife. She did recover here, and together with Kinzō built the original Dai-ichi Takimotokan, a ryokan with an incredible 3,300 square meters of tub. This bath "barn" is open to the public and offers a sensational sensual experience. For a few hundred yen, you get a towel, a locker, and access to a huge hall where you can dabble in thirty tubs, curing whatever you like. If your body's sound, relax in the whirlpools, waterfalls, slippery dips, and multicolored waters. Only the entrances are segregated, so while the women-only tub is set apart from the rest, it's in the same large room. The next day, luxuriate in an outdoor bath beautifully situated in the garden of Noboribetsu Grand Hotel; there are separate baths for men and women. Inside there is a Roman-style bath complete with marble nudes in athletic poses. Admission for the day is cheap.

AROUND AND ABOUT: The resort, white in winter and steamy all year round, is located on the Kusurisanbetsu River—the "stream of hot water," as the Ainu say. But the heat grows especially intense just a bit upriver in Jigokudani, or "Hell Valley." Here the earth rumbles and hot pools roil and people walk gingerly about, not unlike lost souls in a landscape of demonic punishments. The earth is parched, and the crater lake Kuttara is a deep, silent blue that seems to want to coax you down into its bottomless depths. But don't be tempted; look up—above and beyond are fresh, luxuriant green hillsides. The lookout point over the lake boasts a Bear Farm where 180 brown bears scramble about in a pit in the ground nowhere near big enough. Not unlike this pathetic scene is Shiraoi, the Ainu village near Noboribetsu where you see what remains of a proud, creative way of life lost to modernity and the whims of a "superior" civilization.

ACCOMMODATIONS: Dai-ichi Takimotokan has excellent all-around facilities and is a bathing "must." Noboribetsu Grand Hotel has both Japanese and Western rooms and food good enough for the imperial family, who have stayed there. For families, Shimizu Ryokan (inexpensive and without baths *en suite*) is a good choice. It specializes in crab dishes.

FOOD: The choice is clear: small, meaty, tasty steamed crabs called *kegani kōramushi*. If this is hell, the food's sure good!

FESTIVALS: On February 3 and 4 there's the hot-spring festival, which features hot-water fights in the snow. At the end of August, people dressed up as wild blue and red demons are let out of the ground during the Jigoku ("Hell") Festival.

156 Karurusu

LOCATION: Karurusu is south of Sapporo, in western Hokkaidō, very near Noboribetsu Hot Spring (155). From Noboribetsu Station on the Muroran Main Line, take a bus to Noboribetsu Onsen and then transfer to the bus for Karurusu Onsen. In all, the bus trips take 30 minutes.

THE WATERS: Karurusu is within the town limits of Noboribetsu and has long been a popular medicinal spring. In recent years the area has also found favor as a ski resort; its excellent snows make it the best in Hokkaidō. The water contains radium and is classified as simple thermal. This makes it especially good for hard-to-treat complaints like nervous tension and mental disorders, as well as for ordinary fatigue and body aches and pains. Many ryokan here advise patrons to follow special bathing routines that they work out for you according to your ailments and "mental condition" when you arrive. Karurusu is a National Health Resort.

AROUND AND ABOUT: This spring was named after the famous Czechoslovakian spa Kärlsberg. The resemblance extends to the waters and the forests, which presumably reminded some European visitor of home. The path from the spring to Lake Tachibana is a kind of romantic Black Forest walk, particularly where the trees obscure the trappings of Japanese commercialism. The wild flowers make floral carpets, and the upper stretches of the Kusurisanbetsu River are beautiful, but too many people have found this out, and Karurusu isn't the quiet health resort it was when the Europeans first came here. Still, it has a lot to entice you with: the lake, Mount Orofure, a splendid autumn color display, and, as noted, the best skiing on the island.

ACCOMMODATIONS: Suzuki Ryokan is an older inn with atmosphere. Long-term visitors will appreciate Hotel Iwai, which has rooms with cooking facilities as well as ryokan-style accommodations with meals provided. An inexpensive ryokan, Kameya Karurusukan, offers special bathing routines.

157 Tōyako

LOCATION: This spring is on Lake Tōya, southwest of Sapporo, near Noboribetsu (155). From Tōya Station on the Muroran Main Line the spring is a 15-minute bus ride. From Sapporo by bus it takes 2½ hours.

THE WATERS: The name Tōya means "Lake-Hill" in the Ainu language and seems very apt for this lovely body of water ringed by mountains. Part of Shikotsu-Tōya National Park, Lake Tōya is a caldera lake with four islets that can be reached by boat. The thermal water contains sodium chloride and is available at all the ryokan, hotels, and minshuku. It is recommended for skin irritations like eczema and for women going through menopause. The ryokan are ranged around the lake, often with their baths overlooking it—a real bonus at night. No one knows how old the spring is, but it may have been known to the Ainu people living here before the Japanese came.

AROUND AND ABOUT: While the Japanese are now here in force--the area is heavily touristed—the landscape seems vast enough to accommodate all of them, even in summer when the vendors and souvenir shops are at their busiest. Summer, though, is when the lake is lit up by a shower of fireworks, and a time when the streets are alive with the clacking of wooden geta and parades of gaudy dragon floats and blazing lanterns—you can't help but get in the mood and join in the noise and frivolity. In any season you can enjoy a leisurely stroll about the lake front. Afterward, tour this beautiful area—but remember, the beauty here is tinged with danger: there are active volcanoes nearby. These include Shōwa Shinzan, a mountain which rose from the earth in a series of jolts and tremors in 1943-45 to form a lava tower 407 meters high. Another well-known volcano in the area is Mount Usu, which exploded in 1977, covering the town in ash and cracking buildings and roads. The stories of both these eruptions are vividly told in the Kazan Hakubutsukan ("Volcanic Museum") in Tōyako. Seeing the display of a car crushed and covered by spewed-out debris might give you second thoughts about staying on here, but the sun is too bright and the sky and lake are too blue to hurry off. You can ponder the magnificence of nature at one of the enticing cafés with beer gardens looking out over the lake.

ACCOMMODATIONS: The deluxe Hotel Grand Tōya has an inlaid-stone bath for women. Hotel Manseikaku and Tōya Park Hotel are two more fine hotels with Japanese- and Western-style rooms. The former has tennis courts, the latter a jungle bath. Tōya Sansui Hotel has a marble bath. All these hotels front on the lake.

FESTIVALS: At the end of August, fireworks, hot-spring festivals, and volcano festivals make beautiful Tōyako less menacing and a great deal of fun.

158 Sōunkyō

LOCATION: This spring is in Sōunkyō Gorge at the northern end of Daisetsuzan National Park, central Hokkaidō. Get off at Kamikawa Station on the Sekihoku Main Line from Asahikawa. Asahikawa is on the Hakodate Main Line. From Kamikawa it's a 30-minute bus ride to the spring. You can also take a bus directly from Asahikawa to Sōunkyō, which takes about 1¹/₂ hours.

THE WATERS: Although there's evidence that dates this hot spring to the period before Japanese settlement of Hokkaidō, credit for its discovery is usually given to Matsuda Ichitarō, a retainer who came here in 1857 to find the source of the Ishikari River for his samurai lord. Since then it has been very popular, mainly because it sits in a prime position in Hokkaidō's most visited beauty spot: Sōunkyō Gorge. *Sōun* means layers of cloud, and with the peaks of surrounding mountains often swathed in cloud, it's an apt name for this part of Daisetsuzan Park. The spring itself boasts a fair-sized group of ryokan and minshuku, many with their roofs painted red. They cluster together in a valley pinned in by towering cliffs. The water in Sōunkyō is hydrogen sulphide, good for healing rheumatism, neuralgia, external wounds, gout, and paralysis and, when drunk, good for curing constipation.

AROUND AND ABOUT: You might as well join the throngs making their way to Sōunkyō Gorge—they aren't leading you astray. This gorge is one of the highlights of a very beautiful park—the largest in Japan. It is also the most touristy part of the park with a rope-lift way up on Mount Kurodake for superb views, paths and walkways to waterfalls nearby, a ski slope for winter guests, and shops providing every imaginable service. But the natural panoramas easily outweigh any human interventions here, and after your bath you can don your hiking boots and in no time be out in the wilds along one of the many hiking trails into the gorge and beyond. Vistas from places like Ō-bako and Kobako show the gorge at its most spectacular, with vertical cliffs carved into geometrical friezes and torrents of water hurtling down from above. This gorge is but a part of Daisetsuzan National Park. Further south are fields of wild flowers and virgin forests—near Lake Nukabira, for example. Other areas are more mountainous. But wherever you go, you'll find largely untraveled, untouched open countryside, just right if you're looking for log cabins, breathing space, and the scent of deer or bear. You can see a display of the flora and fauna found in Daisetsuzan National Park at the Sōunkyō Museum.

ACCOMMODATIONS: Grand Hotel Sōunkaku is a ryokan with saunas, whirlpool baths, and a marble tub. One of its specialties is trout. Ginsenkaku is a small ryokan that serves fish grilled on a clay slab. Sōunkyō Kanko Hotel has good baths—including a huge, communal outdoor bath. According to the season, they serve either crab (spring) or salmon (winter) for dinner.

FESTIVALS: Kyōkoku Himatsuri, on June 24 and 25, is an Ainu fire festival centered around prayers to the mountain god and the fire god and to the spirits of the hot spring. It begins with a relay of five runners bringing the fire from the Asahi River. This is a very exciting and colorful event with more authenticity than many of the other "Ainu festivals." An ice festival takes place in mid-February. Sculptors construct frames, and the weather does the rest, creating elaborate shapes by the same process that makes hoarfrost on trees in the winter. During the festival, red and blue lights sparkle all over these natural works of art.

159 Akan Kohan

LOCATION: Akan Kohan is on the southern edge of Lake Akan, eastern Hokkaidō. From Kushiro take a direct bus (2 hours), or take the Senmō Main Line to Teshikaga Station. From there the bus to the hot spring takes 1 hour 10 minutes.

THE WATERS: Lake Akan offers one of the best vistas in Hokkaidō. Flanked by Mount Me-Akan and Mount O-Akan, Lake Akan is an irregularly shaped blue-green body of water whose shores are overgrown with tangled trees and bushes. The hot spring is a resort catering to people coming for the view or to sail. Most of the ryokan and a large number of baths overlook the lake. The water is simple thermal or contains sulphur, depending on which tub you enter. Usually sulphurous water doesn't lather, but here it does, and without the usual acrid sulphur smell. It treats rheumatism, neuralgia, skin complaints, and, when imbibed, diabetes and stomach woes.

AROUND AND ABOUT: For starters take a boat out to the islands in the center of the lake. The islands look more like mountaintops, which they are: long ago Mount O-Akan erupted and dammed up a river, making it into a lake wild and beautiful with interesting curves and bends and small mountain peaks for islands. On the biggest island you'll file through a dimly lit museum filled with tanks of bouncing algae, furry, green balls called *marimo*, or "god's fairies," for which the lake is famous. Afterward go to Ainu Kotan Village and see craftsmen at work, or take the bus to Onnetō to view the hot waterfall (*yudaki*) and bathe if it's not too cold out. A wooden-framed outdoor bath has been built at the base of the falls so that the hot water splashes over the bathers. The 1-kilometer walk from the bus stop is worth it; this is a wild, natural spot, off the beaten track. East of Akan Kohan are two lakes well worth a visit. Lake Mashū is for those in love, with its romantic misty vistas and tasty corn on the cob. Lake Kussharo has sand baths on its banks, but you have to dig your own. You can also join the ongoing search for Kusshi—Japan's Nessie—said to inhabit these waters.

ACCOMMODATIONS: New Akan Hotel has Western and Japanese rooms and serves deer meat. Akankosō has a bath on the fifth floor with good views of the lake. It also offers Western-style accommodations for those not partial to the floor. Both of these ryokan are very comfortable.

FOOD: A wide variety of river fish, white and sweet, and deer meat are some of the delicacies offered in Akan. On the lake you can munch on roasted corn or sweet potatoes as you row about.

FESTIVALS: Fireworks burst over the lake on June 19. Later in summer, on August 16, candle-lit lanterns are floated out on the lake as part of the Buddhist Bon Festival.

160 Rausu

LOCATION: Rausu is on the eastern side of Shiretoko Peninsula, eastern Hokkaidō. Take the Shibetsu Line to Nemuro Shibetsu and then it's 1½ hours by bus to Rausu; there board a bus for Rausu Onsen (10 minutes).

THE WATERS: Rausu is a fisherman's town that winds up a valley between steep mountains. From above it looks like a river of red and blue rooftops. The town is a typical Japanese country town, but its beach area is more expansive and cleaner than in many beach towns in southern Japan. There is a public outdoor bath, Kuma-no-yu, which is a rock pool in the river— and that's all. The setting is wild: spindly trees, boulders, rocks, birds, and hot water. The pool is owned by the town and is open to anyone passing through or staying in Rausu. The water contains sodium chloride and is recommended for backaches, nervous diseases, skin problems, pimples, and those who have been overexposed to industrial dust.

AROUND AND ABOUT: Morishige Hisaya, an extremely popular actor-singer, once had a hit song about Rausu and Shiretoko Peninsula. Hence what might seem to you a remote, wild, end-of-the-earth stretch of land is to many Japanese people a place of romance and tender beauty—until they see it. Morishige's statue stands guard over the harbor. Before you take the boat around the tip of Shiretoko, which is the only way to see the peninsula, you can visit Makkausu, a cave lined with yellow moss that used to be inhabited by native tribes and is now protected state property. Or from Rausu Hot Spring you can hike to and climb Mount Rausu—allow at least 5 hours— to see the whole peninsula below you and Lake Rausu in the crater.

ACCOMMODATIONS: Rausu Dai-ichi Hotel is in the gorge. The service is good and the menu features dishes grilled on a clay slab. Sansō Mine features boat-shaped sashimi platters with more than the usual amount of sea urchin (*uni*), a delicacy. Shiretoko Kankō Hotel is a large hotel-ryokan with a rock bath and all kinds of sports facilities.

161 Seseki

LOCATION: Seseki, an open-air seaside pool, is almost at the tip of Shiretoko Peninsula in eastern Hokkaidō, 20 kilometers from Rausu Hot Spring (160). From Rausu take a bus to Aidomari, and get off at Seseki Onsen, a 50-minute ride. Note that buses only run in July and August.

THE WATERS: Seseki's sodium chloride water is very good for wounds that won't heal properly. The bathing pool disappears when the tide comes in.

AROUND AND ABOUT: Until a few years ago the only approach to Seseki used to be on foot, along a wild, lonely beach. You'll see rough, wooden huts and perhaps even some of the brown, wiry men who sometimes use them, out in the water harvesting long tresses of kelp. Shiretoko means "End of the Earth," and there is an air of desolation in these parts, but it's a natural, challenging environment with a vitality as strong and pure as the catlike shrieks of the seagulls who chase along the shoreline.

ACCOMMODATIONS: About all you can do here is pitch your tent on the beach and hope the tide won't wash you away. Masses of wild, red briars make this a very attractive camping spot, but if you plan to spend the night and don't fancy a three-course seaweed dinner, you had better take along your own food.

162 Iwaobetsu

LOCATION: This spring is a little way down the western side of Shiretoko Peninsula and inland toward Rausu. From Shari on the Senmo Main Line take a bus to Iwaobetsu (1½ hours but note that buses do not run in winter, mid-October to mid-April); the route is very picturesque with many views of the coast.

THE WATERS: Iwaobetsu is another small hot spring in untamed terrain, surrounded by forests and near the Okhotsk Sea. There is only one ryokan here and an outdoor river bath that is open to the public. The water contains sodium chloride and is good for aching backs, rheumatism, neuralgia, and travel fatigue. To get to the open-air bath, walk up the river behind the ryokan until you see a pool in the stream. The bathing holes are deep and hot, so test the water first. Other baths you might like to try are 1-by-3-meter wooden tubs made out of tree trunks and located in the ryokan garden near an old water wheel. The water here is transparent, but it's such a lonely spot you needn't worry about prying eyes, except perhaps those of curious squirrels and foxes.

AROUND AND ABOUT: Iwaobetsu is a typical Hokkaidō fishing village, with hardworking boats hauled up onto the gray sandy beach, fish and seaweed hung on lines to dry, and suntanned, clear-eyed inhabitants with few illusions about life. From here you can visit the port of Utoro, 20 minutes by bus, and catch a boat that will take you around or part of the way around the Shiretoko Peninsula, affording you a good view of the coastline. The seaside cliffs are sheer, brown, and rocky, here and there pitted with holes and caves and topped by overhanging unkempt bushes and trees. In places the cliff face sparkles with falling water tumbling into the brine. As the sea washes and pounds the cliffs, gulls squeal about your boat looking for a bite to eat. A guide tells you stories about people who once lived in the cliff caves and what they did there. Back in Utoro, visit the store Shiretokoya Matsumoto to pick up two of the local specialties—mountain cranberry and Hamanasu, a distilled liquor (*shōchū*).

ACCOMMODATIONS: Hotel Chinohate, named after a movie filmed here, is the only place to stay. It is a comfortable hotel-ryokan, but it is only open from mid-April to mid-October.

163 Kamuiwakka

LOCATION: Kamuiwakka comprises a series of thermal rock pools along the Kamuiwakka River near Mount Iō on the Shiretoko Peninsula. It is 15 kilometers from Iwaobetsu Hot Spring (162) or 1 hour 50 minutes on the bus via Iwaobetsu that leaves from Shari Station on the Senmō Main Line. Note that buses only run in summer and early autumn.

THE WATERS: As soon as you get off the bus you'll see—and smell—the river. This sulphur spring with very hot water is good for your skin and nervous diseases like sciatica. To get to the bathing spots, walk upstream alongside the river until you reach a roped-off area of rocky pools, where you climb into a hot hole and soak. There is a steep, steaming hot waterfall—Kamuiwakka no Yudaki—and also places where enough cold river water has mixed with the spring water coming up from the bed to make lukewarm tubs. There are no cabanas for changing, so just choose your spot, shed your garments, and step in.

AROUND AND ABOUT: The scenery here is wild and woolly, and from the top of the waterfall you can see the dots of ships sailing on the Okhotsk Sea.

ACCOMMODATIONS: There is nowhere to stay here. Visit on a day trip from Iwaobetsu, Shari, or Utoro.

3
HELPFUL
INFORMATION

Appendix 1

Mineral Waters and Their Health Benefits

The following chart presents the current official classification system, instituted by the Environment Agency in 1979. Some waters fall neatly into one of the nine basic categories, but others—in fact, most—are a combination of several types. For example, "carbon-dioxated simple thermal" is both simple thermal—i.e., contains at least 1,000 mg of a combination of minerals per kg of water—and carbon-dioxated—i.e., contains at least 1,000 mg of free carbon per kg of water. Such complex waters are written as a string of minerals in order of progressively greater quantities present. A

typical poolside sign announcing mineral content might read:

含 重曹 芒硝 食塩 泉
1　2　3　4　5

1 = contains (gan)　2 = sodium hydrogen-carbonate (jūsō)　3 = sodium sulphate (bōshō)　4 = sodium chloride (shokuen)　5 = springs (sen)

Sodium chloride is present in the highest concentration, and sodium sulphate in the lowest.

Kind of Water	Mineral Content (per kg of water)	Effects on Body	Ailments Treated	Possible Adverse Effects
Sodium Chloride (salty) 食塩泉 shokuen sen	Over 1,000 mg of solid matter, mainly salt. Over 1,500 mg per kg is strong; under 500 mg is weak.	Warms body and helps body retain heat (salt on skin prevents sweat evaporation).	Post-operative rehabilitation, rheumatism, surface wounds, infertility, arthritis, hypertension. When imbibed: aids digestion.	Strong salt, when imbibed, is bad for stomach. Excessive drinking is bad for high blood pressure and heart problems.

Type	Composition	Effects	Good for	Cautions
Simple Thermal 単純泉 tanjun sen	Multiple minerals in small amounts: less than 1,000 mg of any single mineral and/or free carbonate, but at least 1,000 mg in total of solid matter.	Mild stimulation. When imbibed: stimulates urination and secretion of gastric juices.	Rheumatism, neuralgia, broken bones, wounds, post-cerebral apoplexy, hypertension. When imbibed: stomach and gastroenteric problems, and fatigue.	
Carbon-dioxated 炭酸泉 tansan sen	Over 1,000 mg of free carbon. Usually cool (since high temperature releases carbon dioxide).	Bubbles visible on skin. Enlarges capillaries. When imbibed: activates stomach juices.	Poor circulation problems, heart diseases, high blood pressure, impotence, infertility. When imbibed (directly from spring): constipation and digestive problems.	Aggravates diarrhea.
Hydrogen Carbonate 炭酸土類泉 tansan dorui sen				
Calcium (or Magnesium) 重炭酸土類泉 jūtansan dorui sen	Over 1,000 mg of solid matter, mainly calcium hydrogen-carbonate or magnesium hydrogen-carbonate.	Neutralizes gastric juices or excess acid. When imbibed: works as vasodilator for perifery.	Chronic stomach problems, allergies, chronic skin problems. When imbibed: diabetes, urinary calculus, cystitis, gout.	Excessive drinking is not good for high blood pressure or stomach problems.

Kind of Water	Mineral Content (per kg of water)	Effects on Body	Ailments Treated	Possible Adverse Effects
Sodium (alkaline springs) 重曹泉 jūsō sen	Over 1,000 mg of solid matter, mainly sodium hydrogen-carbonate (always occurs with sodium chloride or sodium sulphate).	Softens skin tissue. *When imbibed*: same as above, and stimulates secretion of bile and elimination of uric acid. Inhalation of steam breaks down mucus in bronchial tubes and clears them.	Diabetes, gout, drug addiction, gallstones, bronchial problems. Good for complexion.	
Sulphate 硫酸塩泉 ryūsanen sen	Over 1,000 mg of solid matter (listed below).		Arteriosclerosis, high blood pressure, cuts, rheumatism.	
Sodium 芒硝泉 bōshō sen	Natrium	*When imbibed*: stimulates bile secretion.	Cholecystitis, kidney problems, constipation. *When imbibed*: gout, diabetes, obesity.	Never drink if any part of body is swollen.
Calcium 石膏泉 sekkō sen	Calcium	Soothes. *When imbibed*: stimulates secretion of bile, aids digestion.	High blood pressure, wounds, palsy. *When imbibed*: obesity.	
Magnesium (rare in Japan) 正苦味泉 seikumi sen	Magnesium	Soothes, tightens skin. Helps skin retain moisture. *When imbibed*: same as above.	Same as above. *When imbibed*: liver troubles, constipation.	Don't use soap at all.

Name	Composition	Effect	Benefits	Cautions
Acid-aluminum 明礬泉 myōban sen	Acid-aluminum	Tightens skin tissue.	Skin and muscle problems.	Not for delicate skin.
Sulphur 硫黄泉 iō sen	Over 1 mg of sulphur.	Detoxifies, softens skin.	Metallic poisoning, complexion. *When imbibed:* diabetes.	Not for delicate skin. Don't drink if suffering from diarrhea. Metals (jewelry) may tarnish. Don't use soap.
Hydrogen Sulphide 硫化水素泉 ryūka suiso sen	Over 1 mg of sulphur with hydrogen sulphide and carbonate gas.	Enlarges capillaries, loosens phlegm. *When imbibed:* lowers blood sugar level.	Heart problems, arteriosclerosis, bronchial problems.	
Acidic 酸性泉 sansei sen	Over 1 mg of hydrogen ion (often with acid-aluminum, hydrogen sulphide).	Tightens skin tissue. *When imbibed:* acidifies digestion.	Athlete's foot, Tricomonia's polio, chronic rheumatism. *When imbibed:* anacidity.	Not good for the elderly.
Iron 鉄泉 tessen	Over 10 mg of Fe^{2+} or Fe^{3+} (often with other minerals).	Warms body. *When imbibed:* aids blood production.	Rheumatism, menopause. *When imbibed (directly from spring):* anemia.	
Radioactive 放射能泉 hōshanō sen	Over 8.25 Mache units (3×10^{-9} curies) of radon (radium emanation).	Stimulates urination and elimination of uric acid.	Gout, neuralgia, diabetes. *When imbibed (or when steam is inhaled):* chronic digestive problems, gallstones, fatigue.	

Specific Health Problems and What Helps

This list of health problems and remedies is generally accepted in Japan by balneologists and other specialists on thermal waters and their effects. The list was compiled with the assistance of Dr. Ueda Michihiko, who has conducted extensive research in the field. It must be stressed, however, that the mineral content of every spring is different and that, depending on such factors as the patient's physical condition, the duration of bathing, and the water temperature, the effects of a hot-spring bath will vary. Do not expect a specific water to completely cure a certain ailment, although in most cases you can assume it will help to some degree.

Health Problem	Waters
anemia	Drink: iron carbonate, sulphate.
bronchial problems (e.g., asthma)	Bathe in: sulphur, sodium chloride with sodium hydrogen-carbonate. Inhaling steam and gargling are also effective.
circulation problems	Bathe in: simple thermal, carbon-dioxated, sulphur, hydrogen sulphide. Drink: sulphate, sodium chloride.
diabetes, gout	Bathe in: sulphur, acidic. Drink: sulphate, radioactive.
external wounds	Bathe in: simple thermal, carbon-dioxated, sodium hydrogen-carbonate, calcium sulphate, sodium chloride.
gallstones	Bath in: simple thermal, sodium hydrogen-carbonate, sulphate, radioactive. Drink: sodium hydrogen-carbonate, sulphate, radioactive.
hardening of the arteries, palsy	Bathe in tepid: simple thermal, carbon-dioxated, sulphate, sulphur, radioactive.
hemorrhoids	Bathe in: simple thermal, weak sodium chloride, carbon-dioxated, hydrogen carbonate, sulphate, iron, sulphur, radioactive.
neuralgia, rheumatism	Bathe in hot: simple thermal, sodium chloride, sulphate, iron, radioactive, sulphur, acidic.
neurosis	Bathe in: tepid water for a long time.
obesity	Bathe in: sulphate, sulphur, hydrogen carbonate. Drink: sulphate, sulphur, hydrogen carbonate. A sand bath is also effective.
skin problems	Bathe in: acidic, hydrogen carbonate, sulphur, sulphate, sodium chloride, simple thermal.
stomach problems	Drink: sodium chloride, carbon-dioxated, sodium or calcium sulphate, acidic, sulphur, iron, radioactive.

The Japan Health and Research Institute (Tōkyō [03]3274-2861) offers further advice on hot-spring cures for specific ailments.

Appendix 2

Accommodations Directory

Listed below are the accommodations mentioned in the text and some others which may be useful. When making reservations, it is often necessary to enlist the aid of a Japanese friend since some of the staff in remote areas have difficulty understanding certain kinds of Japanese, let alone English. The following agencies may be able to help with accommodations. (Note that J.T.B. makes reservations, but T.I.C. does not.)

Japan Travel Bureau (J.T.B.): Tōkyō (03)3276-7771
Ōsaka (06)344-0022
Kyōto (075)361-7241

Japan Minshuku Association: Tōkyō (03)3371-8120 or 3988-6688

Tourist Information Center (T.I.C.): Tōkyō (03)3502-1461/2
Kyōto (075)371-5649

From all other areas in Japan: Dial 106 and say "Collect call for T.I.C. (or Tourist Information Center)," and you'll be connected to instant assistance. This service is available during regular office hours. The list below includes local tourist information offices, which can provide more detailed information.

The price system used here is:

A = ¥10,000 and up
B = ¥7,000–¥10,000 (an average ryokan or hotel)
C = under ¥7,000 (M = minshuku, K = kokuminshukusha)

These prices include tax and service charges. Be warned that they may increase, but remember, too, that it's often possible to negotiate directly with the proprietor, especially on weekdays, which are less crowded. When two price ranges are listed for one inn—e.g., "A, B"—the first range listed is the normal range though some rooms at the second price range are available. "A+" indicates prices over ¥25,000.

Where no address is given for an inn, the address is the same as that of the inn(s) preceding it. When addressing correspondence to any of these inns, don't forget to include the hot-spring name after the name of the inn.

1. Kyūshū Island 九州

HOT SPRING	HOTEL/INN	PRICE RANGE	ADDRESS/TELEPHONE
1 Beppu Onsen 別府温泉			
Beppu Proper 別府	Hinago Hotel 日名子ホテル	A	Beppu-shi, Ōita Pref. (0977)22-1111 大分県別府市
	Hakusen 白扇	B	(0977)22-4154
Kannawa 鉄輪	Oniyama Hotel 鬼山ホテル	A	Kannawa, Beppu-shi, Ōita Pref. (0977)66-1121 大分県別府市鉄輪
	Kannawa-en 神和苑	A	(0977)66-2111
Myōban 明礬	Okamotoya Ryokan 岡本屋旅館	B, A	Myōban, Beppu-shi, Ōita Pref. (0977)66-3228 大分県別府市明礬
Kankaiji 観海寺	Suginoi Hotel 杉乃井ホテル	A	Kankaiji, Beppu-shi, Ōita Pref. (0977)24-1141 大分県別府市観海寺
	Tourist information		(0977)22-0401
2 Yunohira Onsen 湯平温泉	Migimaru Ryokan 右丸旅館	B	Yunohira, Yufuin-chō, Ōita-gun, Ōita Pref. (0977)86-2002 大分県大分郡湯布院町湯平
	Shimizu Ryokan 志美津旅館	B	(0977)86-2111
	Tourist Information		(0977)84-3111
3 Yufuin Onsen 由布院温泉	Kamenoi Bessō 亀の井別荘	A	Yufuin-chō, Ōita-gun, Ōita Pref. (0977)84-3166 大分県大分郡湯布院町
	Tamanoyu Ryokan 玉の湯旅館	A	(0977)84-2158
	Tourist information		(0977)84-3111
4 Kabeyu Onsen 壁湯温泉	Fukumotoya 福元屋	C	Machida, Kokonoe-machi, Kusu-gun, Ōita Pref. (09737)8-8754 大分県玖珠郡九重町町田

5 Sujiyu Onsen 筋湯温泉	Sujiyu Kankō Hotel 筋湯観光ホテル	A	Sujiyu, Kokonoe-machi, Kusu-gun, Ōita Pref. (09737)9-2231 大分県玖珠郡九重町筋湯
	Asahiya 朝日屋	B, A	(09737)9-2114
	Tourist information		Machiyakuba (Town Hall) (09737)6-2111
6 Ebino Kōgen Onsen えびの高原温泉	Ebino Kōgen Hotel えびの高原ホテル	A	Suenaga, Ebino-shi, Miyazaki Pref. (0984)33-1155 宮崎県えびの市末長
	Kokuminshukusha Ebino Kōgensō 国民宿舎えびの高原荘	C (K)	(0984)33-0161
	Tourist information		Shiyakusho (City Hall) (0984)35-1111
7 Ibusuki Onsen 指宿温泉	Hakusuikan 白水館	A	Ibusuki-shi, Kagoshima Pref. (09932)2-3131 鹿児島県指宿市
	Ibusuki Kankō Hotel 指宿観光ホテル	A	(09932)2-2131
	Ibusuki Kaijō Hotel 指宿海上ホテル	A	(09932)2-2221
	Takayoshi たかよし	C (M)	3-9-22 Yunohama, Ibusuki- shi, Kagoshima Pref. (09932)2-5982 鹿児島県指宿市湯の浜3-9-22
	Tourist information		Shiyakusho (City Hall) (09932)2-2111
8 Shinyu Onsen 新湯温泉	Shinmoesō 新燃荘	C (K)	Makizono-chō, Aira-gun, Kagoshima Pref. (09957)8-2255 鹿児島県姶良郡牧園町
9 Onoaida Onsen 尾之間温泉	Sasakisō 佐々木荘	C (M)	Onoaida, Yaku-chō, Kumage-gun, Kagoshima Pref. (09974)7-2031 鹿児島県熊毛郡屋久町尾之間
	Tourist information		Machiyakuba (Town Hall) (09974)7-2111

10 Hirauchi Onsen 平内温泉	Iso-no-kaori いその香	B	Hirauchi, Yaku-chō, Kumage-gun, Kagoshima Pref. (09974)7-2867 鹿児島県熊毛郡屋久町平内
11 Yamaga Onsen 山鹿温泉	Seiryūsō 清流荘	B, A	Yamaga-shi, Kumamoto Pref. (09684)3-2101 熊本県山鹿市
	Asanoya 朝の家	B	(09684)3-2936
12 Tarutama Onsen 垂玉温泉	Yamaguchi Ryokan 山口旅館	B, A	Chōyō-mura, Aso-gun, Kumamoto Pref. (09676)7-0006 熊本県阿蘇郡長陽村
13 Hinagu Onsen 日奈久温泉	Kinparō 金波楼	B, A	Hinagu-chō, Yatsushiro-shi, Kumamoto Pref. (0965)38-0611 熊本県八代市日奈久町
	Ichifuji 一ふじ	C, B	(0965)38-0145
14 Unzen Onsen 雲仙温泉	Kyūshū Hotel 九州ホテル	A+	Unzen, Obama-chō, Minami Takaki-gun, Nagasaki Pref. (09577)3-3234 長崎県南高来郡小浜町雲仙
	Miyazaki Ryokan 宮崎旅館	A+	(09577)3-3331
	Kaseya Ryokan かせや旅館	C (M)	(09577)3-3321
	Tourist information		(09577)3-3434
15 Shimabara Onsen 島原温泉	Grand Hotel グランドホテル	A	Ōjimo-chō, Shimabara-shi, Nagasaki Pref. (09576)2-1234 長崎県島原市大下町
	Kunimitsuya 国光屋	A	Hori-chō, Shimabara-shi, Nagasaki Pref. (09576)2-5151 長崎県島原市堀町
	Hotel Nanpūrō ホテル南風楼	A	Benten-chō, Shimabara-shi, Nagasaki Pref. (09576)2-5111 長崎県島原市弁天町

	Hisago ひさご	B	Naka-chō, Shimabara-shi, Nagasaki Pref. (09576)2-3481 長崎県島原市中町
	Shimabara しまばら	C (M)	Sugiyama-chō, Shimabara-shi, Nagasaki Pref. (09576)2-2681 長崎県島原市杉山町
16 Ureshino Onsen 嬉野温泉	Ureshino Kankō Hotel Taishōya 嬉野観光ホテル大正屋	A	Ureshino-machi, Fujitsu-gun, Saga Pref. (09544)2-1170 佐賀県藤津郡嬉野町
	Wataya Bessō 和多屋別荘	A	(09544)2-0210
	Unagiya Ryokan うなぎや旅館	B, A	(09544)3-0170
17 Takeo Onsen 武雄温泉	Takeo Kokusai Hotel Tōkyōya 武雄国際ホテル東京屋	B, A	Takeo, Takeo-shi, Saga Pref. (09542)2-2195 佐賀県武雄市武雄
	Kagetsu 花月	B, A	(09542)2-3108
18 Futsukaichi Onsen 二日市温泉	Enjukan 延寿館	A	Chikushino-shi, Fukuoka Pref. (092)924-1500 福岡県筑紫野市
	Gyokusenkan 玉泉館	A	(092)922-2331
	Tourist information		(092)922-2421

2. Chūgoku Region 中国

HOT SPRING	HOTEL/INN	PRICE RANGE	ADDRESS/TELEPHONE
19 Tawarayama Onsen 俵山温泉	Fukuzumi 福隅	B	Tawarayama, Nagato-shi, Yamaguchi Pref. (08372)9-0014 山口県長門市俵山
	Chikusuien Takeya 竹翠園たけや	B, C	(08372)9-0021
	Tourist information		(08372)9-0001

20 Ofuku Onsen 於福温泉	Ofukusō お福荘	B	Ofuku-chō, Mine-shi, Yamaguchi Pref. (08375)6-0057 山口県美祢市於福町
	Fukuya Ryokan ふくや旅館	B	(08375)6-0061
	Tourist information		Shiyakusho (City Hall) (08375)2-1110
21 Yuki Onsen 湯来温泉	Kajikasō 河鹿荘	A	Yuki-chō, Saeki-gun, Hiroshima Pref. (0829)85-0311 広島県佐伯郡湯来町
	Midorisō みどり荘	A, B	(0829)85-0321
	Kokuminshukusha Yuki Lodge 国民宿舎湯来ロッヂ	C (K)	(08298)5-0111
22 Yunotsu Onsen 湯泉津温泉	Kiunsō 輝雲荘	B, A	Yunotsu-machi, Nima-gun, Shimane Pref. (08556)5-2008 島根県邇摩郡湯泉津町
	Masuya ますや	B, A	(08556)5-2515
	Tourist information		(08556)5-2065
23 Tamatsukuri Onsen 玉造温泉	Chōrakuen 長楽園	A	Tamatsukuri, Yatsuka-gun, Shimane Pref. (0852)62-0111 島根県八束郡玉造
	Hoseikan 保性館	A	(0852)62-0011
	Tourist information		(0852)62-0634
24 Okutsu Onsen 奥津温泉	Kawanishi Hotel 川西ホテル	A	Okutsu-chō, Tomata-gun, Okayama Pref. (08685)2-0046 岡山県苫田郡奥津町
	Okutsusō 奥津荘	A	(08685)2-0021
	Kokuminshukusha Kinzansō 国民宿舎錦山荘	C (K)	(08685)2-0321
(Yunogō Onsen) （湯郷温泉）	Chikutei 竹亭	A	Yunogō, Mimasaka-chō, Aida-gun, Okayama Pref. (08687)2-0090 岡山県英田郡美作町湯郷

25 Iwai Onsen 岩井温泉	Hanaya Ryokan 花屋旅館	B, A	Iwami-chō, Iwami-gun, Tottori Pref. (0857)72-1431 鳥取県岩美郡岩美町
	Akashiya 明石家	B, A	(0857)72-1515
	Tourist information		Machiyakuba (Town Hall) (0857)73-1411
26 Misasa Onsen 三朝温泉	Saiki Bekkan 斉木別館	A, A+	Misasa-chō, Tōhaku-gun, Tottori Pref. (0858)43-0331 鳥取県東伯郡三朝町
	Ryokan Nakaya 旅館中屋	C, B	(0858)43-0859
	Kokuminshukusha Misasa Onsen Kaikan 国民宿舎三朝温泉会館	C (K)	(0858)43-2211
	Tourist information		(0858)43-0431
27 Hawai Onsen 羽合温泉	Asozuen 浅津苑	A	Hawai-chō, Tōhaku-gun, Tottori Pref. (0858)35-3311 鳥取県東伯郡羽合町
	Hagoromo 羽衣	B, A	(0858)35-3628
	Tourist information		(0858)35-4052
28 Sekigane Onsen 関金温泉	Onseirō 温清楼	A	Sekigane-chō, Tōhaku-gun, Tottori Pref. (0858)45-3311 鳥取県東伯郡関金町
	Hotel Sekigane ホテルせきがね	B, A	(0858)45-3331
	Kokuminshukusha Sekiganesō 国民宿舎せきがね荘	C (K)	(0858)45-2211
	Tourist information		Machiyakuba (Town Hall) (0858)45-2111
29 Kaike Onsen 皆生温泉	Hotel Seifūsō ホテル清風荘	A	Kaike, Yonago-shi, Tottori Pref. (0859)22-4141 鳥取県米子市皆生
	Hisagoya ひさご家	A	(0859)22-2248
	Tōkōen 東光園	A	(0859)34-1111

2: ACCOMMODATIONS 245

Itō Ryokan いとう旅館	B, A	(0859)22-4168	
Tourist information		(0859)34-2888	

3. Shikoku Island 四国

HOT SPRING	HOTEL/INN	PRICE RANGE	ADDRESS/TELEPHONE
30 Dōgo Onsen 道後温泉	Funaya Ryokan ふなや旅館	A	Dōgo, Matsuyama-shi, Ehime Pref. (0899)47-0278 愛媛県松山市道後
	Tsubakikan 椿館	A	(0899)43-3251
	Tōuntei 東雲亭	B	(0899)41-0649
	Umenoya Ryokan 梅の家旅館	B	(0899)41-2570
	Tosa Ryokan とさ旅館	C (M)	1-5-32 Dōgo, Matsuyama- shi, Ehime Pref. (0899)21-1223 愛媛県松山市道後1–5–32
	Tourist information		(0899)43-8342
31 Inosawa Onsen 猪野沢温泉	Isuisō 依水荘	B, A	Kahoku-chō, Kami-gun, Kōchi Pref. (08875)8-2248 高知県香美郡香北町
32 Inomisaki Onsen 井ノ岬温泉	Inomisaki Onsen Hotel 井ノ岬温泉ホテル	B, A	Ida, Ōkata-chō, Hata-gun, Kōchi Pref. (08804)4-1111 高知県幡郡大方町伊田
33 Iya Onsen 祖谷温泉	Hotel Iya Onsen ホテル祖谷温泉	A	Matsuo, Ikeda-chō, Miyoshi- gun, Tokushima Pref. (0883)75-2311 徳島県三好郡池田町松尾
	Toshikosō とし子荘	C (M)	(0883)87-2842
34 Aji Onsen 庵治温泉	Aji Onsen Aji Kankō Hotel 庵治温泉庵治観光ホテル	A	Aji-chō, Kita-gun, Kagawa Pref. (0878)71-3141 香川県木田郡庵治町

4. Kinki Region 近畿

HOT SPRING	HOTEL/INN	PRICE RANGE	ADDRESS/TELEPHONE
35 Kinosaki Onsen 城崎温泉	Kobayashiya 小林屋	A	Yushima, Kinosaki-chō, Kinosaki-gun, Hyōgo Pref. (079632)2424 兵庫県城崎郡城崎町湯島
	Tsutaya つたや	A	(079632)2511
	Kataoka かたおか	B	(079632)2317
	Ryokan Hakusan 旅館白山	C	419 Imazu, Kinosaki-chō, Kinosaki-gun, Hyōgo Pref. (079632)3404 兵庫県城崎郡城崎町今津419
	Tourist information		(079632)4141
36 Arima Onsen 有馬温泉	Hashinoya 橋之家	A+	Arima-chō, Kita-ku, Kōbe-shi, Hyōgo Pref. (078)904-0651 兵庫県神戸市北区有馬町
	Goshobō Ryokan 御所坊旅館	A	(078)904-0551
	Takayamasō 高山荘	A, B	(078)904-0744
37 Yumura Onsen 湯村温泉	Yumura Kankō Hotel 湯村観光ホテル	A	Yu, Onsen-chō, Mikata-gun, Hyōgo Pref. (07969)2-1000 兵庫県美方郡温泉町湯
	Izutsuya Ryokan 井筒屋旅館	A	(07969)2-1111
	Sankin Ryokan さんきん旅館	B	(07969)2-0014
38 Kizu Onsen 木津温泉	Ebisuya Ryokan ゑびす屋	A	Kizu, Amino-chō, Takeno-gun, Kyōto (07727)4-0025 京都府竹野郡網野町木津
	Sakamotoya Ryokan 坂本屋旅館	B	(07727)4-0029

39 Arita Onsen 有田温泉	Arita Kankō Hotel 有田観光ホテル	A	Arita-shi, Wakayama Pref. (0737)82-5201 和歌山県有田市
	Yabitsusō やびつ荘	B, A	(0737)83-2772
40 Ryūjin Onsen 竜神温泉	Kamigoten 上御殿	A	Ryūjin-mura, Hidaka-gun, Wakayama Pref. (0739)79-0005 和歌山県日高郡竜神村
	Shimogoten 下御殿	A	(0739)79-0007
	Kokuminshukusha Ryūjin Onsen Lodge 国民宿舎竜神温泉ロッヂ	C (K)	(0739)79-0331
41 Shirahama Onsen 白浜温泉	Hotel Koganoi ホテル古賀の井	A	Shirahama-chō, Nishimuro- gun, Wakayama Pref. (0739)42-2922 和歌山県西牟婁郡白浜町
	Yuzakikan 湯崎館	A	(0739)42-3019
	Kokuminshukusha Meikō Shirahama Lodge 国民宿舎明光白浜ロッヂ	C (K)	(0739)43-5103
	Tourist information		(0739)42-2215
42 Katsuura Onsen 勝浦温泉	Koshinoyu 越之湯	A	Nachi Katsuura-chō, Higashi Muro-gun, Wakayama Pref. (07355)2-1414 和歌山県東牟婁郡那智勝浦町
	Urashima Hotel 浦島ホテル	A	(07355)2-1011
	Hotel Nakanoshima ホテル中の島	A	(07355)2-1111
	Tourist information		(07355)2-5311
43 Yunomine Onsen 湯ノ峰温泉	Azumaya あずまや	A	Hongū-chō, Higashi Muro- gun, Wakayama Pref. (07354)2-0012 和歌山県東牟婁郡本宮町
	Iseya 伊せや	A	(07354)2-0128
	Tourist information		(07354)2-0735

44 Kawayu Onsen 川湯温泉	Fujiya 富士屋	A	Hongū-chō, Higashi Muro-gun, Wakayama Pref. (07354)2-0007 和歌山県東牟婁郡本宮町
	Kameya 亀屋	A	(07354)2-0002
	Ōmuraya 大村屋	C (M)	(07354)2-1066
	Tourist information		(07354)2-0735
45 Wataze Onsen 渡瀬温泉	Watarase Sansō わたらせ山荘	B, A	Hongū-chō, Higashi Muro-gun, Wakayama Pref. (07354)2-0230 和歌山県東牟婁郡本宮町
46 Yoshino Onsen 吉野温泉	Yoshino Onsen Motoyu 吉野温泉元湯	B, A	Yoshinoyama, Yoshino-chō, Yoshino-gun, Nara Pref. (07463)2-3061 奈良県吉野郡吉野町吉野山
47 Tōsenji Onsen 湯泉地温泉	Yado Yunosato やど 湯の里	A	Totsukawa-mura, Yoshino-gun, Nara Pref. (07466)3-0020 奈良県吉野郡十津川村
	Totsukawasō 十津川荘	A	(07466)2-0035
48 Miyano Onsen 宮乃温泉	Miyano Onsen 宮乃温泉	B, A	Kōnan-mura, Kōga-gun, Shiga Pref. (0748)86)2212 滋賀県甲賀郡甲南村
49 Yunoyama Onsen 湯ノ山温泉	Shin-Yunoyama Kankō Hotel 新湯ノ山観光ホテル	A	Komono-chō, Mie-gun, Mie Pref. (0593)92-2151 三重県三重郡菰野町
	Yunoyama Lodge 湯ノ山ロッヂ	B	(0593)92-3155
	Tourist information		(0593)92-2115
50 Nagashima Onsen 長島温泉	Hotel Nagashima ホテル長島	A, A+	Nagashima-chō, Kuwana-gun, Mie Pref. (05944)5-1111 三重県桑名郡長島町

5. Tōkai Region 東海

HOT SPRING	HOTEL/INN	PRICE RANGE	ADDRESS/TELEPHONE
51 Atami Onsen 熱海温泉	Atami Tsuruya Hotel 熱海つるやホテル	A+	Higashi Kaigan-chō, Atami-shi, Shizuoka Pref. (0557)82-1212 静岡県熱海市東海岸町
	Hanamura Ryokan はなむら旅館	A+	Sakimi-chō, Atami-shi, Shizuoka Pref. (0557)81-5503 静岡県熱海市咲見町
	Tōrikyō 桃李境	A+	Izusan, Atami-shi, Shizuoka Pref. (0557)80-2211 静岡県熱海市伊豆山
	Kokuminshukusha Atami Village 国民宿舎熱海ビレーヂ	C (K)	21-7 Baien-chō, Atami-shi, Shizuoka Pref. (0557)81-8295 静岡県熱海市梅園町21-7
	Tourist information		(0557)82-3053
52 Itō Onsen 伊東温泉	Oyado Ryūseki 御やど龍石	A+	Itō-shi, Shizuoka Pref. (0557)45-2266 静岡県伊東市
	Itōen Hotel 伊東園ホテル	A	(0557)37-1101
	Hatoya Hotel ハトヤホテル	A	(0557)37-4126
	Tōkaikan 東海館	A	(0557)37-3114
	Izumien 泉苑	C (M)	(0557)37-2323
	Tourist information		(0557)37-6105
53 Shimoda Onsen 下田温泉	Kurofune Hotel 黒船ホテル	A	Shimoda-shi, Shizuoka Pref. (05582)2-1234 静岡県下田市
	Shimoda Yamatokan 下田大和館	A	(05582)2-2936
	Izumisō いずみ荘	A, B	(05582)2-3080
	Katsura Ryokan 桂旅館	C	(05582)2-3274

54 Rendaiji Onsen 蓮台寺温泉	Seiryūsō 清流荘	A	Rendaiji, Shimoda-shi, Shizuoka Pref. (05582)2-1361 静岡県下田市蓮台寺
	Yubatakan ゆばた館	A	(05582)2-2244
	Tourist information		(05582)2-1531
55 Shuzenji Onsen 修善寺温泉	Asaba Ryokan あさば旅館	A+	Shuzenji-machi, Tagata-gun, Shizuoka Pref. (0558)72-0700 静岡県田方郡修善寺町
	Arai Ryokan 新井旅館	A	(0558)72-2007
	Kikuya Ryokan 菊屋旅館	A	(0558)72-2000
	Tourist information		(0558)-72-0271
56 Yoshina Onsen 吉奈温泉	Tōfuya Ryokan 東府屋旅館	A+	Yoshina, Yugashima-chō, Amagi, Tagata-gun, Shizuoka Pref. (05588)5-1000 静岡県田方郡天城湯ケ島町吉奈
	Hōsensō 芳泉荘	A+	(05588)5-0655
	Tourist information		(05588)5-1056
57 Yugashima Onsen 湯ケ島温泉	Yumotokan 湯本館	A	Yugashima, Yugashima-chō, Amagi, Tagata-gun, Shizuoka Pref. (05588)5-1028 静岡県田方郡天城湯ケ島町湯ケ島
	Ochiairō 落合楼	A	(05588)5-0014
	Izu-no-Satarō 伊豆の佐太郎	C (M)	(05588)5-0534
58 Ōdaru Onsen 大滝温泉	Amagisō 天城荘	A	Kawazu-chō, Kamo-gun, Shizuoka Pref. (05583)5-7711 静岡県賀茂郡河津町
	Urushiya うるしや	C (M)	(05583)5-7289
	Kajiya かじや	C (M)	(05583)5-7189
	Tourist information		(05583)2-0290

59 Ōsawa Onsen 大沢温泉	Ōsawa Onsen Hotel 大沢温泉ホテル	A	Matsuzaki-chō, Kamo-gun, Shizuoka Pref. (05584)3-0121 静岡県賀茂郡松崎町
	Ryokan Nakagawa 旅館那賀川	A, B	(05584)3-0188
	Ōsawasō 大沢荘	B, A	(05584)3-0031
	Kokuminshukusha Izu Matsuzakisō 国民宿舎伊豆まつざき荘	C (K)	(05584)2-0450
60 Yuya Onsen 湯谷温泉	Grand Hotel Hōyō グランドホテル鳳陽	A, B	Hōraichō, Minami Shidara- gun, Aichi Pref. (05363)2-1565 愛知県南設楽郡鳳来町
	Miyako 都	B	(05363)2-1521
	Tourist information		(05363)2-0022
61 Shinhodaka Onsen 新穂高温泉	Imadakan 今田館	A	Nakao, Kamitakara-mura, Yoshiki-gun, Gifu Pref. (0578)9-2011 岐阜県吉城郡上宝村中尾
	Shinzansō 深山荘	B	(0578)9-2031
	Taniguchi たにぐち	C	(0578)9-2468
	Tourist information		(0578)6-2165
62 Fukuchi Onsen 福地温泉	Magokurō 孫九郎	A	Fukuchi, Kamitakara-mura, Yoshiki-gun, Gifu Pref. (0578)9-2231 岐阜県吉城郡上宝村福地
	Yumoto Chōza 湯元長座	A	(0578)9-2146
	Satsuki さつき	B	(0578)9-2211
63 Shinhirayu Onsen 新平湯温泉	Shirakabasō 白樺荘	A	Hirayu, Kamitakara-mura, Yoshiki-gun, Gifu Pref. (0578)9-2114 岐阜県吉城郡上宝村平湯
	Gizan Ryokan 岐山旅館	B	(0578)9-2201
	Tourist information		(0578)6-2165

HOT SPRING	HOTEL/INN	PRICE RANGE	ADDRESS/TELEPHONE
64 Gero Onsen 下呂温泉	Suimeikan 水明館	A	Gero-chō, Masuda-gun, Gifu Pref. (05762)5-2800 岐阜県益田郡下呂町
	Moriyama 森山	C (M)	(05762)5-2607
	Tourist information		(05762)5-4711

6. Kōshinetsu Region 甲信越

HOT SPRING	HOTEL/INN	PRICE RANGE	ADDRESS/TELEPHONE
65 Shimobe Onsen 下部温泉	Gensenkan 源泉館	A	Shimobe-chō, Nishi Yatsushiro-gun, Yamanashi Pref. (0556)36-0101 山梨県西八代郡下部町
	Daiichikan 第一館	B	(0556)36-0211
	Tourist information		Machiyakuba (Town Hall) (0556)36-0011
66 Masutomi Onsen 増富温泉	Kinsentō 金泉湯	B, A	Masutomi, Sudama-chō, Kita Koma-gun, Yamanashi Pref. (0551)45-0211 山梨県北巨摩郡須玉町増富
	Furōkaku 不老閣	B, A	(0551)45-0311
67 Yumura Onsen 湯村温泉	Hotel Yuden ホテル湯伝	A, B	Yumura-chō, Kōfu-shi, Yamanashi Pref. (0552)53-3191 山梨県甲府市湯村町
	Tsuruya Ryokan つるや旅館	B	(0552)52-2232
68 Oshino Onsen 忍野温泉	Oshino Fujikyū Hotel 忍野富士急ホテル	A	Oshino-mura, Minami Tsuru-gun, Yamanashi Pref. (055584)3131 山梨県南都留郡忍野村
	Oshino Onsen 忍野温泉	B	(055584)2014
	Tourist information		Machiyakuba (Town Hall) (055584)3111

69 Bessho Onsen 別所温泉	Kashiwaya Bessō 柏屋別荘	A	Ueda-shi, Nagano Pref. (0268)38-2345 長野県上田市
	Hanaya Hotel 花屋ホテル	A	(0268)38-3131
	Katsurasō 桂荘	B	(0268)38-2047
	Tourist information		(0268)38-3230
70 Kakeyu Onsen 鹿教湯温泉	Kakeyu Sansō 鹿教湯山荘	B, A	Maruko-machi, Chiisagata-gun, Nagano Pref. (0268)44-2041 長野県小県郡丸子町
	Shikanoya 鹿乃屋	B, C	(0268)44-2141
	Kokuminshukusha Kagetsusō 国民宿舎鹿月荘	C (K)	(0268)44-2206
	Tourist information		(0268)44-2331
71 Shirahone Onsen 白骨温泉	Shirafunesō Shintaku Ryokan 白船荘新宅旅館	A	Azumi-mura, Minami Azumi-gun, Nagano Pref. (0263)93-2201 長野県南安曇郡安曇村
	Yumoto Saitō Ryokan 湯元斉藤旅館	A	(0263)93-2311
	Awanoyu Ryokan 泡の湯旅館	B, A	(0263)93-2101
	Tourist information		Machiyakuba (Town Hall) (0263)94-2301
72 Nakabusa Onsen 中房温泉	Nakabusa Onsen 中房温泉	B, A	Hotaka-chō, Minami Azumi-gun, Nagano Pref. (0263)35-9704 長野県南安曇郡穂高町
73 Shimosuwa Onsen 下諏訪温泉	Minatoya みなとや	A	Shimosuwa-chō, Suwa-gun, Nagano Pref. (0266)27-8144 長野県諏訪郡下諏訪町
	Kameya Hotel かめやホテル	A, B	(0266)27-8023
	Kokuminshukusha Sannōkaku 国民宿舎山王閣	C (K)	(0266)27-9113
	Tourist information		Machiyakuba (Town Hall) (0266)27-1111

74 Kamisuwa Onsen 上諏訪温泉	Nunohan ぬのはん	A, A+	Kamisuwa, Suwa-shi, Nagano Pref. (0266)52-5500 長野県諏訪市上諏訪
75 Goshiki Onsen 五色温泉	Goshiki-no-yu 五色の湯	A	Takayama-mura, Kamitakai- gun, Nagano Pref. (02624)2-2500 長野県上高井郡高山村
76 Jigokudani Onsen 地獄谷温泉	Kōrakukan 後楽館	C, B	Yamanouchi-chō, Shimotakai-gun, Nagano Pref. (0269)33-4376 長野県下高井郡山ノ内町
77 Yudanaka 湯田中温泉	Yorozuya よろずや	A	Yamanouchi-chō, Shimotakai-gun, Nagano Pref. (0269)33-2111 長野県下高井郡山ノ内町
	Otanisō おたに荘	B	(0269)33-3271
78 Hoppo Onsen 発哺温泉	Tengu-no-yu 天狗の湯	A, B	Yamanouchi-chō, Shimotakai-gun, Nagano Pref. (0269)34-2411 長野県下高井郡山ノ内町
	Yakushi-no-yu 薬師の湯	A, B	(0269)34-2511
	Shiga Swiss Inn 志賀スイスイン	B, A	(0269)34-2834
	Tourist information		(0269)34-2404
79 Echigo Yuzawa Onsen 越後湯沢温泉	Takahan Hotel 高半ホテル	A	Yuzawa-machi, Minami Uonuma-gun, Niigata Pref. (0257)84-3331 新潟県南魚沼郡湯沢町
	Yuzawa Tōei Hotel 湯沢東映ホテル	A	(0257)84-2150
	Ikariya Ryokan いかりや旅館	B (M)	(0257)84-2141
	Kanda 神田	C (M)	(0257)84-2164
	Tourist information		(0257)84-3435

80 Tochiomata Onsen 栃尾又温泉	Jizaikan 自在館	C, B	Yunotani-mura, Kita Uonuma-gun, Niigata Pref. (02579)5-2211 新潟県北魚沼郡湯之谷村
	Jinpūkan 神風館	C, B	(02579)5-2821
	Hōgandō 宝厳堂	C, B	(02579)5-2216
	Tourist information		Machiyakuba (Town Hall) (02579)2-1122
81 Renge Onsen 蓮華温泉	Renge Onsen 蓮華温泉	C	Renge, Ōtokoro-aza, Itoigawa-shi, Niigata Pref. (0255)52-1063 新潟県糸魚川市大所字蓮華
82 Senami Onsen 瀬波温泉	Taikansō 大観荘	A	Murakami-shi, Niigata Pref. (0254)53-2131 新潟県村上市
	Senami Garden Miharashi 瀬波ガーデン見はらし	A, B	(0254)53-3131
83 Katakami Onsen 潟上温泉	Hōsenkan 宝泉館	C, B	Niibo-mura, Sado-gun, Niigata Pref. (02592)2-3125 新潟県佐渡郡新穂村
	Tourist information		(02592)3-3300
84 Yawata Onsen 八幡温泉	Yawatakan 八幡館	A	Sawada-machi, Sado-gun, Niigata Pref. (02595)7-2141 新潟県佐渡郡佐和田町

7. Kantō Region 関東

HOT SPRING	HOTEL/INN	PRICE RANGE	ADDRESS/TELEPHONE
85 Ikaho Onsen 伊香保温泉	Chigira Jinsentei 千明仁泉亭	A	Ikaho-machi, Kita Gunma-gun, Gunma Pref. (0279)72-3355 群馬県北群馬郡伊香保町
	Hotel Kindayū ホテル金太夫	A	(0279)72-3232

	Matsumotorō 松本楼	A	(0279)72-3306
	Kanedaya Ryokan 金田屋旅館	C (M)	48 Kō, Ikaho-machi, Kita Gunma-gun, Gunma Pref. (0279)72-2047 群馬県北群馬郡伊香保町甲48
	Tourist information		(0279)72-3151
86 Kusatsu Onsen 草津温泉	Yamamotokan 山本館	B	Kusatsu, Agatsuma-gun, Gunma Pref. (027988)3244 群馬県吾妻郡草津
	Kirishimaya Ryokan 桐島屋旅館	B	(0279)88-2871
	Yamamotosō 山本荘	C (M)	(0279)88-4184
	Tourist information		(0279)88-3722
87 Yunotaira Onsen 湯ノ平温泉	Shōsenkaku 松泉閣	B	Yunotaira, Iriyama, Kuni-mura, Agatsuma-gun, Gunma Pref. (02799)5-3221 群馬県吾妻郡六合村入山湯ノ平
88 Shima Onsen 四万温泉	Sekizenkan せきぜん館	A, C	Shima, Nakanojō-machi, Agatsuma-gun, Gunma Pref. (0279)64-2101 群馬県吾妻郡中之条町四万
	Yamaguchikan 山口館	A	(0279)64-2011
	Tamura Ryokan 田村旅館	B, A	(0279)64-2111
	Tourist information		(0279)64-2321
89 Hōshi Onsen 法師温泉	Chōjukan 長寿館	B, A	Nagai, Niiharu-mura, Tone-gun, Gunma Pref. (02786)6-0005 群馬県利根郡新治村永井
	Tourist information		(02786)4-0111
90 Takaragawa Onsen 宝川温泉	Ōsenkaku 汪泉閣	A	Fujiwara, Minakami-chō, Tone-gun, Gunma Pref. (0278)75-2121 群馬県利根郡水上町藤原

91 Nasu Yumoto Onsen 那須湯本温泉	Hanaya はなや	B	Yumoto, Nasu-machi, Nasu-gun, Tochigi Pref. (02877)6-3018 栃木県那須郡那須町湯本
	Shimizuya Ryokan 清水屋旅館	B	(02877)6-3023
	Takakuya Ryokan 高久屋旅館	B	(02877)6-2760
	Tourist information		(02877)6-2619
92 Shinnasu Onsen 新那須温泉	Sanraku 山楽	A+	Yumoto, Nasu-machi, Nasu-gun, Tochigi Pref. (02877)6-3010 栃木県那須郡那須町湯本
	Wakaki Ryokan 若喜旅館	A	(02877)6-3170
93 Benten Onsen 弁天温泉	Benten Onsen Ryokan 弁天温泉旅館	A	Benten, Yumoto Okunasu, Nasu-machi, Nasu-gun, Tochigi Pref. (02877)6-2211 栃木県那須郡那須町湯本奥那須弁天
	Nasu Kokumin Kyūka Mura 那須国民休暇村	C	(02877)6-2467
94 Ōmaru Onsen 大丸温泉	Ōmaru Onsen Ryokan 大丸温泉旅館	A	Ōmaru, Yumoto Okunasu, Nasu-machi, Nasu-gun, Tochigi Pref. (02877)6-3050 栃木県那須郡那須町湯本奥那須大丸
95 Sandogoya Onsen 三斗小屋温泉	Daikokuya Ryokan 大黒屋旅館	C	Sandogoya, Kuroiso-shi, Tochigi Pref. (02876)3-2988 栃木県黒磯市三斗小屋
	Tabakoya Ryokan 煙草屋旅館	C	(02876)9-0218
96 Nikkō Yumoto Onsen 日光湯本温泉	Kamaya Ryokan 釜屋旅館	B, A	Yumoto, Nikkō-shi, Tochigi Pref. (0288)62-2141 栃木県日光市湯本
	Yunoya Ryokan 湯の家旅館	B, A	(0288)62-2431
	Tourist information		(0288)54-1111

97 Kaniyu Onsen 加仁湯温泉	Kaniyu Onsen 加仁湯温泉	C	Okukinu, Kuriyama-mura, Shioya-gun, Tochigi Pref. (0288)96-0153 栃木県塩谷郡栗山村奥鬼怒
98 Meotobuchi Onsen 女夫渕温泉	Meotobuchi Onsen Hotel 女夫渕温泉ホテル	A	Meotobuchi, Kuriyama-mura, Shioya-gun, Tochigi Pref. (0288)96-0002 栃木県塩谷郡栗山村女夫渕
99 Araki Onsen 新木温泉	Araki Kōsen 新木鉱泉	B, A	Yamada, Chichibu-shi, Saitama Pref. (0494)23-2641 埼玉県秩父市山田
100 Fukuroda Onsen 袋田温泉	Fukuroda Onsen Hotel 袋田温泉ホテル	A	Fukuroda, Daigo-machi, Kuji-gun, Ibaraki Pref. (02957)2-3111 茨城県久慈郡大子町袋田
	Takimisō 多き美荘	B	(02957)2-3245
	Tourist information		(02957)2-0285
102 Ōshima Onsen 大島温泉	Ōshima Onsen Hotel 大島温泉ホテル	A	Senzu, Ōshima-chō, Tōkyō (04992)2-1673 東京都大島町泉津
	Tourist information		Machiyakuba (Town Hall) (04992)2-1441
103 Jinata Onsen 地鉈温泉	Mimatsuya 美松屋	C	Shikinejima, Niijima Honson, Tōkyō (04992)7-0037 東京都新島本村式根島
104 Ashitsuki Onsen 足付温泉	Ashitsukiya 足付屋	C	Shikinejima, Niijima Honson, Tōkyō (04992)7-0030 東京都新島本村式根島
	Ebisu 恵美須	C (M)	Shikinejima, Niijima Honson, Tōkyō (04992)7-0035 東京都新島本村式根島
105 Shioma Onsen 汐間温泉	Nangoku Onsen Hotel 南国温泉ホテル	B, A	Sueyoshi, Hachijō-machi, Hachijōjima, Tōkyō (04996)8-0211 東京都八丈島八丈町末吉

106 Hakone Yumoto Onsen 箱根湯本温泉	Tenseien 天成園	A+	Yumoto, Hakone-machi Ashigara Shimo-gun, Kanagawa Pref. (0460)5-5521 神奈川県足柄下郡箱根町湯本
	Bansuirō Fukuzumi 萬翠楼福住	A, A+	(0460)5-5531
	Hōeisō 豊栄荘	A+	(0460)5-5763
	Hatsuhanasō 初花荘	A	(0460)5-7321
	Tourist information		(0460)5-5700
107 Tōnosawa Onsen 塔ノ沢温泉	Kansuirō 環翠楼	A, A+	Tōnosawa, Hakone-machi, Ashigara Shimo-gun, Kanagawa Pref. (0460)5-5511 神奈川県足柄下郡箱根町塔ノ沢
	Fukuzumirō 福住楼	A	(0460)5-5301
108 Miyanoshita Onsen 宮ノ下温泉	Naraya Ryokan 奈良屋旅館	A+	Miyanoshita, Hakone-machi, Ashigara Shimo-gun, Kanagawa Pref. (0460)2-2411 神奈川県足柄下郡箱根町宮ノ下
	Fujiya Hotel 富士屋ホテル	A, A+	(0460)2-2211
109 Dōgashima Onsen 堂ケ島温泉	Yamatoya Hotel 大和屋ホテル	A	Miyanoshita, Hakone-machi, Ashigara Shimo-gun, Kanagawa Pref. (0460)2-2261 神奈川県足柄下郡箱根町宮ノ下
	Taiseikan 対星館	A	(0460)2-2281
110 Ubako Onsen 姥子温泉	Shūmeikan 秀明館	A	Moto-Hakone, Hakone-machi, Ashigara Shimo-gun, Kanagawa Pref. (0460)4-8478 神奈川県足柄下郡箱根町元箱根

8. Hokuriku Region 北陸

HOT SPRING	HOTEL/INN	PRICE RANGE	ADDRESS/TELEPHONE
111 Awara Onsen 芦原温泉	Kaikatei 開花亭	A+	Awara-machi, Sakai-gun, Fukui Pref. (0776)77-2525 福井県坂井郡芦原町
	Beniya べにや	A+	(0776)77-2333
	Kameya かめや	B	(0776)77-2011
	Kimuraya きむらや	C (M)	(0776)77-2229
	Tourist information		(0776)77-2040
112 Yuwaku Onsen 湯涌温泉	Haku-unrō 白雲楼	A, A+	Yuwaku-machi, Kanazawa-shi, Ishikawa Pref. (0762)35-1111 石川県金沢市湯涌町
	Kanaya かなや	A	(0762)35-1211
	Tourist information		(0762)35-1040
113 Yamanaka Onsen 山中温泉	Yoshinoya よしのや	A+	Yamanaka-chō, Enuma-gun, Ishikawa Pref. (07617)8-1001 石川県江沼郡山中町
	Kayōtei かよう亭	A+	(07617)8-1410
	Kajikasō 河鹿荘	A+	(07617)8-0015
	Tourist information		(07617)8-0330
114 Yamashiro Onsen 山代温泉	Araya あらや	A+	Yamashiro-chō, Kaga-shi, Ishikawa Pref. (07617)7-0010 石川県加賀市山代町
	Yamashiro Grand Hotel 山代グランドホテル	A, A+	(07617)7-2323
	Shiroganeya 白銀屋	A, A+	(07617)7-0025
	Tourist information		(07617)7-1144

115 Awazu Onsen 粟津温泉	Hōshi 法師	A+	Komatsu-shi, Ishikawa Pref. (0761)65-1111 石川県小松市
	Tsujinoya 辻のや	A	(0761)65-1311
	Tourist information		(0761)65-1834
116 Chūgū Onsen 中宮温泉	Miyamura Ryokan 宮村旅館	B	Chūgū, Yoshinodani-mura, Ishikawa-gun, Ishikawa Pref. (07619)6-7124 石川県石川郡吉野谷村中宮
	Yamada Ryokan 山田旅館	B	(07619)6-7131
	Tourist information		Machiyakuba (Town Hall) (07619)5-5011
117 Wakura Onsen 和倉温泉	Kagaya 加賀屋	A, A+	Wakura-chō, Nanao-shi, Ishikawa Pref. (0767)62-2111 石川県七尾市和倉町
	Ryosō Hamanasu 旅荘はまなす	B, A	(0767)62-2320
	Tourist information		(0767)62-2536
118 Ogawa Onsen Motoyu 小川温泉元湯	Hotel Ogawa ホテル小川	A, C	Yunose, Asahi-chō, Shimoniikawa-gun, Toyama Pref. (0765)84-8111 富山県下新川郡朝日町湯ノ瀬
119 Unazuki Onsen 宇奈月温泉	Hotel Kurobe ホテル黒部	A	Unazuki-chō, Shimoniikawa-gun, Toyama Pref. (0765)62-1331 富山県下新川町郡宇奈月町
	Entaijisō 延対寺荘	A	(0765)62-1231
	Enraku 延楽	A	(0765)62-1211
	Tourist information		(0765)62-1021
120 Kanetsuri Onsen 鐘釣温泉	Miyamasō 美山荘	B	Kanetsuri, Unazuki-chō, Shimoniikawa-gun, Toyama Pref. (0765)62-1634 富山県下新川郡宇奈月町鐘釣

HOT SPRING	HOTEL/INN	PRICE RANGE	ADDRESS/TELEPHONE
121 Ōmaki Onsen 大牧温泉	Ōmaki Onsen Ryokan 大牧温泉旅館	A	Ōmaki, Toga-mura, Higashi Tonami-gun, Toyama Pref. (0763)82-0363 富山県東砺波郡利賀村大牧
122 Rindō Onsen 林道温泉	Kagaya 加賀屋	B	Rindō, Jōhana-machi, Higashi Tonami-gun, Toyama Pref. (0763)62-0027 富山県東砺波郡城端町林道

9. Tōhoku Region 東北

HOT SPRING	HOTEL/INN	PRICE RANGE	ADDRESS/TELEPHONE
123 Higashiyama Onsen 東山温泉	Mukaidaki 向滝	A	Yumoto, Higashiyama-chō, Aizu Wakamatsu-shi, Fukushima Pref. (0242)27-7501 福島県会津若松市東山町湯本
	Arimaya 有馬屋	B	(0242)26-2001
	Tourist information		(0242)27-7051
124 Yunokami Onsen 湯野上温泉	Tōsenkaku 塔泉閣	A, B	Yunokami, Shimogō-machi, Minami Aizu-gun, Fukushima Pref. (0241)68-2513 福島県南会津郡下郷町湯野上
	Kasuikan 花水館	C	(0241)68-2512
	Tourist information		Machiyakuba (Town Hall) (0241)67-2111
125 Shirabu Onsen 白布温泉	Higashiya 東屋	A, B	Ōaza Seki, Yonezawa-shi, Yamagata Pref. (0238)55-2011 山形県米沢市大字関
	Nakaya 中屋	B, A	(0238)55-2111
	Nishiya 西屋	B	(0238)55-2211
	Tourist information		Shiyakusho (City Hall) (0238)22-5111

126 Atsumi Onsen 温海温泉	Tachibanaya たちばなや	A	Nishi Tagawa-gun, Yamagata Pref. (0235)43-3111 山形県西田川郡
	Atsumi Grand Hotel 温海グランドホテル	A	(0235)43-2150
	Tourist information		Machiyakuba (Town Hall) (0235)43-2111
127 Tendō Onsen 天童温泉	Futamikan 二見館	A, B	Tendō-shi, Yamagata Pref. (0236)53-5181 山形県天童市
	Tōshōkan 東松館	B, A	(0236)53-6151
	Tourist information		(0236)53-6146
128 Zaō Onsen 蔵王温泉	Matsukaneya 松金屋	B, A	Yamagata-shi, Yamagata Pref. (0236)94-9411 山形県山形市
	Ōhira Hotel 大平ホテル	B, A	(0236)94-9422
	Ōhira Sansō 大平山荘	C (M)	(0236)94-9137
	Tourist information		(0236)94-9328
129 Ginzan Onsen 銀山温泉	Notoya Ryokan 能登屋旅館	B	Obanazawa-shi, Yamagata Pref. (0237)28-2327 山形県尾花沢市
	Fujiya 藤屋	B	(0237)28-2141
	Tourist information		Shiyakusho (City Hall) (0237)22-1111
130 Imagami Onsen 今神温泉	Imagami Onsen 今神温泉	C	Tsunokawa, Tozawa-mura, Mogami-gun, Yamagata Pref. (02337)3-2311 山形県最上郡戸沢村角川
131 Naruko Onsen 鳴子温泉	Narugo View Hotel 鳴子ビューホテル	A	Naruko-chō, Tamazukuri-gun, Miyagi Pref. (02298)3-2329 宮城県玉造郡鳴子町
	Yokoya Hotel 横屋ホテル	A	(02298)3-3155

	Yusaya Ryokan ゆさや旅館	B	(02298)3-2565
	Tourist information		(02298)3-3441
132 Sakunami Onsen 作並温泉	Iwamatsu Ryokan 岩松旅館	A	Miyagi-chō, Miyagi-gun, Miyagi Pref. (02239)5-2211 宮城県宮城郡宮城町
	Hotel Ichinobō ホテル一の坊	A	(02239)5-2131
	Senzansō　仙山荘	B, A	(02239)5-2041
133 Kamasaki Onsen 鎌先温泉	Kimuraya Ryokan 木村屋旅館	A, B	Kuramoto, Fukuoka Kamasaki, Shiroishi-shi, Miyagi Pref. (02242)6-2161 宮城県白石市福岡蔵本
	Ichijō Ryokan 一条旅館	B, A	(02242)6-2151
	Mogamiya Ryokan 最上屋旅館	B, A	(02242)6-2131
	Tourist information		Shiyakusho (City Hall) (02242)5-2111
134 Aone Onsen 青根温泉	Yumoto Fubōkaku 湯元不忘閣	A, B	Kawasaki-chō, Shibata-gun, Miyagi Pref. (02248)7-2011 宮城県柴田郡川崎町
	Seireikaku 青嶺閣	B, A	(02248)7-2014
	Aone Onsen Hotel 青根温泉ホテル	B, A	(02248)7-2211
135 Getō Onsen 夏油温泉	Getō Onsen Hotel 夏油温泉ホテル	B	Waga, Waga-gun, Iwate Pref. (0197)64-1981 岩手県和賀郡和賀
	Kankōsō 観光荘	B	(0197)64-1982
	Kokuminshukusha Getō Sansō 国民宿舎夏油山荘	C (K)	(0197)64-1980
136 Sukawa Onsen 須川温泉	Sukawa Kōgen Onsen Hotel 須川高原温泉ホテル	B	Genbi-chō, Ichinoseki-shi, Iwate Pref. (0191)23-9337 岩手県一の関市厳美町

137 Ōsawa Onsen 大沢温泉	Sansuikaku 山水閣	B, C	Yuguchi Ōsawa, Hanamaki- shi, Iwate Pref. (0198)25-2021 岩手県花巻市湯口大沢
138 Tōshichi Onsen 藤七温泉	Saiunsō 彩雲荘	C	Matsuo-mura, Iwate-gun, Iwate Pref. (0195)78-3962 岩手県岩手郡松尾村
	Hōraisō 蓬莱荘	C	(0195)78-3961
139 Inazumi Onsen 稲住温泉	Inazumi Onsen 稲住温泉	A	Akinomiya, Ogachi-machi, Ogachi-gun, Akita Pref. (0183)56-2131 秋田県雄勝郡雄勝町秋ノ宮
140 Doroyu Onsen 泥湯温泉	Ogura Ryokan 小椋旅館	C	Doroyuzawa, Takamatsu, Yuzawa-shi, Akita Pref. (0183)79-3035 秋田県湯沢市高松泥湯沢
	Okuyama Ryokan 奥山旅館	C	(0183)79-3021
	Hōmeikan 豊明館	C	(0183)79-2362
141 Yuze Onsen 湯瀬温泉	Yuze Hotel 湯瀬ホテル	A	Yuze, Hachimantai, Kazuno- shi, Akita Pref. (0186)33-2311 秋田県鹿角市八幡平湯瀬
	Hime-no-yu Hotel 姫の湯ホテル	A	(0186)33-2011
	Hotel Taki-no-yu ホテル滝の湯	A, B	(0186)33-2331
142 Tamagawa Onsen 玉川温泉	Tamagawa Onsen 玉川温泉	C	Tazawako-machi, Senboku- gun, Akita Pref. (0187)49-2352 秋田県仙北郡田沢湖町
143 Goshogake Onsen 後生掛温泉	Hotel Sansui ホテル山水	B	Hachimantai, Kazuno-shi, Akita Pref. (0186)31-2311 秋田県鹿角市八幡平
	Goshogake Onsen 後生掛温泉	C	(0186)31-2221

144 Kuroyu Onsen 黒湯温泉	Kuroyu Onsen 黒湯温泉	B	Tazawako-machi, Senboku-gun, Akita Pref. (0187)46-2214 秋田県仙北郡田沢湖町
145 Magoroku Onsen 孫六温泉	Magoroku Onsen 孫六温泉	C, B	Tazawako-machi, Senboku-gun, Akita Pref. (0187)46-2224 秋田県仙北郡田沢湖町
146 Oga Onsen 男鹿温泉	Hakuryūkaku 白龍閣	B, A	Yumoto, Kitaura, Oga-shi, Akita Pref. (0185)33-2101 秋田県男鹿市北浦湯本
	Hotel Yūzankaku ホテル雄山閣	B	(0185)33-3121
	Kokuminshukusha Oga 国民宿舎男鹿	C (K)	(0185)33-3181
	Oga Pension 男鹿ペンション	C	(0185)33-2413
	Tourist information		(0185)24-4700
147 Soma Onsen 杣温泉	Soma Onsen 杣温泉	C	Moriyoshi-machi, Kita Akita-gun, Akita Pref. (0186)76-2210 秋田県北秋田郡森吉町
148 Aoni Onsen 青荷温泉	Aoni Onsen 青荷温泉	C	Kuroishi-shi, Aomori Pref. (0172)54-8588 青森県黒石市
149 Sukayu Onsen 酸ヶ湯温泉	Sukayu Onsen Ryokan 酸ヶ湯温泉旅館	A, C	Hakkōda-Sanchū, Aomori-shi, Aomori Pref. (0177)38-6573 青森県青森市八甲田山中
150 Osorezan Onsen 恐山温泉	Entsūji Temple 円通寺	C	Shin-machi, Mutsu-shi, Aomori Pref. (0175)22-1091 青森県むつ市新町
151 Shimoburo Onsen 下風呂温泉	Kakuchō Ryokan 角長旅館	B	Kazamaura-mura, Shimokita-gun, Aomori Pref. (0175)36-2221 青森県下北郡風間浦村
	Shimoburo Kankō Hotel 下風呂観光ホテル	B	(0175)36-2311

10. Hokkaidō Island 北海道

HOT SPRING	HOTEL/INN	PRICE RANGE	ADDRESS/TELEPHONE
152 Yunokawa Onsen 湯川温泉	Wakamatsu 若松	A+	Yunokawa-chō, Hakodate-shi, Hokkaidō (0138)59-2171 北海道函館市湯川町
	Chikuba 竹葉	A	(0138)57-5171
	Tourist information		(0138)57-0166
153 Raiden Onsen 雷電温泉	Kankō Katō 観光かとう	B, A	Shikishimanai, Iwanai-chō, Iwanai-gun, Hokkaidō (0135)62-1425 北海道岩内郡岩内町敷島内
	Hotel Raiden ホテル雷電	B, A	(0135)62-1451
	Tourist information		Machiyakuba (Town Hall) (0135)62-1011
154 Jōzankei Onsen 定山渓温泉	Jōzankei Grand Hotel 定山渓グランドホテル	A	Minami-ku, Sapporo-shi, Hokkaidō (011)598-2211 北海道札幌市南区
	Shōgetsu Grand Hotel 章月グランドホテル	A	(011)598-2231
	Hotel Shika-no-yu ホテル鹿の湯	A	(011)598-2311
	Shiraito Hotel 白糸ホテル	B, C	(011)598-3351
	Tourist information		(011)598-2029
155 Noboribetsu Onsen 登別温泉	Noboribetsu Grand Hotel 登別グランドホテル	A	Noboribetsu-shi, Hokkaidō (01438)4-2101 北海道登別市
	Dai-ichi Takimotokan 第一滝本館	A	(01438)4-2111
	Shimizu Ryokan 清水旅館	B	(01438)4-2145
	Shin Noboribetsu Onsensō 新登別温泉荘	C (M)	(01438)4-3045
	Tourist information		(01438)4-3311

156 Karurusu Onsen カルルス温泉	Kameya Karurusukan かめやカルルス館	B, C	Karurusu, Noboribetsu-shi, Hokkaidō (01438)4-2851 北海道登別市カルルス
	Hotel Iwai ホテル岩井	B, C	(01438)4-2281
	Suzuki Ryokan 鈴木旅館	C, B	(01438)4-2285
	Tourist information		(01438)4-3311
157 Tōyako Onsen 洞爺湖温泉	Tōya Park Hotel 洞爺パークホテル	A	Abuta-chō, Abuta-gun, Hokkaidō (01427)5-2445 北海道虻田郡虻田町
	Hotel Manseikaku ホテル万世閣	A	(01427)5-2171
	Hotel Grand Tōya ホテルグランドトーヤ	A, B	(01427)5-2288
	Tōya Sansui Hotel 洞爺山水ホテル	B, A	(01427)5-2361
	Tourist information		(01427)5-2446
158 Sōunkyō Onsen 層雲峡温泉	Grand Hotel Sōunkaku グランドホテル層雲閣	A	Sōunkyō, Kamikawa-chō, Kamikawa-gun, Hokkaidō (01658)5-3111 北海道上川郡上川町層雲峡
	Hotel Taisetsu ホテル大雪	B, A	(01658)5-3211
	Sōunkyō Kankō Hotel 層雲峡観光ホテル	B, A	(01658)5-3101
	Ginsenkaku 銀泉閣	B, C	(01658)5-3003
	Tabi no House 旅のハウス	C (M)	(01658)5-3402
159 Akan Kohan Onsen 阿寒湖畔温泉	New Akan Hotel ニュー阿寒ホテル	A, B	Akankohan, Akan-chō, Akan-gun, Hokkaidō (0154)67-2121 北海道阿寒郡阿寒町阿寒湖畔
	Akankosō 阿寒湖荘	A, B	(0154)67-2231
	Kumaya Hotel くまやホテル	B, C	(0154)67-2831
	Tourist information		(0154)67-2254

160 Rausu Onsen 羅臼温泉	Shiretoko Kankō Hotel 知床観光ホテル	B, A	Yunosawa, Rausu-chō, Menashi-gun, Hokkaidō (01538)7-2181 北海道目梨郡羅臼町湯ノ沢
	Sansō Mine 山荘峰	B	(01538)7-3001
	Rausu Dai-ichi Hotel らうす第一ホテル	B	(01538)7-2259
162 Iwaobetsu Onsen 岩尾別温泉	Hotel Chinohate ホテル地の涯	B, A	Iwaobetsu, Shari-chō, Shari-gun, Hokkaidō (01522)3-2188 北海道斜里郡斜里町岩尾別

Appendix 3

Mini-Language Guide

The following words and phrases provide a bare minimum for communicating on your own at Japanese hot springs. Where language is a problem, ask a Japanese friend to make your reservations for you by telephone or to join you if your destination is a particularly remote spot. When you're on your own, smile, try hard, and point to the Japanese writing below. Whatever you do, don't let language deter you from bathing: you may miss an experience of a lifetime.

USEFUL WORDS

Types of Bath

bath   *furo/ofuro*   風呂/御風呂
main bath (signboard; usually men only, but sometimes mixed)
   daiyokujō   大浴場
bath for men   *otokoburo*   男風呂
   or   *otokoyu*   男湯
bath for women   *onnaburo*   女風呂
   or   *onnayu*   女湯
   or   *fujin yokushitsu*   婦人浴室
cascade bath   *takiyu*   滝湯
family bath   *kazoku buro*   家族風呂
mixed bathing   *kon-yoku*   混浴
mud bath   *doroyu*   泥湯
open-air (outdoor) bath   *rotenburo*   露天風呂
sand bath   *sunayu*   砂湯
steam bath   *mushiyu*   蒸湯

Important Places

dining room   *shokudō*   食堂
reception desk   *uketsuke*   受付
station   *eki*   駅
toilet   *otearai*   御手洗
tourist information office   *kankō annaijo*   観光案内所

Other Words

(Japanese-style) bedding   *futon*   布団

(Japanese) clogs   *geta*   下駄
cold water   *mizu*   水
hot water   *oyu*   お湯
lightweight kimono   *yukata*   浴衣
overcoat for kimono   *haori*   羽織
sash   *obi*   帯
umbrella   *kasa*   傘
washcloth (or hand towel)   *tenugui*   手拭い

USEFUL PHRASES

Directions

Where is (name of) Hot Spring?   ____ *onsen wa doko desu ka?*   …温泉はどこですか?
Where is (name of lodgings)?   ____ *wa doko desu ka?*   …はどこですか?
  Straight ahead.   *Massugu desu.*   まっすぐです.
  To the left.   *Hidari desu.*   左です.
  To the right.   *Migi desu.*   右です.
(to taxi driver) Please take me to (name of hot spring or lodgings).   ____ *made onegai-shimasu.*   …までお願いします.
(to bus driver) Please let me off at (name of hot spring or lodgings).   ____ *de oroshite kudasai.*   …で降ろしてください.
Thank you.   *Dōmo arigatō.*   どうもありがとう.

About Bathing

Where are the baths?   *Ofuro wa doko desu ka?*   お風呂はどこですか?
  On the first floor.   *Ikkai desu.*   一階です.
  In the basement.   *Chika desu.*   地下です.
Is it a mixed bath?   *Naka wa kon-yoku desu ka?*   中は混浴ですか?
  Yes.   *Hai.*   はい.
  No, it's separated into men's and women's baths.   *Iie, danjo betsu-betsu desu.*   いいえ、男女別々です.
Where is the public bath?   *Kyōdō yokujō wa doko desu ka?*   共同浴場はどこですか?
  Is it a nice place?   *Ii tokoro desu ka?*   いい所ですか?
Can I just bathe here (without staying at your inn)?   *Ofuro dake hairemasu ka?*   お風呂だけ入れますか?
How much does it cost?   *Oikura desu ka?*   おいくらですか?
Where can I change clothes?   *Kigae wa doko desu ka?*   着替えはどこですか?

What time does the bath close? *Ofuro wa nanji made desu ka?* お風呂は何時
までですか?

What time does the bath open? *Ofuro wa nanji kara desu ka?* お風呂は何時か
らですか?

(about the water temperature)

It's hot. *Atsui desu.* 熱いです.

It's just right. *Chōdo ii desu.* ちょうどいいです.

It's tepid (not hot). *Nurui desu.* ぬるいです.

About Dining

What time is dinner? *Shokuji wa nanji desu ka?* 食事は何時ですか?

What time is breakfast? *Asagohan wa nanji desu ka?* 朝ごはんは何時ですか?

Japanese food will be fine. *Washoku ga ii desu.* 和食がいいです.

Western food would be preferable. *Yōshoku no hō ga ii desu.* 洋食の方がい
いです.

Where are meals served? *Shokuji wa doko de torimasu ka?* 食事はどこでとり
ますか?

Here. *Koko desu.* ここです.

In the dining room. *Shokudō desu.* 食堂です.

In your room. *Oheya desu.* お部屋です.

It tastes good. *Oishii desu.* おいしいです.

Thank you for the meal. *Gochisō-sama deshita.* ごちそうさまでした.

Index

Note: Numbers in boldface are the reference numbers of the hot springs with entries in this book.

おんせん
温泉ガイド
A Guide to
JAPANESE HOT SPRINGS

1986年 3 月15日　第 1 刷発行
2000年10月 2 日　第13刷発行

著　者　　アン・ホッタ
　　　　　いしぐろようこ
　　　　　石黒陽子

発行者　　野間佐和子

発行所　　講談社インターナショナル株式会社
　　　　　〒112-8652 東京都文京区音羽 1-17-14
　　　　　電話 : 03-3944-6493

印刷所　　株式会社　平河工業社

製本所　　株式会社　堅省堂

GUIDES TO DISCOVER JAPAN

GATEWAY TO JAPAN 3rd Edition
June Kinoshita and Nicholas Palevsky

The premier guide to Japan, offering a comprehensive survey of every region of the country, complete with historical and cultural notes.

Paperback: 808 pp, 128 x 188 mm, ISBN 4-7700-2018-X

TOKYO FOR FREE
Susan Pompian

A "priceless" guide to over 400 attractions of traditional and modern Japan—all absolutely free. Perfect for visitors and long-term residents alike.

Paperback: 464 pp, 128 x 182 mm, ISBN 4-7700-2053-8

ANA'S CITY GUIDE TOKYO
ANA / Kodansha International

Handy, ready-to-use information on Tokyo with concise overviews and detailed, bilingual maps.

Paperback: 144 pp, 148 x 210 mm, ISBN 4-7700-1527-5

NEW JAPAN SOLO Expanded Fourth Edition
Eiji Kanno and Constance O'Keefe

From two experienced travel professionals, a dependable, easy-to-use companion for all visitors to Japan, and of special appeal to the first-time visitor.

Paperback: 528 pp, 128 x 188 mm, ISBN 4-7700-2187-9

OLD KYOTO
A Guide to Traditional Shops, Restaurants, and Inns
Diane Durston

Explore the elusive charms and hideaways of one of the world's most enchanting cities.

Paperback: 240 pp, 128 x 182 mm, ISBN 4-7700-1257-8

JAPAN: BUDGET TRAVEL GUIDE Updated
Ian L. McQueen

The classic guide to getting there and enjoying it more—with minimum hassle and expense. Perfect for the independent traveler.

Paperback: 658 pp, 128 x 188 mm, ISBN 4-7700-2047-31

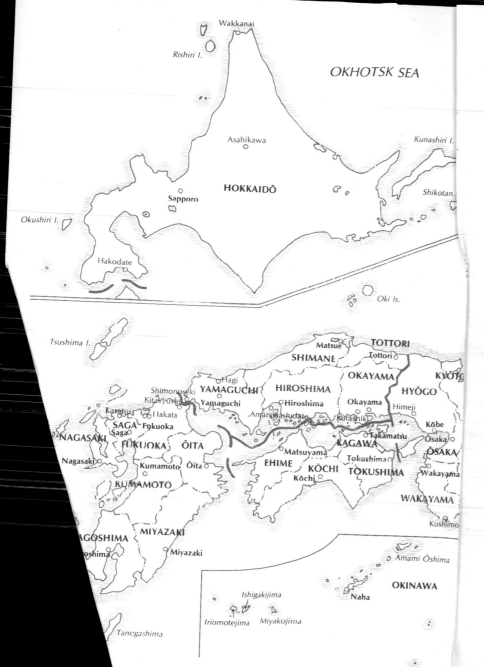

GUIDES FOR EXPLORING JAPAN'S NATURAL BEAUTY

DAY WALKS NEAR TOKYO Revised Edition
Gary D'A. Walters

One-day treks of scenic beauty and cultural interest in the Tokyo area. Twenty-five different walks.

Paperback: 160 pp, 128 x 182 mm, ISBN 4-7700-1620-4

TRAILS OF TWO CITIES
A Walker's Guide to Yokohama, Kamakura and Vicinity
John Carroll

A memorable series of guided walking tours through the cosmopolitan port of Yokohama and the ancient capital of Kamakura.

Paperback: 320 pp, 128 x 182 mm, ISBN 4-7700-1837-1

HIKING IN JAPAN
An Adventurer's Guide to the Mountain Trails
Paul Hunt

Discover some of the most beautiful, unspoiled scenery in Japan. Hikes for the novice to the most experienced.

Paperback: 208 pp, 128 x 182 mm, ISBN 4-7700-1393-0

SKI JAPAN!
T. R. Reid

A complete guide to over 100 exotic ski areas, including 20 world-class resorts, the site of the 1972 Olympics in Hokkaido, or the 1998 Olympics in the Japanese Alps.

Paperback: 328pp, 128 x 182 mm, ISBN 4-7700-1680-8

A BIRD WATCHER'S GUIDE TO JAPAN
Mark Brazil and the Wild Bird Society of Japan

Sixty of the best bird-watching sites in Japan. Includes maps, field notes and travel information.

Paperback: 220 pp, 128 x 182 mm, ISBN 0-87011-849-8

A FIELD GUIDE TO THE WATERBIRDS OF ASIA
Noritaka Ichida, et al.

The first illustrated, English reference to the rich variety of aquatic bird species found in Asian wetlands.

Paperback: 224 pp, 116 x 182 mm, ISBN 4-7700-1740-5

BILINGUAL MAPS AND ATLASES

JAPAN: A Bilingual Atlas

The entire country of Japan is covered, from Hokkaido to Okinawa, in more than 50 color maps.

Paperback: 128 pp, 150 mm x 212 mm, ISBN 4-7700-1536-4

JAPAN: A Bilingual Map

A fold-out national map indicating major travel routes, plus detailed maps of seven major metropolitan areas.

Folder: 138 mm x 264 mm, Map: 770 mm x 1058 mm, ISBN 4-7700-1621-2

TOKYO CITY ATLAS: A Bilingual Guide

A comprehensive guide to Metropolitan Tokyo, featuring 21 area maps with both chome and banchi numbers, subway station exit guides, 18 detailed maps, details of surrounding urban centers, and an exhaustive index of 3600 place names and landmarks.

Paperback: 124 pp, 150 mm x 212 mm, ISBN 4-7700-2314-6

TOKYO RAIL AND ROAD ATLAS: A Bilingual Guide

This bilingual atlas for Metropolitan Tokyo provides clear, detailed maps of all major railways, subways, bus lines, expressways, and international airports.

Paperback: 96 pp, 150 mm x 212 mm, ISBN 4-7700-1781-2

TOKYO: A Bilingual Map

A fold-out wall map of central Tokyo, plus detailed maps of major downtown areas.

Folder: 111 mm x 228 mm, Map: 611 mm x 840 mm, ISBN 4-7700-1478-3

TOKYO METROPOLITAN AREA: A Bilingual Map

A fold-out wall map of the Kanto region, plus area maps of cities outside of central Tokyo.

Folder: 111 mm x 228 mm, Map: 606 mm x 856 mm, ISBN 4-7700-1522-4

KYOTO-OSAKA: A Bilingual Atlas

The first bilingual reference for the Kansai region. 36 maps of all major metropolitan areas, transportation, and tourist areas.

Paperback: 96 pp, 150 mm x 212 mm, ISBN 4-7700-1610-7